MW00450957

How Firm a Foundation

Studies in Biblical Literature

Hemchand Gossai
General Editor

Vol. 63

PETER LANG
New York • Washington, D.C./Baltimore • Bern
Frankfurt am Main • Berlin • Brussels • Vienna • Oxford

Hal Harless

How Firm a Foundation

The Dispensations in the Light of the Divine Covenants

PETER LANG
New York • Washington, D.C./Baltimore • Bern
Frankfurt am Main • Berlin • Brussels • Vienna • Oxford

Library of Congress Cataloging-in-Publication Data

Harless, Hal.
How firm a foundation: the dispensations
in the light of the divine covenants / Hal Harless.
p. cm. — (Studies in biblical literature; v. 63)
Includes bibliographical references and indexes.
1. Covenants—Biblical teaching.
2. Dispensationalism. I. Title. II. Series.
BS680.C67H37   231.7′6—dc22   2003016262
ISBN 0–8204–6931–9
ISSN 1089–0645

Bibliographic information published by **Die Deutsche Bibliothek**.
Die Deutsche Bibliothek lists this publication in the "Deutsche
Nationalbibliografie"; detailed bibliographic data is available
on the Internet at http://dnb.ddb.de/.

The paper in this book meets the guidelines for permanence and durability
of the Committee on Production Guidelines for Book Longevity
of the Council of Library Resources.

© 2004 Peter Lang Publishing, Inc., New York
275 Seventh Avenue, 28th Floor, New York, NY 10001
www.peterlangusa.com

All rights reserved.
Reprint or reproduction, even partially, in all forms such as microfilm,
xerography, microfiche, microcard, and offset strictly prohibited.

Printed in Germany

for LOIS ANN
who is the wind beneath my wings

TABLE OF CONTENTS

PART II: THE DIVINE COVENANTS

PART III: THE DISPENSATIONS IN THE LIGHT OF THE DIVINE COVENANTS

◆ ILLUSTRATIONS

TABLES

EDITOR'S PREFACE

More than ever the horizons in biblical literature are being expanded beyond that which is immediately imagined; important new methodological, theological, and hermeneutical directions are being explored, often resulting in significant contributions to the world of biblical scholarship. It is an exciting time for the academy as engagement in biblical studies continues to be heightened.

This series seeks to make available to scholars and institutions, scholarship of a high order, and which will make a significant contribution to the ongoing biblical discourse. This series includes established and innovative directions, covering general and particular areas in biblical study. For every volume considered for this series, we explore the question as to whether the study will push the horizons of biblical scholarship. The answer must be *yes* for inclusion.

In this volume Hal Harless explores an understanding of the biblical idea of covenant in light of archaeological, anthropological and ancient Near Eastern evidence. While much has been written on *Covenant*, Harless pursues this theme in terms of its connection with, and relationship to Dispensationalism. He argues for the complementarity between Covenants and Dispensations, noting that they both work in bringing about the divine plan. For both scholars and laity alike who have an evangelical inclination, this study will prove to be particularly useful.

The horizon has been expanded.

Hemchand Gossai
Series Editor

ACKNOWLEDGMENTS

I would like to express my gratitude to several people whose support and encouragement have been invaluable throughout the process of completing this work. First of all, I am grateful to my wife, Lois Ann, for her love and understanding through long hours of research and writing. I am very grateful to Mrs. Jody Cunningham for proofreading the manuscript. I would also like to thank my pastor, Rev. Matthew Dodd, for his encouragement and enthusiasm for the work.

Grateful acknowledgment is hereby made to copyright holders for permission to use the following copyrighted material:

Hal Harless, "The Cessation of the Mosaic Covenant," *Bibliotheca Sacra* 160, July–September 2003. Reprinted by permission of the publisher. All rights reserved.

David H. Lane, "Theological Problems with Theistic Evolution," *Bibliotheca Sacra* 151, April–June 1994. Reprinted by permission of the publisher. All rights reserved.

Darrell L. Bock, "The Son of David and the Saint's Task: The Hermeneutics of Initial Fulfillment," *Bibliotheca Sacra* 150, October–December 1993. Reprinted by permission of the publisher. All rights reserved.

F. F. Bruce, "Colossian Problems—Part 4: Christ as Conqueror and Reconciler," *Bibliotheca Sacra* 141, October–December 1984. Reprinted by permission of the publisher. All rights reserved.

John F. Walvoord, "Part 3: Does the Church Fulfill Israel's Program," *Bibliotheca Sacra* 137, July–September 1980. Reprinted by permission of the publisher. All rights reserved.

Walter C. Kaiser, Jr., "The Promise Theme and the Theology of Rest," *Bibliotheca Sacra* 130, April–June 1973. Reprinted by permission of the publisher. All rights reserved.

Gordon R. Lewis, "Theological Antecedents of Pretribulationism," *Bibliotheca Sacra* 125, April–June 1968. Reprinted by permission of the publisher. All rights reserved.

Roy L. Aldrich, "A New Look at Dispensationalism," *Bibliotheca Sacra* 120, January–March 1963. Reprinted by permission of the publisher. All rights reserved.

J. Dwight Pentecost, "The Godly Remnant of the Tribulation Period," *Bibliotheca Sacra* 117, April–June 1960. Reprinted by permission of the publisher. All rights reserved.

Roy L. Aldrich, "Has the Mosaic Law Been Abolished," *Bibliotheca Sacra* 116, October–December 1959. Reprinted by permission of the publisher. All rights reserved.

Roy L. Aldrich, "An Apologetic for Dispensationalism," *Bibliotheca Sacra* 112, January–March 1955. Reprinted by permission of the publisher. All rights reserved.

John F. Walvoord, "Series in Christology—Part 4: The Preincarnate Son of God," *Bibliotheca Sacra* 104, October–December 1947. Reprinted by permission of the publisher. All rights reserved.

Lewis Sperry Chafer, "Soteriology," *Bibliotheca Sacra* 103, July–September 1946. Reprinted by permission of the publisher. All rights reserved.

John F. Walvoord, "Eschatological Problems X: The New Covenant with Israel," *Bibliotheca Sacra* 103, January–March 1946. Reprinted by permission of the publisher. All rights reserved.

John F. Walvoord, "Eschatological Problems VII: The Fulfillment of the Davidic Covenant," *Bibliotheca Sacra* 102, April–June 1945. Reprinted by permission of the publisher. All rights reserved.

Scripture taken from the NEW AMERICAN STANDARD BIBLE®, Copyright © 1960, 1962, 1963, 1971, 1972, 1973, 1975, 1977, 1995 by

The Lockman Foundation. Used by permission.

Quotations designated (NIV) are from THE HOLY BIBLE: NEW INTERNATIONAL VERSION®. NIV®. Copyright © 1973, 1978, 1984 by International Bible Society. Used by permission of Zondervan Publishing House. All rights reserved.

Most of all I am grateful to our covenant keeping God "for His lovingkindness is everlasting" (Ps 118).

✦ ABBREVIATIONS

ABD	*Anchor Bible Dictionary*
ALGNT	*Analytical Lexicon to the Greek New Testament*
ASV	American Standard Version
BDAG	*A Greek-English Lexicon of the New Testament and Other Early Christian Literature, 3rd ed.*
BAR	*Biblical Archaeology Review*
BBCNT	*The IVP Bible Background Commentary: New Testament*
BBCOT	*The IVP Bible Background Commentary: Old Testament*
BDB	*A Hebrew and English Lexicon of the Old Testament*
BJ	La Bible de Jerusalem
BKCOT	*The Bible Knowledge Commentary: Old Testament*
BSac	*Bibliotheca Sacra*
COT	Commentary on the Old Testament (Keil and Delitzsch)
CTJ	*The Conservative Theological Journal*
DBI	*Dictionary of Biblical Imagery*
DJG	*Dictionary of Jesus and the Gospels*
DLNT	*Dictionary of the Later New Testament & Its Developments*
DPT	*Dictionary of Premillennial Theology*
EBC	The Expositor's Bible Commentary
EvDT	*Evangelical Dictionary of Theology*
GELNT	*Thayer's Greek-English Lexicon of the New Testament*
GTJ	*Grace Theological Journal*
HALOT	*The Hebrew and Aramaic Lexicon of the Old Testament*
IDB	*The Interpreter's Dictionary of the Bible*
ISBE	*International Standard Bible Encyclopedia*
ISBErev	*International Standard Bible Encyclopedia Revised*
JB	Jerusalem Bible
JETS	*Journal of the Evangelical Theological Society*
KJV	King James Version
LSJ	*Liddell and Scott's Greek-English Lexicon*

LXX	Septuagint
MM	*Vocabulary of the Greek Testament (Moulton and Milligan)*
MSJ	*Master's Seminary Journal*
NASB	New American Standard Bible
NBC	*The New Bible Commentary*
NBD	*The New Bible Dictionary*
NDBT	*New Dictionary of Biblical Theology*
NEB	New English Bible
NIDNTT	*New International Dictionary of New Testament Theology*
NIDOTTE	*New International Dictionary of Old Testament Theology & Exegesis*
NIV	New International Version
NLT	New Living Translation
NRSV	New Revised Standard Version
NSRB	*The New Scofield Reference Bible*
NT	New Testament
OT	Old Testament
RSB	*The Ryrie Study Bible*
RSV	Revised Standard Bible
TDOT	*Theological Dictionary of the Old Testament*
TJ	*Trinity Journal*
TLOT	*Theological Lexicon of the Old Testament*
TWOT	*Theological Wordbook of the Old Testament*
UBD	*Unger's Bible Dictionary*
WBC	*Wycliffe Bible Commentary*
WBE	*Wycliffe Bible Encyclopedia*
WTJ	*Westminister Theological Journal*
WUED	*Webster's Universal Encyclopedic Dictionary*
YLT	Young's Literal Translation
ZPBD	*Zondervan's Pictorial Bible Dictionary*
ZPEB	*The Zondervan Pictorial Encyclopedia of the Bible*

CHAPTER ONE
Introduction

Due to recent archaeological discoveries, there has been an explosion in our understanding of ancient Near Eastern covenants. Excavations of the city of Boğazköy (ancient Hittite *Hattusha*) in Turkey have unearthed thousands of cuneiform tablets from the third millennium BC. These tablets contained many covenant documents including a treaty between the Hittite King Hattusili III and Pharaoh Ramses II.[1] G. Herbert Livingston, a biblical historian, explains that

> the new knowledge about the covenants current in the ancient Near East during the patriarchal and Mosaic time span has aided our understanding of the Scriptures. *Scholars of all theological persuasions have admitted their debt to this new information, for it is not too strong to say that the religious faith and life of the Old Testament men and women cannot be understood apart from a careful study of the covenant relationship in the Old Testament* (emphasis mine).[2]

This wealth of information has illuminated the relational world of the ancient Near East.

Covenants could take many forms in the ancient world. Two friends might covenant together to always be faithful each to the other. Marriage was a covenant binding a couple together before God. Moreover, a king might impose a covenant of loyalty on his subjects. Men related to each other by means of covenant, but, more importantly, humankind related to God by covenant. The concept of covenant was foundational and integral to all of life in the ancient Near East. Therefore, the concept of covenant is critical to the understanding of the cultural and historical context of the Scriptures.

When God promised Abraham an heir, he simply believed and God "reckoned it to him as righteousness" (Gen 15:1–6).[3] However, in the next verse, when God made a grant of the land of Canaan to Abraham, he responded with an intriguing question, "O Lord GOD, how may I *know* that I will possess it?" (Gen 15:8, emphasis mine). God's response was to perform a well-known ritual, the covenant. In that culture this was the most solemn and binding of commitments. It was in the context of a covenant that God confirmed to Abraham that he could "know for certain" (Gen 15:13) that God's promises were true.

In 1954 George E. Mendenhall introduced the importance of the Hittite covenants to biblical understanding in a seminal article entitled "Law and Covenant in Israel and the Ancient Near East."[4] Four years later J. Dwight Pentecost published his important dispensational work, *Things to Come.*[5] In his section "The Biblical Covenants and Eschatology" no mention is made of the Hittite discoveries and only the Abrahamic, Palestinian, Davidic, and new covenants are dealt with. Mal Couch comments concerning this dispensational dispensing with the covenants:

> Few writers have addressed the relationship between the dispensations and the biblical covenants. Rarely do you find dispensationalists discussing this issue. Because of this, often there are statements that seem to miss the mark and confuse the specifics that make dispensations and covenants different.[6]

Unfortunately, dispensationalists have often shown a lack of interest in the light that archaeology has shed on the biblical covenants. Dispensational scholars, such as Pentecost, have done a wonderful job of deducing from the text many of the theological characteristics of biblical covenants. However, the Hittite treaty documents and other discoveries can reinforce or modify their conclusions. Since the first element of the *sine qua non* of dispensationalism is a consistent literal-grammatical-historical hermeneutic, dispensationalists must consider this evidence.

This body of evidence has largely been abandoned to liberal scholars, such as Mendenhall, or covenant theologians, such as Meredith G. Kline[7] or O. Palmer Robertson[8]. This information is invaluable and should not be neglected. Therefore, I will seek to examine the biblical covenants and relate them to the dispensations. First, I will consider the concept of covenant in the cultural context of the ancient Near East and more specifically the cultures of the Bible. Then I will explore the biblical covenants exegetically. Finally, I will investigate the dispensations in light of the biblical covenants and offer some conclusions.

NOTES

1. Howard F. Vos, *Archaeology in Bible Lands* (Chicago: Moody, 1977) 337–39.
2. G. Herbert Livingston, *The Pentateuch In Its Cultural Environment* (Grand Rapids, MI: Baker, 1978) 154.
3. Unless otherwise noted, Scripture quotes will be from the New American Standard Bible.
4. George E. Mendenhall, "Law and Covenant in Israel and the Ancient Near East," *The Biblical Archaeologist* [article on-line] 17, no. 2 (May 1954): 26–44 and 17, no. 3 (September 1954): 49–76, accessed 26 February 2001, available from http://members.cftnet.com/chrishum/Law_Cov_Mendenhall_TITLE.htm; Internet.
5. J. Dwight Pentecost, *Things to Come: A Study in Biblical Eschatology* (n.p.: Dunham, 1958; Grand Rapids, MI: Zondervan, 1974) 65–128.
6. Mal Couch, "The Relationship Between the Dispensations and Covenants," *The Conservative Theological Journal* (hereafter referred to as *CTJ*) 2, no. 7 (December 1998): 405–31.
7. Meredith G. Kline, *The Structure of Biblical Authority*, 2nd ed. (Eugene, OR: Wipf and Stock, 1989); Meredith G. Kline, *Treaty of the Great King* (Grand Rapids, MI: Eerdmans, 1963); and Meredith G. Kline, *By Oath Consigned* (Grand Rapids, MI: Eerdmans, 1968).
8. O. Palmer Robertson, *The Christ of the Covenants* (Phillipsburg, NJ: Presbyterian and Reformed, 1980).

PART ONE

The Meaning of Covenant

CHAPTER TWO

Ancient Near Eastern Covenants

The Antiquity and Nature of Covenant

The Origin of Covenant

The concept of covenant is older, in all probability, than recorded history. Covenant was already a well-developed form by the time of the Hittites. Mendenhall explains

> that covenants most probably originated in remote prehistoric times is indicated by the fact that they were already well-developed political instruments by the 3rd millennium BC. To judge from later parallels and from the modern observations of anthropologists, covenants may very well have developed at least in part out of marriage contracts between exogamous tribes or bands; i.e., those groups that stayed within the required patterns of intermarriage. Whether or not this was the case, the most important functions of covenants for 1,000 years before the 13th-century BC Sinai covenant ... had to do with the creation of new relationships, both familial and political.[1]

Thus, covenants may originally have been seen as a means of extending the tribe or family.[2] Mendenhall and Gary Herion note that covenants in the form of treaties are nearly as old as writing itself.[3] They also note that the large number of treaty texts preserved from all over the ancient Near East spectacularly shows the importance of covenants in ancient culture.[4] The idea of covenant shaped much of the ancient world that was the larger historical and cultural context of the Scriptures.

The first covenants were probably seen as a way to mingle bloods and so join families and peoples together in new relationships. Although these earliest covenants are shrouded in the mists of prehistory, many have seen similarities in more contemporary primitive rituals. George R. Berry echoes the same thought and draws a parallel to the ancient Arab custom of blood-brotherhood.[5] H. Clay Trumbull, who surveyed the customs concerning blood covenants in multitudes of primitive societies, relates a similar example of this rite in Syria. Public oaths of loyalty were exchanged, blood was drawn, and wiped on the covenant documents. The bond formed by this ritual is considered indissoluble. Trumbull notes that "the compact thus made, is called *Mʿâhadat ed-Dam* ... the 'Covenant of Bloods.' The two persons thus conjoined, are *Akhwat el-Mʿâhadah* ... 'Brothers of the Covenant.' The rite itself is recognized, in Syria, as one of the very old customs of the land, as *ʿâdah qadeemeh* ... 'a primitive rite.'"[6] These rites establish by means of a covenant a blood brotherhood as strong or stronger than familial and tribal ties. Although we should exercise caution when dealing with anthropological data so far removed from antiquity, these covenant rites, coming from the Middle East and said to be primitive or ancient in that culture, are certainly suggestive.

Covenant Terminology

The terms used in the ancient Near East for covenant seem to suggest a binding obligation. Gleason L. Archer notes concerning the Hebrew בְּרִית that "the original meaning was probably 'fetter' or 'obligation' coming from a root *bārâ*, 'to bind.' This root does not occur as a verb in Hebrew, but it does occur in Akkadian as *bārù*, 'to bind,' and appears as a noun in the Akkadian *birîtu, which means 'bond' or 'fetter.'"[7] Moshe Weinfeld agrees that

> the most plausible solution seems to be the one that associates *berith* with Akk. *birītu*, "clasp," "fetter" (cf. the Talmudic *byryt*). This is supported by the Akkadian and Hittite terms for treaty: Akk. *riksu*, Hitt. *išḫiul*, both meaning "bond." The concept of a binding settlement also stands behind Arab. *ʿaqd*, Lat. *vinculum fidei*, "bond of faith," *contractus*, "contract," and is likewise reflected in the German *Bund*.... The "bond" metaphor explains the use of "strengthening" or "fastening" to convey the idea of the "validity" or "reliability" of the treaty. Thus we find in Akk. *dunnunu riksāte*, "to fasten the bonds" (= to validate the treaty), or *riksu dannu*, "strong persistent bond" (= a valid and reliable treaty), and similarly in Aram. *le-thaqqapah ʾesar*, "strengthen the bond" (Dnl. 6:8). The Greek term for annulling the pact is *lyein*, "to loosen," which also points to the understanding of the treaty as a bond.[8]

However, Weinfeld contends that the meaning of the Akkadian *riksu* and Hittite *išḫiul* is not an "agreement or settlement between two parties," as is commonly argued. *berith* implies first and foremost the notion of "imposition," "liability," or "obligation," as might be learned from the "bond" etymology discussed above....

The same applies to the Akk. *riksu* and Hitt. *išḫiul*. The formulas *riksa irkus* in Akkadian and *išḫiul išḫiya* in Hittite occur in connection with a set of commandments imposed by the king on his officials, his soldiers or citizens, as well as his vassals.[9]

Although the concept of covenant seems to entail the idea of a bond or obligation, some have presented other explanations.

There have been three main alternatives to the bond etymology as suggested by Weinfeld *et al.* Gordon J. McConville summarizes the positions:

> There have been three main attempts to explain בְּרִית by reference to Akk. The first relates בְּרִית to the nom. *biritu*, clasp, fetter, and thus thinks of covenant essentially as a bond (Weinfeld). A second refers to a use in a text from Mari of the Akk. preposition *birit*, between, and thus sees the covenant as an arrangement between two parties (Noth). The third option, which postulates a vb. בָּרָה, has been influential because of the work of E. Kutsch. Finding a connection with the Akk. *barû*, see, he argues for an extended meaning in Heb., "select for a task," hence "obligation," on the basis of the form בְּרוּ in 1 Sam 17:8 (apparently "choose," but the text is disputed; see McCarter, 287). A fourth explanation (not connected with Akk.) is Gerleman's proposal of the meaning "something specially set apart," deriving בְּרִית from the root בָּרַר.[10]

E. Kutsch objects to the bond concept of covenant since "according to etymology the expression *krt bᵉrît*, lit. 'to cut a *bᵉrît*,' would mean 'to cut (off) a band/fetter,' which hardly fits the (generally accepted) meaning 'to make a covenant' for *krt bᵉrît*...."[11] This objection is hardly telling if the concept of "binding agreement" arose first and was later combined with "cutting" due to covenant rituals. It is noteworthy that, although he derives בְּרִית from the Akkadian *barû* ("to see, choose, select, designate (for a particular task)"), Kutsch also sees the concept of "obligation" as basic to the idea of covenant. He rightly rejects Martin Noth when he

> compared *bᵉrît* with the Akk. prep. *birīt* "between" (cs. of *birītu* "space between") on the strength of ARM II:37.13f. But in the Akk. phrase *salīmam birīt ... u ... aškun*, "I brought about an agreement between ... and ...," *birīt* corresponds not to the Hebr. *bᵉrît* ... but to the prep. *bên*.[12]

Kutsch also finds the suggestion that the covenant derived from a verb *brh* to be "out of the question" because the root is only in Arabic and related words. In Hebrew it refers only to the food of the "unfortunate and ailing."[13] Other concepts, such as a covenantal meal or cutting a sacrifice, do not change the basic concept of covenant as a binding obligation.

Oath: The Sine Qua Non of Covenant

The ancient Near Eastern concept of covenant/treaty was a binding obligation based on a religious oath. Delbert R. Hillers explains this connection between oath and covenant:

> In the desire to achieve some kind of good faith among nations, to replace a state of constant war by peace, recourse was to the oath, to the gods....
>
> An ancient treaty then is essentially an elaborate oath. There are two fundamental components: the thing to be performed, and the oath, the invoking of divine vengeance in case the promise is not kept. These basic features are discernibly present in extremely early texts....[14]

In Akkadian the stipulations were the bond (*riksu*) that was accepted by oath (*mamitu*). Therefore, they referred to a treaty as an "oath and bond (*riksu u mamitu*)."[15] Mendenhall contrasts covenant with law. In making a solemn binding covenant, oaths were sworn before the gods. In the case of law, the sanctions were imposed by society. In the case of a covenant, the gods would avenge themselves directly on the one who broke his oath.[16]

The oath was not necessarily a verbal act. Symbolic acts can also take on the character of an oath. Gordon P. Hugenberger explains this and notes that Mendenhall expanded his definition to include symbolic acts:

> As implied in our definition, one important misunderstanding to be avoided is the tendency to equate oaths exclusively with verbal acts. As elsewhere in the ancient Near East, oaths in the Old Testament are not infrequently symbolic rather than verbal, or at least not just verbal. In particular, such symbolic oaths, or "oath-signs" as they have been termed, were frequently employed in the ratification of covenants. So, for example, G. E. Mendenhall defines a covenant as "a solemn promise made binding by an oath, which may be either a verbal formula or a symbolic action."[17]

The ritual associated with a covenant should be seen as a means of acting out the oath of the covenant.

Since, as Mendenhall asserts, "A covenant is a promise that is sanctioned by an oath," there are implications as to the nature of covenants. Mendenhall explains that

> because a person can bind only himself by an oath, covenants in the ancient world were usually unilateral. In circumstances in which it was desirable to establish a par-

ity (equivalence) treaty, such as in rare cases in political life, the parity was obtained by the simple device of what might be termed a double covenant, in which both parties would bind themselves to identical obligations, and neither was therefore subjected to the other.[18]

The fact is that all covenants are essentially unilateral. If the Great King wished to leave himself an escape clause, it had to be an explicit part of the oath. In the covenant between Suppiluliuma I (1375–1335 BC) and Huqqana (ca. 1350 BC), Suppiluliuma swears, "But if you in any way do evil, then I, My Majesty, shall be free from this oath before the gods."[19] As we shall see later, the unilateral nature of covenants will have an impact on our understanding of the biblical covenants.

Covenant Rituals

Various rituals accompanied covenants. The most common appears to be a sacrifice. Livingston gives the example of a covenant tablet between a Great King and his vassals from Alalakh (northern Syria) in which he binds himself with an oath and sacrifices a sheep to seal the oath.[20] In the Mari documents (ca. 18th century BC), the phrase, "to kill an ass" is equivalent to "to make a covenant."[21] Mendenhall explains that the ritual slaughter of a sacrificial animal dramatically portrayed the fate of the oath-breaker.[22] Thus, the sacrifice did not merely solemnize the oath, but also had a self-maledictory function. Hugenberger cites an example:

> As an especially vivid illustration of the use of such an oath rite, M. G. Kline cites the eighth-century treaty of Ashurnirari V and Mati'ilu, the King of Arpad. According to the treaty a ram was to be removed from its herd, and "If Mati'ilu [sins] against the treaty sworn by the gods, just as this ram is broug[ht here] from his herd and to his herd will not return [and stand] at its head, so may Mati'ilu with his sons, [his nobles,] the people of his land [be brought] far from his land and to his land not return [to stand] at the head of his land." Not content with this malediction of exile, the treaty goes on to specify that the ram was to be decapitated: "This head is not the head of a ram; it is the head of Mati'ilu, the head of his sons, his nobles, the people of his land. If those named [sin] against this treaty, as the head of this ram is c[ut off,] his leg put in his mouth [...] so may the head of those named be cut off." Finally, the shoulder of the ram is torn off, and once again the treaty threatens that the shoulder of Mati'ilu, and his sons, etc., would similarly be torn out if Mati'ilu sins against the treaty.[23]

The parties of the covenant were identified with the sacrificial victim and, if they broke the oath, they invited the fate of the sacrifice on themselves.

A ritual meal or eating of salt might accompany the covenant. H. William F. Gesenius notes in his comments on בְּרִית that eating together in the Near East is almost equivalent to making a covenant of friendship.[24] James M. Freeman mentions that the Arab custom of eating salt together was tantamount to making a covenant.[25] Trumbull remarks on the Arab custom of eating together a covenant meal, called a *casâma*. The *casâma* consisted of first killing a lamb or calf, pouring out its blood as a offering, and sharing a meal of the flesh of the peace offering.[26] The sacrifice establishes the relationship and the meal celebrates the established relationship.

There may be an even deeper meaning in the show of hospitality. Morroe Berger explains that the Bedouin right of protection is part of the ritual of hospitality.[27] Dennis J. McCarthy sees this custom in antiquity:

> The significance of the meal as seal of the alliance seems to stem from Bedouin culture. It is a sign that the weaker is taken into the family of the stronger, a reassuring gesture on the part of the superior toward the inferior and not a pledge by the latter. This rite with its echo of nomad life reinforces the impression of antiquity.... This is an authentic gesture of covenant making, and it is ancient....[28]

Although it is not certain that contemporary Bedouin culture retains elements of the ancient Near Eastern culture, it does present the possibility that the covenant meal was an expression of protection as well as hospitality.

The covenant was a means of forming new relationships both personal and political. A covenant may be defined as *a solemn unilateral obligation made binding by an oath*. The oath is often of a self-maledictory character and may be verbal, symbolic, or both. In its verbal form, the gods were invoked to punish the oath-breaker. In its symbolic form, a sacrifice was identified with the oath-taker and its fate represented his should he become an oath-breaker. Although this is the basic concept, it resulted in varieties of covenants.

Types of Covenants

The single word "covenant" encompasses several different kinds of relationships. Mendenhall and Herion classify these categories as treaties, loyalty oaths, and charters.[29] However, this classification does not distinguish between suzerainty treaties and parity treaties. Additionally, the loyalty oath can be considered for our purposes as a late form of the suzerainty treaty from the vassal's point of view. Mendenhall had earlier classified covenants as suzerainty, parity, patron, and promissory.[30] I largely follow this classification with the exception that, since there is not a clear distinction between patron and promissory types, I combine them into the category of grant covenants. Therefore, the three categories of covenants are suzerainty, parity, and grant.

Suzerainty Covenants

The suzerainty covenant delineates the relationship between a vassal and a king. It is perhaps the best-attested covenant form of antiquity.[31] Please note that we do not have in our documents the actual covenant ceremonies. Rather the documents record the details that the ancients considered important about the covenants. This evidence gives us a clear picture of the nature of suzerainty covenants.

The Great King would impose oaths upon his vassals. The vassal swore an oath in the presence of multitudes of the gods, who were expected to enforce blessings or curses based on obedience. The oath was unilateral, although it concerned the Great King, because the vassal was the one bound by oath. Occasionally, we even find explicit statements in suzerainty covenants that they are not to be taken as reciprocal.[32] As previously observed, covenants are essentially unilateral. In the case of a suzerainty covenant, the vassal is unilaterally binding himself.

The form of the suzerainty covenant is well known and consistently followed. The Hittite suzerainty treaty/covenant form consisted of six sections:

1. The Preamble: This section contains the name, titles, and lineage of the Great King and does not contain mention of the vassal.
2. The Historical Introduction: This section recounts the prior history of relations with the vassal and demonstrates the reasons for the vassal's loyalty.
3. The Provisions: These are the stipulations of the covenant consisting of obligations, such as tribute, military assistance, renouncing of all independent foreign diplomatic contacts, the extradition of fugitives, guarantees of succession, and delimiting the frontiers of the vassal's realm.
4. The Instructions for Deposition: These might stipulate that the tablet on which the treaty was written is to be kept in the temple of a deity

under the watchful eyes of the gods and that it be read aloud before
the vassal at regular intervals.

5. The List of Divine Witnesses: The gods of both partners are called to
    act as witnesses to the stipulations and oaths.

6. The Curses and Blessings: In this section the vassal recites various
    self-curses before the gods guaranteeing the covenant. The Great
    King pronounces a number of blessings on the vassal, based on his
    keeping his obligations.[33]

This form is easily recognizable in all the Hittite treaty/covenant documents.

Examples of the elements of the suzerainty covenant abound. From the
treaty between Mursili II of Hatti (ca. 1350 BC) and Tuppi-Teshshup of
Amurru (ca. 1350 BC), an example of the preamble is, "[Thus says] My
Majesty, Mursili, [Great King, King of Hatti], Hero, Beloved of the Storm-
god; [son of] Suppiluliuma, [Great King, King of Hatti, Hero]...."[34] An historical introduction follows emphasizing the reasons the vassal has for gratitude:

> But when your father died, according to [the request of your father], I did not
> cast you off. Because your father had spoken your name before me during his life-
> time (?), I therefore took care of you.... I nonetheless installed you [in] place of your
> father. I made your [...] brothers and the land of Amurru swear an oath to you.[35]

Mursili begins the section of provisions in this manner, "And as I took care
of you according to the request of your father, and installed you in place of
your father, I have now made you swear an oath to the King of Hatti. Observe the oath and the authority of the King. I, My Majesty, will protect
you."[36] Mursili continues to stipulate succession, tribute, extradition, defen-
sive, and offensive alliances:

> [Whoever] is [My Majesty's] enemy shall be your enemy. [Whoever is My
> Majesty's friend] shall be your friend....
>   As I, My Majesty, protect you, Tuppi-Teshshup, be an auxiliary army for My
> Majesty and [for Hatti].[37]

There is no explicit provision for the deposition of this particular covenant.
However, we have an example of this in another covenant/treaty between
Shattiwaza of Mittanni (ca. 1350 BC) and Suppiluliuma I of Hatti:

> [A duplicate of this tablet is deposited] in the land [of Mittanni before the
> Storm-god, Lord of the kurinnu of Kahat. It shall be read repeatedly, for ever and
> ever], before the king of the land [of Mittanni and before the Hurrians. Whoever, be-

fore the Storm-god, Lord of the kurinnu of Kahat, alters] this tablet, [or sets it in a secret location—if he breaks it, if he changes the words of the text of the tablet]—in regard to this treaty we have summoned the gods of secrets and the gods who are guarantors of the oath.[38]

Paragraphs 16 through 20 from the treaty between Mursili II of Hatti and Tuppi-Teshshup of Amurru contain a long list of divine witnesses in an attempt to cover any possible interested deities:

> [... The thousand Gods shall now stand] for this [oath]. They shall observe [and listen]....
> [The Sun-god of Heaven, the Sun-goddess] of Arinna, the Storm-god of Heaven, the Storm-god of Hatti, ... [the Moon-god, Lord of the Oath, Ishhara], Queen of the Oath, [Hebat, Queen of Heaven, Ishtar, Ishtar of the Countryside, Ishtar of Nineveh, ...] ... the mountain-dweller gods, the mercenary gods, ... the male deities and female deities of Hatti, ... of Amurru, [all] the primeval deities ... the mountains, the rivers, the springs, the great sea, heaven and earth, the winds, and the clouds. They shall be witnesses to this treaty [and] to the oath.[39]

Lastly, we come to the curse:

> All the words of the treaty and oath [which] are written [on] this tablet—if Tuppi-Teshshup [does not observe these words] of the treaty and of the oath, then these oath gods shall destroy Tuppi-Teshshup, [together with his person], his [wife], his son, his grandsons, his household, his city, his land, and together with his possessions.[40]

And the blessing:

> But if Tuppi-Teshshup [observes] these [words of the treaty and of the oath] which [are written] on this tablet, [then] these oath gods [shall protect] Tuppi-Teshshup, together with his person, his wife, his son, his grandsons, [his city, his land], his(!) household, his subjects, [and together with his possessions].[41]

Thus, we see in these covenant examples all of the elements of the suzerainty covenant.

In differing order and with possible omissions, one can expect to see the following elements in a suzerainty covenant: a preamble, an historical introduction, provisions, deposition, list of divine witnesses, and curses and blessings.[42] The suzerainty covenant appears to be the basic form for other covenant types. Since many of its elements appear in other covenant forms, we must distinguish between forms by consideration of the context and purpose of the covenant.

Parity Covenants

Parity covenants are covenants between equals. Great Kings formed relationships with other kings of equal rank by means of parity covenants. In parity
covenants there is full equity between the parties. Each king voluntarily assumes reciprocal obligations. A superior does not impose the oaths.[43]
Mendenhall subdivides this sort of covenant into two classes: those that impose obligations and those that impose no obligation except to keep the
peace.[44] Thus, the parity covenant form involves a continuum of relationships
ranging from friendships to an international peace treaties. The main
identifying feature of the parity covenant form is the mutuality of obligation.

We have a record of the parity covenant/treaty between Hattusili III of
Hatti (ca. 1300 BC) (Hittite) and Ramses II of Egypt (ca. 1250 BC). The sur-
viving record is from the perspective of Ramses' oath but it is reasonable to
assume that Hattusili swore a similar oath. In this document Ramses takes on
himself only the obligations of "good peace and good brotherhood"; none are
laid on Hattusili.[45] We would expect to find similar obligations in Hattusili's
covenant document that he would swear to unilaterally.

Another example of a parity covenant is the treaty between a king of
Hatti and Paddatissu of Kizzuwatna (ca. 1500 BC). This covenant explicitly
lists the separate oaths one after the other:

> [If a subject of the Great King plots against his lord....
> If a subject of Paddatissu plots against his lord....
> [If] the Great [King] sends either his son or his subject to Paddatissu, Paddatissu
> shall not harm him. And if Paddatissu sends either his son or his subject [to] the
> Great King, the Great King shall not harm him....
> [If the population of a settlement] of the Great King.... And if the population of a
> settlement of Paddatissu....[46]

Here again we have the unilateral nature of the covenant form displayed.
Each party unilaterally swears an oath to their respective obligations.

Grant Covenants

Ancient kings bestowed grants of land and privilege on their vassals by
means of covenants. In Babylon *kudurru* stones witnessed royal land grants
that were a type of covenant.[47]   Kline describes the characteristics of the
Babylonian *kudurru*, that were used to establish property rights:

The *kudurru* inscriptions were written on roughly oval shaped stones and on stone tablets, the former serving as public monuments and the latter as permanent private records. They were copied from original deeds on clay tablets, the records of royal grants of land and, occasionally, of related privileges. Along with the boundary description and, usually, the list of witnesses to the transaction copied from the original deed, the *kudurru's* had engraved on them divine symbols and curses against anyone who would contest the title or molest the stone inscription. Other reliefs found on the stones depict in various combinations the figures of the king, the recipient, and a deity. These additional features were clearly intended to place the private property and other rights of the owner under divine protection. The *kudurru* pillar set up in the midst of the property thus confirmed the recipient's title to it and protected his land from encroachment. [48]

Although used to establish property rights, the grant covenant form has broader application. These covenants can also function as royal charters and not merely property guarantees, as Kline notes.[49] Thus, by means of the grant covenant the Great King can establish the rule of his vassal king and grant privileges beyond land.

A Hittite example of a royal charter covenant is the treaty between Suppiluliuma I of Hatti and Niqmaddu II (ca. 1350 BC) of Ugarit:

Thus says His Majesty, Suppiluliuma, Great King, King of Hatti, Hero....

Niqmaddu, king of Ugarit, turned to Suppiluliuma, Great King, writing: "May Your Majesty, Great King, my lord, save me from the hand of my enemy! I am the subject of Your Majesty, Great King, my lord. To my lord's enemy I am hostile, [and] with my lord's friend I am at peace...." The Great King heard these words of Niqmaddu....

Now Suppiluliuma, Great King, King of Hatti, has made the following treaty with Niqmaddu, king of the land of Ugarit, saying ... Furthermore, all of the land of Ugarit, together with its border districts, together with [its] mountains, together with its fields, together with I ...] ...

[... up to Mount] Igari-ayali, together with Mount Hadamgi, [...] itkitiya, Panishtai, Nakhati, Halpi and Mount Nana, Shalma, Gulbata, Zamirti, Sulada, Maraili, and Himulli....

[Now] Suppiluliuma, Great King, King of Hatti, Hero, has deeded by means of a sealed document these [border districts], cities, and mountains to Niqmaddu, [king] of the land of Ugarit, and to his sons and grandsons forever. Now Niqmaddu is hostile to my enemy and at peace with my friend. He has put himself out greatly for My Majesty, Great King, his lord, and has observed the treaty and state of peace with Hatti. Now My Majesty, Great King, has witnessed the loyalty of Niqmaddu....

And whoever alters the words of this treaty tablet will transgress the oath. The Thousand Gods shall be aware (of the perpetrator, beginning with) the Storm-god of Heaven, the Sun-god of Heaven, the Storm-god of Hatti, the Sun-goddess of Arinna,

Hebat of Kizzuwatna, Ishtar of Alatah, Nikkal of Nubanni, and the Storm-god of Mount Hazzi.[50]

The royal charter form of covenant was well known both in Babylon and the Hittite Empire and profoundly influences biblical covenants as well.

Finally, as in the suzerainty covenants, the grant covenant form sometimes employs an historical prologue. Kline notes that the historical prologue of the grant covenant emphasizes the worthiness of the one receiving the grant rather than the beneficence of the suzerain. Kline argues that the existence of historical prologues in *kudurru's* indicates a close interrelationship between them and treaty/covenants.[51] Although the form is similar to the suzerainty covenant, there are subtle differences in the context and purpose of the grant covenant form.

The pattern for the grant covenant form then consists with some variation in the following:

1. The Preamble: Here the grantor is identified.
2. The Historical Prologue: This differs from the suzerainty covenant form in that the deeds of the vassal are emphasized rather than the king. This section explains why the king has been moved to grant a benefit to this vassal.
3. The Provisions of the grant or charter: This section would include not only boundary descriptions, but also a description of privileges and promises concerning succession.
4. The Instructions for Deposition: A public marker such as a *kudurru* stone could accomplish this.
5. The Witnesses: The witnesses may be divine, human, or both.
6. The Curses: The covenant pronounces curses on those who would violate the grant. The covenant promises the vassal both divine and royal protection. This section lacks the parallel emphasis on blessings since the grant is the blessing for services already rendered.

The superior party binds himself in this covenant form, not the inferior. Mendenhall observes that this category of covenant, that he designates a patron covenant, "is a type in which the party in superior position binds himself to some obligation for the benefit of an inferior."[52] McCarthy notes that the Great King is himself bound by oath to the vassal, "The sovereignty of the lesser prince was subordinated and not eliminated. He was not a simple agent of the overlord. The overlord recognized certain rights in the subordinate which he was to respect."[53] In a footnote McCarthy adds that "the treaty texts too testify indirectly to the fact that the sovereign as well as the vassal was bound by oath, for he could be freed from it in certain instances of vassal infidelity and one cannot be freed without first being bound...."[54] In fact, there are no implied conditions. If the King wished to stipulate a condition that would free him from his oath, he had to make it explicitly.[55] Mendenhall explains the grant form of covenant, which he designates the promissory type:

> This type, which is extremely important in secular as well as religious tradition, shows a considerable change from older patterns of behavior and thought, and may well have derived from age-old legal practices. A promissory oath is not primarily intended to establish a new relationship between two parties, but simply guarantees future performance of stipulated obligations. There is thus really one party to this type of covenant, which differs from a vow only in that the vow conditions future stipulated action upon action of deity, whereas the type here termed "promissory oath" is unconditioned.[56]

This form of covenant is also unilateral in nature, the king swearing the oath for the benefit of the vassal. However, even more importantly for the student of biblical prophecy, it is unconditional since it is the sovereign unilateral promise of the Great King.

Type of Covenant	Purpose of Covenant	Oath taken by	Unilateral?	Conditional?
Suzerainty	Imposed by king on a vassal	Inferior	Yes	Yes
Parity	Equals each swear oath of obligation	Equals	Yes	Either
Grant	Give land and/or privileges	Superior	Yes	No

Table 1. Unilateral Nature of Covenants

Summary

In the ancient Near East relationships both political and personal, were formed by means of covenants. A covenant may be defined as *a solemn uni-*

lateral obligation made binding by an oath. The oath is often of a self-maledictory character and may be verbal, symbolic, or both. The main form of covenant is the suzerainty covenant that a Great King imposed on a vassal. The following elements characterize the suzerainty covenant: a preamble, a historical introduction, provisions, deposition, list of divine witnesses, and curses and blessings. The other two main covenant forms derive from the suzerainty covenant: parity and grant covenants. Parity covenants are covenants between equals where both parties swore their individual oath of obligation. Grant covenants are unilateral oaths of the Great King granting unconditionally land and/or privileges to a vassal. Most importantly, we must remember that, in the ancient Near East, all covenants were essentially unilateral (see table 1).

NOTES

1. George E. Mendenhall, "Covenant," *Encyclopaedia Britannica* [book on-line] (n.p.: Britannica.com, Inc., 2001, accessed 3 May 2001); available from http://www.britannica.com/eb/article?eu=117214&tocid=34041; Internet.

2. Frank Moore Cross, *From Epic to Canon* (Baltimore: Johns Hopkins University Press, 1998).

3. George E. Mendenhall and Gary A. Herion, "Covenant," *The Anchor Bible Dictionary* (hereafter referred to as *ABD*), ed. David Noel Freedman, 6 vols. (New York: Doubleday, 1992) 1:1179–202.

4. Ibid.

5. George Ricker Berry, "Covenant, in the Old Testament," *International Standard Bible Encyclopedia* (hereafter referred to as *ISBE*), gen. ed. James Orr, 10 vols. (Peabody, MA: Hendrickson, 1939), in The Master Christian Library v. 8.0 [CD-ROM] (Rio, WI: AGES Software, 2000) 2:1245–46.

6. H. Clay Trumbull, *The Blood Covenant: A Primitive Rite and Its Bearings on Scripture*, 2nd ed. (n.p.: 1893; reprint, Kirkwood, MO: Impact Christian Books, 1975) 4–7.

7. Gleason L. Archer, Jr., "Covenant," *Evangelical Dictionary of Theology* (hereafter referred to as *EvDT*), 2nd ed., ed. Walter A. Elwell (Grand Rapids, MI: Baker, 2001) 299.

8. Moshe Weinfeld, "בְּרִית *bᵉrîth*," *Theological Dictionary of the Old Testament* (hereafter referred to as *TDOT*), ed. G. Johannes Botterweck and Helmer Ringgren, trans. John T. Willis, 12– vols. (Grand Rapids, MI: Eerdmans, 1975–) 2:253–79. See also Ludwig Koehler, Walter Baumgartner, "בְּרִית," *The Hebrew and Aramaic Lexicon of the Old Testament: Study Edition* (hereafter referred to as *HALOT*), trans. M. E. J. Richardson, 2 vols. (Boston: Brill, 2001) 1:157–59.

9. Weinfeld, *TDOT* 2:255.

10. Gordon J. McConville, "בְּרִית," *New International Dictionary of Old Testament Theology & Exegesis* (hereafter referred to as *NIDOTTE*), gen. ed. Willem A. VanGemeren, 5 vols. (Grand Rapids, MI: Zondervan, 1997) 1:747–55.

11. E. Kutsch, "בְּרִית *bᵉrît* obligation," *Theological Lexicon of the Old Testament* (hereafter referred to as *TLOT*), eds. Ernst Jenni, Claus Westermann, trans. Mark E. Biddle from the *Theologisches Handwörterbuch zum Alten Testament*, 3 vols. (Peabody, MA: Hendrickson, 1997) 1:256–66.

12. Kutsch, *TLOT* 1:257.

13. Ibid. Köhler actually thought that the phrase "cut a covenant" derived from the necessity of cutting up the food for a sacrificial meal (Dennis J. McCarthy, *Old Testament Covenant: A Survey of Current Opinions* [Atlanta, GA: John Knox, 1972] 3).

14. Delbert R. Hillers, *Covenant: The History of a Biblical Idea* (Baltimore: The Johns Hopkins University Press, 1969) 28.

15.   J. Arthur Thompson, "Covenant (OT)," *The International Standard Bible Encyclo-pedia* (hereafter referred to as *ISBErev*), rev. ed., gen. ed. Geoffrey W. Bromiley, 4 vols. (Grand Rapids, MI: Eerdmans, 1994) 1:790–93.

16.   Mendenhall, "Covenant," *Encyclopaedia Britannica.*

17.   Gordon P. Hugenberger, *Marriage as a Covenant: Biblical Law and Ethics as Developed from Malachi* (Grand Rapids, MI: Baker, 1994) 194.

18.   Mendenhall, "Covenant," *Encyclopaedia Britannica.*

19.   Gary Beckman, *Hittite Diplomatic Texts*, Writings from the Ancient World: Society of Biblical Literature, ed. Harry A. Hoffner, Jr. (Atlanta, GA: Scholars, 1996) 7:29.

20.   Livingston, *Pentateuch* 154.

21.   Thompson, "Covenant (OT)," *ISBErev* 1:790.

22.   Mendenhall, "Covenant," *Encyclopaedia Britannica.*

23.   Hugenberger 194–95; see also Mendenhall, "Covenant," *ABD* 1:1182. I am reminded of Jesus' saying, "This is My body.... This ... My blood ..." (Luke 22:19–20). If the Last Supper is viewed as a covenant ceremony establishing the new covenant, then this would mean identification not transubstantiation.

24.   H. W. F. Gesenius, *Gesenius' Hebrew and Chaldee Lexicon to the Old Testament Scriptures*, trans. Samuel Prideaux Tregelles (n.p.: 1847; reprint, Grand Rapids, MI: Baker, 1979) 141–42.

25.   James M. Freeman, *Manners and Customs of the Bible: A Complete Guide to the Origin and Significance of Our Time-honored Biblical Tradition* (Plainfield, NJ: Logos, 1972) 86.

26.   Trumbull, *Blood Covenant* 351.

27.   Morroe Berger, *The Arab World Today* (Garden City, NY: Doubleday, 1962) 50–51.

28.   Dennis J. McCarthy, *Treaty and Covenant: A Study in Form in the Ancient Oriental Documents and in the Old Testament*, 2nd ed. (Rome: Biblical Institute Press, 1981) 254.

29.   Mendenhall and Herion, "Covenant," *ABD* 1:1179.

30.   George E. Mendenhall, "Covenant," *The Interpreter's Dictionary of the Bible: An Illustrated Encyclopedia* (hereafter referred to as *IDB*), ed. George Arthur Buttrick, 5 vols. (Nashville, TN: Abingdon, 1962) 1:714–23.

31.   Livingston, *Pentateuch* 153.

32.   Beckman, *Hittite Diplomatic Texts* 7:2.

33.   Ibid. 7.2–3.

34.   Ibid. 7:55, no. 8.1.

35.   Ibid. no. 8.2–4.

36.   Ibid. 7:55–6, no. 8.5.

37.   Ibid. 7:55, no. 8.7–8.

38.   Ibid. 7:47, no. 6B.8.

39.   Ibid. 7:58–9, no. 8.16–20.

40.   Ibid. 7:59, no. 8.21.

41. Ibid. no. 8.22.
42. Mendenhall, "Covenant," *IDB* 1:714–15 and Mendenhall and Herion, "Covenant," *ABD* 1:1180–82.
43. Beckman, *Hittite Diplomatic Texts* 7:4.
44. Mendenhall, "Covenant," *IDB* 1:717.
45. Beckman, *Hittite Diplomatic Texts* 7:92, no. 15.4, 5.
46. Ibid. 7:12, no. 1.1–5.
47. Kline, *Structure* 31.
48. Ibid. 32.
49. Ibid. 32–33.
50. Beckman, *Hittite Diplomatic Texts* 7:30–2, 4.1–7.
51. Kline, *Structure* 34.
52. Mendenhall, "Covenant," *IDB* 1:717.
53. McCarthy, *Treaty* 128.
54. Ibid. 128–29.
55. Beckman, *Hittite Diplomatic Texts* 7:29.
56. Mendenhall, "Covenant," *IDB* 1:717.

CHAPTER THREE

✦ Biblical Covenants

Covenant Terminology

Covenant

The main word for covenant in the OT is בְּרִית. בְּרִית is used two hundred eighty-six times from the first use in Gen 6:18 to the last in Mal 3:1.[1] The Scriptures use בְּרִית for divine covenants, human covenants, and even promises made to oneself.[2] As I have indicated, an ancient Near Eastern covenant is defined as *a solemn unilateral obligation made binding by an oath*.[3] The oath is often of a self-maledictory character and may be verbal, symbolic or both. Brown, Driver, and Briggs define בְּרִית as a *"pact, compact, covenant."*[4] This definition emphasizes the treaty aspect but does not do justice to the unilateral oath aspect of covenants. As discussed above, it is preferable to define בְּרִית, as Archer does, as an "obligation."[5] Weinfeld indicates that בְּרִית should be associated with the Akkadian *birītu* ("clasp," "fetter.").[6] In Ezek 20:37 a covenant relationship is called מָסֹרֶת הַבְּרִית ("the bond of the covenant"). Therefore, as in other ancient Near Eastern cultures, a covenant in the Scriptures is a binding obligation.

Although covenants are a source of obligation, they are not contracts. Daniel J. Elazar explains that

> the moral commitment supporting a covenant is undergirded by a transcendent power.... unlike contracts which are private agreements between private parties to further the respective interests of each. In a contract, each side pursues his own advantage and attempts to limit what he has to give the other party(s) to the contract to make it work. Moreover, when the advantage disappears, it is legitimate for the parties to the contract to dissolve it.[7]

Weinfeld notes that

the original meaning of the Heb. *berith* (as well as of Akk. *riksu* and Hitt. *išhiul)* is not "agreement or settlement between two parties," as is commonly argued. *berith* implies first and foremost the notion of "imposition," "liability," or "obligation," as might be learned from the "bond" etymology discussed above. Thus we find that the *berith* is commanded *(tsivvah beritho,* "he has commanded his covenant," Ps. 111:9; Jgs. 2:20), which certainly cannot be said about a mutual agreement.[8]

Because the basis for the covenant is an oath, each individual is responsible for what they have sworn. The lack of performance on the part of the other party does not release the first party from their obligation unless specifically stipulated. This confirms the unilateral nature of the covenant form.

A rich vocabulary exists for covenant activities in the OT. The main technical phrase for making a covenant is כָּרַת בְּרִית ("to cut a covenant").[9] The earliest instance in Genesis sheds light on the subsequent uses. Genesis 15:10 relates that Abraham took the animals for the sacrifice and "cut them in two, and laid each half opposite the other." The record summarizes, "On that day the LORD made a covenant with Abram (כָּרַת יְהוָֹה אֶת־אַבְרָם בְּרִית)" (Gen 15:18). This is reminiscent of the covenant of Ashurnirari V and Mati'ilu.[10] The parties of the covenant are identified with the animals and invite the animals' fate to be their own, if they violate their oaths. The cutting in half of the sacrificial animals forms the basis for the phrase כָּרַת בְּרִית ("cut a covenant"). Eventually, כָּרַת ("cut") came to be used even without בְּרִית to mean "to make a covenant" (1 Sam 22:8).

Some see significance in the prepositions used with כָּרַת. F. C. Fensham asserts that, when כָּרַת is used with the prepositions לְ or עִם, it indicates a covenant contracted by a superior.[11] Kutsch has an even more elaborate scheme.[12] McCarthy sees less precision in the use of the Hebrew prepositions than Kutsch:

> KUTSCH works out a scheme where *krt bᵉrit* with *ʾet* or *ᶜim* must mean "impose a bond upon another," and with *lᵉ-* "bind oneself to another," while with *ûbên ... ûbên* it means "bind one another." This is neat and satisfying. It is also misleading in many cases. In general it is dangerous to fix hard and fast meanings to prepositions. Here it is impossible. Even the use of *bên,* which is probably the most consistent, shows irregularities (compare the equation with *ʾet* in I Kgs 15,19 and with *ᶜim* in 2 Kgs 11,17 and 2 Chron 23,3), while *ᶜim* and *ʾet* are not carefully distinguished (cf. Gen 26,28 [*ᶜim* parallel with *bên*]; I Kgs 20,34 [MT]: one imposes a *bᵉrit* on another with *lᵉ-*; 2 Kgs 11,4: *lᵉ-* involves coming to terms, making a deal; Hos 12,2: *ᶜim* involves submitting oneself to another.[13]

While there might be some basis to Fensham and Kutsch's approach,

McCarthy's critique is valid. The many exceptions make too strong a conclusion unwise. As always, the context must be determinative.

New covenants can be established or old covenants strengthened. In Deut 8:18 Yahweh is said to "cause His covenant to stand (הָקִים אֶת־בְּרִיתוֹ)." God told Noah that the rainbow was the "sign of the covenant which I give (נֹתֵן אוֹת־הַבְּרִית אֲשֶׁר־אֲנִי)" (Gen 9:12). Covenants are established (שָׂם בְּרִית) (Gen 17:19), entered into (עָבַר בִּבְרִית)[14] and (בוֹא בִּבְרִית)[15], commanded (צִוָּה בְרִית)[16]), and raised up (נָשָׂא בְרִית) (Ps 50:16). The coming Roman prince will "cause a covenant to be strengthened (הִגְבִּיר בְּרִית)" (Dan 9:27). This suggests the renewal of an already existing covenant.

There is a great deal of flexibility in the biblical uses of covenant. McConville observes that covenants between human parties include friendship, treaties between rulers or powerful individuals, treaties in which the more powerful dictate terms to the weaker, treaties where the weaker party seeks terms, and marriage.[17] McCarthy agrees that there is variety in ancient Near Eastern covenants. However, he sees a generalized, but not rigid, uniformity. The two essentials are the obligations and the divine sanctions.[18]

The LXX consistently translates בְּרִית with διαθήκη. The NT follows that translation with διαθήκη being used thirty-three times. Adolf Deissmann, although his understanding of the term "covenant" was that of a bilateral agreement, asserts the unilateral nature of διαθήκη:

> Now as the new texts help us generally to reconstruct Hellenistic family law and the law of inheritance, so in particular our knowledge of Hellenistic wills has been wonderfully increased by a number of originals on stone or papyrus. There is ample material to back me in the statement that no one in the Mediterranean world in the first century A.D. would have thought of finding in the word διαθήκη the idea of "covenant." St. Paul would not, and in fact did not. To St. Paul the word meant what it meant in his Greek Old Testament, "a unilateral enactment," in particular "a will or testament." This one point concerns more than the merely superficial question whether we are to write "New Testament" or "New Covenant" on the title-page of the sacred volume; it becomes ultimately the great question of all religious history: a religion of grace, or a religion of works? It involves the alternative, was Pauline Christianity Augustinian or Pelagian?[19]

Walter Bauer, F. W. Danker, W. F. Arndt, and F. W. Gingrich also maintain that διαθήκη, as a translation of בְּרִית, is "the declaration of one person's will, not the result of an agreement betw[een] two parties, like a compact or contract."[20] A διαθήκη is a unilateral disposition, but is it a testament or a covenant?

A will or testament is a διαθήκη because it is a unilateral enactment. However, a will is not the only kind of διαθήκη. Moulton and Milligan explain that, although universally used in the papyri and inscriptions to mean "testament" or "will," διαθήκη is used in place of συνθήκη ("compact"), since διαθήκη is best described as a *"disposito*, an 'arrangement' made by one party with plenary power, which the other party may accept or reject, but cannot alter." Although they acknowledge the possibility of a play on words, the fact that God and humankind are not on equal terms makes διαθήκη the perfect term.[21] Robertson strongly objects to the "last will and testament" concept. He explains that a last will and testament assumes an inevitable death. However, a covenant presents the option of life or death. Only the covenant violator need die. Robertson insists that Christ's death must be understood in a covenantal context. He sees Christ's death as a substitutionary sacrifice in place of the covenant breaker. Humankind is doomed to death because of covenant violations and Christ died in our place. In a last will and testament, the testator dies for himself.[22] These distinctions are convincing that it is best to see Christ's death in a covenantal way. J. Barton Payne notes the appropriateness of διαθήκη to describe God's sovereign disposition, as opposed to συνθήκη. He observes that salvation comes from a behest from of covenant.[23] Merrill F. Unger and William White contend that the unilateral nature of the covenant is the reason for the choice of διαθήκη, since Israel did not mutually agree on terms with God.[24] Although the Greek term adds the possibility of some word play on will or testament, the central sense of a unilateral commitment is prominent.

Other terms are used briefly for covenant. As part of the covenant renewal in Neh 9–10, "making a binding agreement (כֹּרְתִים אֲמָנָה)" (Neh 9:38 NIV) is mentioned. We should note the use of כָּרַת ("to cut") normally found with בְּרִית in this verse. McConville defines אֲמָנָה as "covenant, binding agreement...."[25] In Isa 28:15, 18 the terms חֹזֶה and חָזוּת are used. McConville observes that these both have meanings associated with seeing. However, in Isa 28:15, 18 they are used in parallel with בְּרִית.[26] None of these instances modifies our basic understanding of covenant as *a solemn unilateral obligation made binding by an oath.*

Oath

The *sine qua non* of a covenant is the oath. As indicated, a covenant is *a sol-*

emn unilateral obligation made binding by an oath. Therefore, we would expect that the oath would be a major component of the covenant in biblical usage. Indeed, this is the case. The ancients took oaths much more seriously than we do today. As Philo (15 BC–AD 50) explains that

> an oath is nothing else but the testimony of God invoked in a matter which is a subject of doubt, and to invoke God to witness a statement which is not true is the most impious of all things.
>
> For a man who does this, is all but saying in plain words (even though he hold his peace), "I am using thee as a veil for my iniquity; do thou co-operate with me, who am ashamed to appear openly to be behaving unjustly. For though I am doing wrong, I am anxious not to be accounted wicked, but thou canst be indifferent to thy reputation with the multitude, having no regard to being well spoken of." But to say or imagine such things as these is most impious, for not only would God, who is free from all participation in wickedness, but even any father or any stranger, provided he were not utterly devoid of all virtue, would be indignant if he were addressed in such a way as this.
>
> A man, therefore, as I have said, must be sure and give effect to all oaths which are taken for honourable and desirable objects, for the due establishment of private or public objects of importance, under the guidance of wisdom, and justice, and holiness.[27]

Again, Philo states that "an oath is the calling of God to give his testimony concerning the matters which are in doubt; and it is a most impious thing to invoke God to be witness to a lie."[28] Any exceptions to the oath had to be explicit. Abraham's servant required an escape clause when he swore an oath to Abraham (Gen 24:5, 8). The oath, taken with the full expectation that God would punish the oath-breaker, was foundational to covenant making.

The Hebrew word אָלָה ("swear," "oath," or "curse"[29]) appears in obvious parallel to בְּרִית (Gen 26:28; Ezek 16:59; 17:13–19).[30] Robert P. Gordon defines the *qal* of אָלָה as "swear, curse," the *hipʿil* as "put under oath," and the noun form as "oath, curse." He explains that the אָלָה is a curse that binds one to an obligation.[31] The same verbs are used with אָלָה as with בְּרִית, "enter into" (עָבַר),[32] and "cut" (כָּרַת).[33] Don Garlington comments on the connection between the concepts of covenant and oath:

> But notwithstanding the multiplicity of the oaths, the "glue" which held them all together was the loyal Israelite's determination to keep Yahweh's covenant. The oaths were thus emblems of the righteous person's commitment to maintain faith with his God. This is why "oath" (שבועה and אלה) could be equated with "covenant" (e.g., Gen 26:3, 28; Josh 9:20; 2 Chr 15:15; Neh 6:18; Ezek 17:13, 16, 18–19) and why Israel's covenant with God involved the people in oath-like sanctions (e.g., Le-

viticus 26 and Deuteronomy 27–28), even though the covenant stipulations are in-
frequently termed an "oath" as such (2 Chr 15:12–15; Neh 10:30). The oath, in point
of fact, was a vehicle of confessing the one God of Israel: "You shall fear the Lord
your God; you shall serve him, and swear by his name" (Deut 6:13); and: "You shall
fear the Lord your God; you shall serve him and cleave to him, and by his name you
shall swear" (Deut 10:20).

So closely associated was the oath with the service of God that swearing by
him could be used as a synonym for adhering to and trusting in him (Ps 63:12; Isa
19:18; 48:1; Jer 44:26; Zeph 1:5).[34]

This is a case of synecdoche in that the oath, a crucial part of the covenant,
came to refer to the entire covenant.

We see the same phenomenon with the other Hebrew terms for oath: the
verb שָׁבַע and the noun שְׁבוּעָה (שְׁבָעָה). T. W. Cartledge defines שָׁבַע in the *nipᶜal*
as "swear, make an oath, bind oneself by an oath," in the *hipᶜil* as "cause to
swear, adjure," and the noun שְׁבוּעָה as simply "oath." He explains that the OT
oath is a promise fortified by adding a curse that appeals to a deity to enforce
the curse. Cartledge cites 1 Sam 3:17, "May God do so to you, and more
also, if you hide anything from me of all the words that He spoke to you,"
and 2 Kgs 6:31, "May God do so to me and more also, if the head of Elisha
the son of Shaphat remains on him today," as typical examples of the oath
formula. He observes that the initial clause ("May God do so to you, and
more ...") came over time to be understood and was occasionally omitted
(e.g., Gen 14:23; Num 14:23; 1 Sam 3:14; 19:6; 2 Kgs 2:2; 3:14; Job 6:28; Ps
132:3–4; Isa 22:14). This has been taken as an emphatic negative in translation, which obscures the nature of the oath. Also, as Cartledge noted, God's
promises are equivalent to oaths and, since there is no higher power, God
swears by Himself (Ps 89:35; Isa 45:23; 62:8; Jer 44:26; 49:13; 51:14).
Cartledge explains that, although oaths appear to be conditional, actually the
curse is the conditional part of the statement. There is no question of the intent of the promisor to fulfill his word.[35] Therefore, it should clearly understood that the curses are conditional, not the obligations. Here also the oath
stands for the entire process of covenanting.

In the LXX ἀρά ("wish, prayer, curse"[36]) normally translates אָלָה (twenty-
one times[37] out of thirty-four uses).[38] The verbal form ἀράομαι ("to invoke
evil on someone, wish evil, imprecate"[39]) is used three times (Judg 17:2; 1
Kgs 8:31; 2 Chr 6:22) and the related term κατάρα ("supernatural curse, wish
evil on someone, curse, imprecation"[40]) is used twice (Jer 44:12; Dan 9:11).
Three times אָלָה is not translated in the LXX (Jer 23:10; 29:18; Ezek 16:59).

אָלָה is translated once by ὅρκος ("oath"⁴¹—Prov 29:24), twice by ὁρκισμός ("administration of an oath"⁴²—Gen 24:41; Lev 5:1), once by ὁρκωμοσία ("taking of an oath, swearing, confirmation by oath, an oath"⁴³—Ezek 17:18), and once by λόγος ("word"—2 Chr 34:24). Ἀρά is used only once in the NT (Rom 3:14) with the sense of "curse." The Greek word κατάρα ("supernatural curse, wish evil on someone, curse, imprecation") is used five times (Gal 3:10, 13; Heb 6:8; Jas 3:10; 2 Pet 2:14). The verb ἀράομαι is not used in the NT. Significantly, the ἀρά family of words are never used in the LXX to translate the Hebrew words שָׁבַע, שְׁבוּעָה, and שְׁבָעָה with their more positive connotations. As with the Hebrew אָלָה, although ἀρά means "oath" and by extension "covenant," the emphasis is on the curse aspect of the oath and not the blessing.

In the LXX שָׁבַע is translated most often by the verb ὀμνύω (ὄμνυμι) (literally "grasping a sacred object," "swear, affirm, confirm by an oath"⁴⁴) one hundred forty-three of one hundred seventy-eight instances.⁴⁵ Next in frequency (twenty-five times)⁴⁶ is the Greek verb ὁρκίζω ("cause to swear an oath, put someone under oath, solemnly command, adjure"⁴⁷). The words ἐξορκίζω ("cause to swear, adjure, put under oath"⁴⁸—Gen 24:3); ἀποκρίνομαι ("answer"—1 Sam 20:3); λέγω ("speak"—Isa 14:24); and ἐπίορκος ("one who violates his oath, perjured, swearing falsely"⁴⁹—Zech 5:3) are only used once each. The LXX does not translate שָׁבַע on six occasions (Josh 2:17, 20; 6:22; 23:7; 1 Kgs 18:10; Ezek 21:23). The word ὄμνυμι ("swear") is used in conjunction with ὅρκος ("oath"—Num 30:3; Lev 5:4; 2 Chr 15:15; Eccl 9:2; Jer 11:5) and ὁρκίζω ("cause to swear an oath, put someone under oath, solemnly command, adjure"—Ezra 10:5). The related term ὁρκισμός ("administration of an oath") is used with ὄμνυμι ("swear") in Gen 21:31 and 26:3. In fact, Gen 21:31 in the LXX reads, "Therefore he named the name of that place, The Well of the Oath (Φρέαρ ὁρκισμοῦ), for there they both swore (ἐκεῖ ὤμοσαν)."⁵⁰ It would appear that the action of both the verbs ὁρκίζω and ὄμνυμι result in an ὅρκος ("oath").

The LXX translates שְׁבוּעָה (שְׁבָעָה) as ὅρκος in most cases (twenty-five of thirty).⁵¹ The LXX does not translate שְׁבוּעָה (שְׁבָעָה) in Ezek 21:28 and Hab 3:9. It is translated by ὁρκισμός ("administration of an oath") in Gen 21:31, ἔνορκος ("bound by oath"⁵²) in Neh 6:18, and πλησμονή ("satisfaction, gratification"⁵³) in Isa. 65:15. In the NT ὅρκος, ὁρκίζω, and ὁρκωμοσία are used with the sense of "swearing an oath" (Matt 5:33; 14:7, 9; 26:72; Mk 5:7; 6:26; Luke 1:73; Acts 2:30; 19:13; Heb 6:16–17; 7:20, 21, 28; Jas 5:12).

Therefore, there are two shades of meaning that we can discern in the terminology of the oath. The Hebrew אָלָה and the Greek ἀρά family of terms mainly represent the curse or sanction aspect of the oath. The Hebrew שָׁבַע family of terms, normally translated by the Greek ὄμνυμι or the ὁρκίζω family of words, focus more on the oath itself. It is interesting that, although curse became synonymous with oath and covenant, blessing did not. The punishment is more in view than the reward.

Promise

The blessing aspect of the covenant relates to the concept of promise. Walter C. Kaiser remarks that

> no other theme provides such a comprehensive insight into the plan and program of our Lord in both testaments as the "promise." Beginning with the promise of a victorious "seed" in Genesis 3:15, the content of this single, all encompassing theme builds. A constellation of terms is used in the Old Testament to teach that the promise is God's "word," "blessing," and "oath," to his chosen "seed," while the New Testament focuses the now enlarged picture by limiting the terminology to that of God's "promise," *epangelia*. Both testaments can also depict the promise doctrine under one of the most ubiquitous formulas in the canon: "I will be your God, you shall be my people, and I will dwell in the midst of you."[54]

Biblical Hebrew seems to lack a specific word for "promise." In the NASB "promise" usually translates דָּבָר ("a word"—e.g., 1 Kgs 8:56; 2 Chr 1:9; Hag 2:5) or אָמַר ("a saying"—e.g., Ps 77:8). Haggai 2:5 actually uses דָּבָר with כָּרַת, אֶת־הַדָּבָר אֲשֶׁר־כָּרַתִּי ("the promise which I made" or "the word that I covenanted" ASV). The LXX normally uses λόγος or ῥῆμα in these cases. The Hebrew word בְּרָכָה ("a blessing") is used often in a covenantal context (e.g., Deut 11:26, "See, I am setting before you today a blessing and a curse"). The LXX normally translates בְּרָכָה by εὐλογία ("the act or benefit of blessing"[55]). In the NT εὐλογία is used of covenant blessings in 1 Cor 10:16; Gal 3:14; Heb 12:17.

The NT Greek word for "promise" is ἐπαγγελία ("declaration to do someth[ing] with implication of obligation to carry out what is stated, *promise, pledge, offer*"[56]). It is found mostly in Paul's letters (twenty-five references), Hebrews (thirteen references), Luke (nine references), two references in Peter's letters, and one in 1 John. In the LXX it is used only three times. The two instances (Ps 55:9; Amos 9:6) that refer to God's promise do not actually translate any Hebrew words. The other instance (Esth 4:7) refers to a human promise and translates אָמַר. In the NT ἐπαγγελία refers to all the covenants in general (Acts 13:32; Rom 9:4; 15:8; 2 Cor 1:20), the Abrahamic covenant (Acts 7:17; Rom 4:13–14, 16, 20; 9:8–9; Gal 3:16–29; 4:23, 28; Eph 3:6; Heb 4:1; 6:12, 15, 17; 7:6; 11:9, 13, 17), the Davidic covenant (Acts 13:23), and the new covenant (Heb 8:6; 9:15; 1 John 2:25). In Gal 3:17 and Eph 2:12 ἐπαγγελία is equated with διαθήκη. Acts 7:17 is interesting in that ὁ χρόνος τῆς ἐπαγγελίας ("time of the promise") refers to the Abrahamic covenant's promise of the Exodus. However, χρόνος in other contexts is often used in a dispensational sense (Acts 1:7; 3:21; 17:30; Gal 4:4; 1 Thess 5:1; 1 Pet 1:13; Jude 1:18). This hints at the connection we shall see later between the covenants and the dispensations.

Testimony

The Hebrew word, normally translated "testimony" (עֵדֻת/עֵדָת) is derived from עֵד ("witness"). Brown, Driver, and Briggs define עֵדוּת as a testimony and note that the testimony is the law, i.e., covenant stipulations.[57] Carl Schultz notes that

> this word is always used in reference to the testimony of God. It is most frequently connected with the tabernacle (Exo 38:21; Num 1:50, 53), resulting in the expression "tabernacle of the testimony," and with the ark (Exo 25:22; Exo 26:33, 34; Exo 30:6, 26), resulting in the phrase "ark of the testimony." In fact in several instances this word stands alone to indicate the ark (Exo 16:34; Exo 27:21; Exo 30:36; Lev 16:13). Moses was instructed to put the testimony in ("before," Exo 16:34; Exo 27:21) the ark (Exo 25:21) and he did so (Exo 40:20; cf. Heb 9:4). Here the meaning is made quite clear. It designates the two tables of stone upon which the Ten Words (commandments) were written (Exo 24:12; Exo 31:18; Exo 32:15; Exo 34:29). These two tables represented God's covenant with Israel (Exo 34:27, 28) and as such are called the "tables of the covenant" (Deut 9:9; Deut 11:15).[58]

Peter Enns also takes עֵדוּת to be the written record of the covenant stipulations. He agrees with Hillers that it would be better translated "part" or "covenant" than "testimony."[59] The word עֵדוּת is found fifty-seven times in the OT.[60] The first thirty-three instances are in the Pentateuch and refer to the actual tablets deposited in the ark of the covenant. The meaning of עֵדוּת evolved so that by synecdoche in the book of Psalms it is parallel with תּוֹרָה ("law"—Ps 19.7; 78.5; 119:14, 31, 36, 88, 99, 111, 129, 144, 157). Therefore, עֵדוּת refers to the stipulations of a covenant that are engraved on tablets and deposited for a testimony in a holy place under divine oversight.[61]

Apparently, other objects are used as a witness in addition to engraved tablets. Abraham made a gift of seven lambs to Abimelech for a testimony in Gen 21:30. In Gen 31:45–52 Jacob and Laban use a heap of stones as a testimony to their covenant. Joshua 8:30–35 also uses stones for a similar testimony. Ruth 4:7 mentions the gift of a sandal as a legal testimony, "Now this was *the custom* in former times in Israel concerning the redemption and the exchange *of land* to confirm any matter: a man removed his sandal and gave it to another; and this was the *manner of* attestation in Israel (הַתְּעוּדָה בְּיִשְׂרָאֵל וְזֹאת)" (Ruth 4:7).

The LXX consistently translates עֵדוּת as μαρτύριον ("an objective act, circumstance, or statement which serves as a means of proof *evidence, testimony, witness*"[62]). A. A. Trites notes that

> it is immediately apparent in the LXX that the commonest member of the word-group is the noun *martyrion* (in total over 290 instances), by far the greater part of these cases being found in Exod. and Num., and 45 in Lev. Here as in some passages in the Chronicler (e.g. 1 Chr. 9:21; 23:32; 2 Chr. 5:5; 24:6), it may refer to the two tablets with the Sinaitic commandments (*dyo plakes tou martyriou*, Exod. 31:18; 32:15). It is also frequently used of the *skēnē tou martyriou*, the tent of the testimony (AV, "the tabernacle of the congregation"; Exod. 29:4, 10 f. ; 40:2 ff. ; Lev. 4:4 ff. ; Num. 4:25 ff. ; cf. also the *kibōtos tou martyriou*, the box or ark of the testimony, Exod. 40:3; 5:21; Lev. 16:2; Num. 4:5). *Martyrion* has here a sense which accords with its later usage in cl. Gk., namely that of the piece of evidence which calls to mind a particular event, or of the deeds (such as the founding of the covenant or of the Law).[63]

Both in Greek and in Hebrew, the concept of testimony is fundamentally legal. The testimony serves as a reminder and evidence of covenant obligation.

Law

The ancient Near Eastern covenant contained stipulations that the party or parties were bound by oath to perform. In biblical terminology these stipulations were the law. The main Hebrew term for "law" is תּוֹרָה ("direction, instruction, law"[64]). The Hebrew word תּוֹרָה is derived from יָרָה ("to teach"). John E. Hartley explains the connection between instruction and stipulation in the term תּוֹרָה:

> The word *tôrâ* means basically "teaching" whether it is the wise man instructing his son or God instructing Israel…. So too God, motivated by love, reveals to

man basic insight into how to live with each other and how to approach God. Through the law God shows his interest in all aspects of man's life which is to be lived under his direction and care. Law of God stands parallel to word of the Lord to signify that law is the revelation of God's will (e.g. Isa 1:10)....

Covenant precedes law; and the law was given only to the nation which had entered into covenant with God.... The law specifically is the stipulations of the covenant. But in the broad sense of law, namely God's teaching, covenant plays the central part. Law and covenant may parallel one another (e.g. Psa 78:10). Since they are so closely tied together, to break one is to break both.[65]

G. Liedke and C. Petersen note that תּוֹרָה occurs in a non-theological sense mainly in Proverbs and Job.[66] After considering these few exceptions, they conclude that in all other texts תּוֹרָה is used in a theological context.[67] Enns sees תּוֹרָה as a divine standard of conduct.[68] The LXX normally (two hundred of two hundred twenty three instances) translates תּוֹרָה as νόμος ("law, norm"). Therefore, תּוֹרָה is mainly to be seen as the entirety of the covenant stipulations.

Most scholars divide the law into two broad categories: case law and apodictic law. Apodictic law, sometimes referred to as categoric law, is couched in terms of "thou shalt" or "thou shalt not" whereas case law assumes the form of "if X, then Y." The Ten Commandments are all in the form of apodictic law but the remainder of the law of Moses is a mixture of case law and apodictic law. R. A. Cole notes that case law is common in Mesopotamian law codes.[69]

The OT employs a number of synonyms for law. J. A. Motyer explains:

With the law so central to life, it is understandable that the OT should develop a rich legal vocabulary. In logical order, the first word descriptive of God's law is "testimonies" (‘ēdâ, e.g., Ps. 119:2 KJV). In his law the Lord has "testified" regarding himself and his requirements. This self-revelation was given in "teaching" (tôrâ, e.g., Ps. 119:1), such as a loving parent would impart (cf., e.g., Prov. 3:1; 6:20). Once given, the teaching is a "word" (dābār, e.g., Ps. 119:28) to live by, an intelligible body of truth to be pondered and applied. But the Lord's testimony is also imperative, taking the form of "statute" (ḥōq, a permanent enactment, e.g., Ps. 119:5 KJV), "judgment" (mišpāṭ, authoritative decision, e.g., Ps. 119:7), "precept" (piqqûd, e.g., Ps. 119:4), and "commandment" (miṣwâ, e.g., Ps. 119:10), applying the law to the details of life. As a whole, God's law is a "way" (derek, e.g., Ps. 119:37 KJV) or characteristic lifestyle.[70]

The richness of the OT vocabulary for "law" shows the importance of the concept.

The word חק is closely related to the concept of covenant.[71] Jack P. Lewis explains that the Hebrew term חק

> is from the root ḥāqaq which means "to scratch" or "to engrave," hence "to write." It occurs 128 times, and its feminine counterpart ḥuqqâ occurs 102 times.
>
> It was a common practice among the ancients to engrave laws upon slabs of stone or metal and to set them up in a public place (e.g. the code of Hammurabi, engraved on diorite stone). But this root is not limited to the writing of laws on stone. The LXX chiefly used three words to render ḥōq prostagma "order" or "injunction," dikaiōma "regulation" or "requirement," and nomimon "commandment." The use of ḥōq in Qumran is similar to that in the OT.
>
> ḥōq occurs in sequences with other words for law: dᵉbārîm (words), tôrâ (law), mishpāṭ (judgment), ᶜēdût (testimony), and miṣwâ (commandment). These words are used almost indiscriminately. In a few cases ḥōq and mishpāṭ are used as if intended to summarize two kinds of Israelite law (Exo 15:25; Josh 24:25; Ezr 7:10). But efforts to distinguish clearly between their connotations have not been entirely successful. Albrecht Alt has suggested such a distinction in his categories of casuistic and apodictic laws. But he admits that ḥōq is not limited to the apodictic form.[72]

Liedke agrees with Alt that חק originally designated apodictic law.[73] Ringgren claims that חק is the result of the action of a superior that affects an inferior. However, he disagrees with Liedke that מִשְׁפָּט is used for case law and חק for apodictic law.[74] H. Ringgren notes that חק is commonly seen as referring to cultic law rather than civil. However, in the final analysis, Ringgren concludes that the distinction between חק and מִשְׁפָּט was lost.[75] Enns argues that חק is a more generic term for law.[76] From the above it would appear that, while it originally referred to the literal engraving on the tablets that witnessed to a covenant (e.g., Jer 32:11), חק became a generic term for law.

The LXX normally (fifty-two instances) translates חק as δικαίωμα ("ordinance, regulation, commandment"[77]), πρόσταγμα ("an official directive, order, command(ment), injunction"[78]—thirty-eight instances), or νόμιμος ("constitutional or statutory legal system, law"[79]—eighteen cases). The Greek word νόμος ("law") is used four times (Lev 6:22; Josh 24:25; Neh 10:29; Jer 31:36), γράφω ("write"—Isa 10:1), and ὅριον ("boundary"—Job 38:10; Jer 5:22) are both used twice. The words συντάξις ("a covenant, previous arrangement"[80]—Exod 5:14), δόμα ("gift"—Gen 14:22), ἐντολή ("command"[81]—Deut 16:12), ἐξικνέομαι ("to reach, arrive at"[82]—Judg 5:15), μαρτύριον ("evidence"—2 Kgs 17:15), χρόνος ("time"—Job 14:5), ἔνταλμα ("commandment"[83]—Job 23:12), αὐτάρκης ("content, self-sufficient"[84]—Prov 30:8), and ἔργον ("work"—Prov 31:15) are used once each. The LXX does not translate חֹק on seven occasions. The variety that exists in the Greek translation of חֹק reinforces the conclusion that חֹק became a generic term for legal decrees.

As indicated above, the word מִשְׁפָּט ("judgment," "sentence," "decision"[85]) probably refers to the concept of case law. B. Johnson cautiously suggests that the basic meaning of מִשְׁפָּט is decision making.[86] Enns contends that מִשְׁפָּט has definite judicial connotations and is most often concerned with dispute resolution.[87] Liedke considers מִשְׁפָּט to describe case law and case law to be derived from the arbitration process.[88] Robert D. Culver explains that ancient Israel's concept of judging encompassed more than mere judicial functions, including all rule and governance.[89] The concept of מִשְׁפָּט then includes both judicial decisions and administrative regulations that apply the stipulations of a covenant.

The LXX normally translates מִשְׁפָּט by κρίμα ("dispute, lawsuit, decision, decree, judging, judgment, judicial verdict"[90]—one hundred fifty one times) or κρίσις ("judging, judgment"[91]—one hundred and thirty seven instances). It is translated as δικαίωμα ("ordinance, regulation, commandment") in sixty-three cases and δίκαιος ("*upright, just, fair*"[92]—Prov 16:33; 21:7; 29:4, 26). Outside of these terms, other terms are used in only twenty-eight cases: σύγκρισις ("decision"[93]—nine times), πρόσταγμα ("order, commandment, injunction"—seven instances), καθήκω ("*it is fitting* or *proper*"[94]—four times), συντάξις ("a previous arrangement"—three instances), διάταξις ("*command, ... testamentary disposition, compact*"[95]—twice), ἀρχὴ ("an authority figure who initiates activity or process, *ruler, authority*.... the sphere of one's official activity, *rule office ... domain, sphere of influence*"[96]—once), ἐθισμός ("*accustoming, habituation*"[97]—once), and δικαίωσις ("*justification, vindication, acquittal*"[98]—once). As with the Hebrew, so also the Greek terminology also has a judicial cast.

The term מִצְוָה ("*charge, command*"[99]) brings to mind the concept of apodictic law. Liedke notes that מִצְוָה involves both commands ("thou shalt") and prohibitions ("thou shalt not").[100] Thus, the essence of מִצְוָה is command and is couched in apodictic terms of "thou shalt" or "thou shalt not."

The LXX overwhelmingly (one hundred fifty-four instances out of one hundred eighty-one) translates מִצְוָה by ἐντολή ("command"). The related terms ἐντέλλω ("*command, order, give orders*"[101]) and ἔνταλμα ("commandment") are used twice each. The Greek word πρόσταγμα ("order, commandment, injunction") is used six times, and its related verb, προστάσσω ("to issue an official directive or make a determination, *command, order, give in-structions, determine*"[102]) is used once. The word δικαίωμα ("ordinance, regu-lation, commandment") is used twice. The unusual word θεσμός (*"that which is laid down, law, ordinance"*[103]) is used once. The remaining terms concern speech: λέγω ("to speak"—three cases), λόγος ("word"—three cases), ῥῆμα ("saying"—three cases), and φωνή ("voice"—once). The LXX does not translate מִצְוָה on two occasions. The LXX supports the understanding of מִצְוָה as command and therefore apodictic law.

The word פִּקּוּד ("precept, ... *thing appointed, charge*"[104]) is used exclu-sively in the Psalms. Victor P. Hamilton defines פִּקּוּד as a general term for God given responsibilities.[105] Enns agrees that it is a general term for God's commands.[106] The LXX translates פִּקּוּד by ἐντολή ("command"—eighteen of twenty-four uses) and δικαίωμα ("ordinance, regulation, commandment"—six times).

There are several shades of meaning in the vocabulary of the law. The word עֵדוּת calls to mind the actual tablets that the covenant was inscribed on. That inscription was expressed by חקק. The inscribed tablets record the cove-nant stipulations as a whole (תּוֹרָה) consisting of covenant obligations (פִּקּוּד). Those obligations could be in apodictic form (מִצְוָה) or case law (מִשְׁפָּט) (see figure 1). Caution should be exercised in interpreting these terms, since, by means of synecdoche, any of them could be used for the entire law. This ap-pears to be especially the case in Psalms. Therefore, one should be both aware of and careful concerning the connotations of these legal terms (see table 2).

Since the term "law" refers to the stipulations of a covenant, it is a much broader term than it is normally taken to be. For example, Jer 31:33 reads, "'But this is the covenant which I will make with the house of Israel after those days,' declares the LORD, 'I will put My law within them and on their heart I will write it'." The term "law" in this context need not be equated with the Mosaic covenant. This is especially the case since Jeremiah explic-itly says that the new covenant is "not like the covenant which I made with their fathers in the day I took them by the hand to bring them out of the land of Egypt" (Jer 31:32). Jeremiah is saying that God would write the stipula-tions of the new covenant on the hearts of His people instead of inscribing them on a stone tablet, as indeed the stipulations of most covenants were (in-cluding the Mosaic law). One should not assume that "law" means the law of Moses without considering the covenantal context.

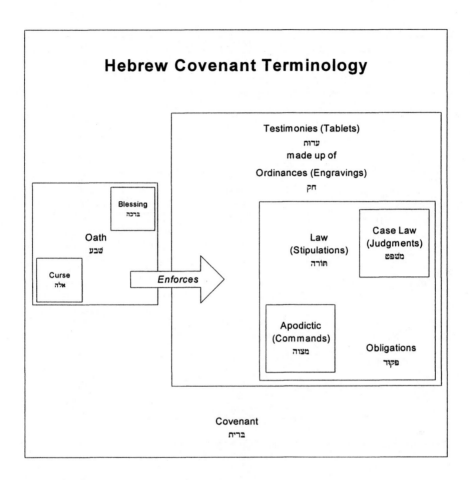

Figure 1. Hebrew Covenant Terminology

Concept	Hebrew	Greek
Covenant	בְּרִית כרת	διαθήκη
Oath	שָׁבַע שבועה	ὄμνυμι ὁρκίζω ἐξορκίζω ὅρκος ἔνορκος ἐπίορκος ὁρκισμός ὁρκωμοσία

Continued on the next page

Table 2 (*Continued*)

Concept		Hebrew	Greek
Blessing		בְּרָכָה	εὐλογία
			ἐπαγγελία
Curse		אָלָה	ἀρά
Testimony		עֵדוּת	μαρτύριον
Ordinances		חֹק	δικαίωμα
			πρόσταγμα
			νόμιμος
			νόμος
			γράφω
Law		תּוֹרָה	νόμος
Obligations		פִּקּוּד	ἐντολή
			δικαίωμα
Apodictic Law		מִצְוָה	ἐντολή
			ἐντέλλω
			ἔνταλμα
			πρόσταγμα
			προστάσσω
			δικαίωμα
			λόγος
			λέγω
			ῥῆμα
			φωνή
			θεσμός
Case Law		מִשְׁפָּט	κρίμα
			κρίσις
			δικαίωμα
			δικαίος
			σύγκρισις

Table 2. Comparison of Hebrew and Greek Covenant Terminology

Covenant Rituals

All of the rituals mentioned above as part of ancient Near Eastern covenants are attested in the OT. In Gen 31:44–54 we see the oath (Gen 31:53), the divine witness (Gen 31:44–53), the sacrifice, and the ritual meal (Gen 31:54). Salt is mentioned in a covenantal context in three cases (Lev 2:13; Num 18:19; 2 Chr 13:5). In Num 18:19 and 2 Chr 13:5 the term בְּרִית מֶלַח is used to signify a perpetual covenant relationship. King Zedekiah held a covenant renewal ceremony (Jer 34:8–20), with an emphasis on keeping the Mosaic commands concerning Hebrew slaves. In Jer 34 the prophet condemns those who then went back on their word and kept their slaves (Jer 34:10–20). Jeremiah 34:18–19 (cp. Gen 15:9–11, 17) clearly refers to the cutting of a calf and passing between its parts. As they had acted out a self-maledictory curse and then broken the covenant, so God pronounces their destruction (Jer 34:20). Similar covenant renewals are mentioned under kings Jehoash (2 Kgs 11:17) and Josiah (2 Kgs 23:1–3). These covenant rituals are clearly ancient, but also continued at least to the period of the Babylonian exile.

Covenant Types

Suzerainty Treaties

The suzerainty treaty type is well represented in the OT. The main example is, of course, the Mosaic law, as we shall see later. David made a suzerainty covenant with Abner making him his vassal (2 Sam 3:12–13). Abner then led the elders of Israel to make a suzerainty covenant with David (2 Sam 3:20–21; 5:3; 1 Chr 11:3). The priest Jehoiada made the royal guard make a suzerainty covenant with Jehoash when he revealed to them that the young king was still alive (2 Kgs 11:4). This was done to protect him from the murderous queen Athaliah (2 Kgs 11:1). Therefore, there are examples of suzerainty covenants from the days of Moses to the days of the monarchy in Judah.

However, there is an unfortunate tendency today to force all covenants into the suzerainty covenant form. Since the suzerainty covenant form is conditional in nature, it would be erroneous to interpret grant covenants, which are unconditional, or even parity covenants, which may be either, as suzerainty covenants. Wrong conclusions will inevitably result. Indeed, this could even amount to the difference between law (conditional) and grace (unconditional). Therefore, we must not assume that all covenants are suzerainty covenants.

Parity Covenants

There are numerous instances of parity covenants of various sorts in the Scriptures. In Gen 14:13 Mamre, Eschol, and Aner are mentioned as allies with Abraham. Literally, the text says, "And they [were] possessors of a covenant with Abram (וְהֵם בַּעֲלֵי בְרִית־אַבְרָם)" (my translation). In Gen 21:22–34 Abraham and Abimelech conclude a mutual non-aggression pact at Beersheba following the parity covenant form, complete with mutual oaths (Gen 21:23–24, 31) and sacrifices (Gen 21:27). In Gen 31:44–54 Jacob and Laban also made a mutual non-aggression agreement using a parity covenant form.

As discussed above, many covenant rituals are employed in this instance. Of main importance are the mutual oaths (Gen 31:50, 52). Exodus 34:12 forbids the Israelis from making parity covenants with the inhabitants of the land. However, Joshua was tricked into disobeying this command by the subterfuge of the Gibeonites (Josh 9:1–27). In 1 Kgs 5:12 Hiram and Solomon form a peace treaty according to the parity covenant form. Marriage, with its mutual obligations, is spoken of as a covenant in Mal 2:14. This is important, since disappointment with one's spouse does not remove one's covenant obligation before God. Although we see many parity covenants between human beings, the Scriptures never present God as making a parity covenant, since God has no equal.

Grants

Aside from the Abrahamic (Gen 15:8–21) and Davidic (2 Sam 7:4–17) covenants, which I will examine in more detail later, grant covenants are less explicit in the Hebrew Bible. We may have elements of grant covenants in the patriarchal blessings (Gen 27:27–29; 49:7–33). The entire process of the patriarchal blessing is referred to as charging, e.g., "When Jacob finished charging his sons" (Gen 49:33). The word translated as "charging" is צָוָה, which is the root for מִצְוָה ("commandment"). So, grant terminology is in use.

In the light of the contemporary ancient Near Eastern culture, many other events in Scripture may be assumed to have involved grant covenants. In 1 Sam 17:25 King Saul promised three grants to whoever defeats Goliath: riches, freedom from taxation, and marriage with the royal family. This is similar to the statement of Suppiluliuma I of Hatti to Huqqana of Hayasa, "I have now elevated you, Huqqana, a lowly dog, and have treated you well. In Hattusa I have distinguished you among the men of Hayasa and have given you my sister in marriage."[107] Achish granted the city of Ziklag to David in 1 Sam 27:5–6. This is reminiscent of the treaty between Suppiluliuma I of Hatti and Niqmaddu II of Ugarit.[108] Cyrus claimed a grant from God to rule (Ezra 1:2). David granted all of Saul's property to Mephibosheth (2 Sam 9:9–13) and Nebuzaradan gave grants of vineyards and fields to the poor after the exile (Jer 39:10). In keeping with the custom of that age and region, these transactions almost certainly involved grant covenants.

Summary

The covenants of Israel differ from the surrounding region in one important respect. The covenants of Israel invoked the one true God or His creation as witness. They did not invoke polytheistic lists of multitudes of gods. However, in all other respects, the covenants of Israel are the same genre as the ancient Near Eastern treaties. I have considered the terminology for biblical covenants and demonstrated that it coincides with the covenant practices of other ancient Near Eastern peoples. Biblical covenant rituals are all attested to in the surrounding culture as well. Finally, I have demonstrated that the types of covenants observed elsewhere in the ancient Near East are also represented in the Hebrew Scriptures. Therefore, I conclude that the ancient Near Eastern covenant forms provide a valid historical context for interpreting the biblical covenants.

NOTES

1. Mal 3:1–2 contains a pun: The "Messenger of the covenant (בְּרִית *berith*)" is coming, but His coming will be like "fuller's soap (ברית *borith*)!"
2. Cf. Job 31:1; Walter Brueggemann, *The Covenanted Self: Explorations in Law and Covenant*, ed. Patrick D. Miller (Minneapolis, MN: Fortress, 1999) 12–13.
3. See above chapter 2.
4. Francis Brown, S. R. Driver, and Charles A. Briggs, *A Hebrew and English Lexicon of the Old Testament: With an Appendix Containing the Biblical Aramaic, Based on the Lexicon of William Gesenius* (hereafter referred to as *BDB*) (Oxford: Clarendon, 1953; reprint, New York: Oxford University Press, 1977) 136–37.
5. G. L. Archer, Jr., "Covenant," *EvDT* 299–301.
6. Weinfeld, *TDOT* 2:255.
7. Daniel J. Elazar, *HaBrit V'HaHesed: Foundations of the Jewish System* [paper online] (Jerusalem: Jerusalem Center for Public Affairs, accessed 8 July 2001), available from http://www.jcpa.org/dje/articles2/britvhesed.htm.
8. Weinfeld, *TDOT* 2:255.
9. Cf. Gen 15:18; Exod 34:10; Deut 4:23; 5:2; 29:24; 1 Sam 11:1; 1 Kgs 8:21; 2 Chr 6:11; Jer 34:8–20; Hos 10:4.
10. See p. 11.
11. F.C. Fensham, "Covenant, Alliance," *The New Bible Dictionary* hereafter referred to as *NBD*, [CD-ROM] (Wheaton, IL: Tyndale House Publishers, Inc., 1962), available Logos Library System. Köhler has a similar scheme. See McCarthy, *Old Testament Covenant* 3.
12. E. Kutsch, *TLOT* 1:61.
13. McCarthy, *Treaty* 18.
14. עָבַר בִּבְרִית means "cross over into covenant," i.e., "enter into" (Deut 29:12) but בְּרִית עָבַר has the meaning of "transgress (cross over away from) the covenant" (Deut 17:2; Josh 7:11, 15; 23:16; Judg 2:20; 2 Kgs 18:12; Jer 34:18; Hos 6:7; 8:1). Thus Jer 34:18–20 has a play on the word עָבַר, "I will give the men who have transgressed My covenant (הָעֹבְרִים אֶת־בְּרִתִי), who have not fulfilled the words of the covenant which they made before Me, *when* they cut the calf in two and passed between (עָבַר) its parts— the officials of Judah and the officials of Jerusalem, the court officers and the priests and all the people of the land who passed between (עָבַר) the parts of the calf— I will give them into the hand of their enemies and into the hand of those who seek their life. And their dead bodies will be food for the birds of the sky and the beasts of the earth" (Jer 34:18–20).
15. Cf. 1 Sam 20:2, 8; 2 Chr 15:12; Jer 34:10; Ezek 16:8; 20:37.
16. Cf. Deut 4:13; 28:69; Josh 7:11; 23:16; Judg 2:20; 1 Kgs 11:11; 2 Kgs 17:35; 18:12; 1 Chr 16:15; Ps 105:8; 111:9; Jer 11:8.
17. Gordon J. McConville, "בְּרִית," *NIDOTTE* 1:747–55.

18. McCarthy, *Treaty* 81.

19. Adolf Deissmann, *Light From The Ancient East: The New Testament Illustrated by Recently Discovered Texts of the Graeco-Roman World*, trans. Lionel R. M. Strachan (Peabody, MA: Hendrickson Publishers, Inc., 1995) 337–8.

20. Bauer, W., F. W. Danker, W. F. Arndt, F. W. Gingrich, *A Greek-English Lexicon of the New Testament and Other Early Christian Literature* (hereafter referred to as *BDAG*), 3rd ed. (Chicago: The University of Chicago Press, 1999) 228–29.

21. J. H. Moulton, G. Milligan, *Vocabulary of the Greek Testament* (hereafter referred to as *MM*) (Peabody, MA: Hendrickson Publishers, 1997) 148–49.

22. Robertson, *Christ* 12.

23. J. Barton Payne, "Testament," *Wycliffe Bible Encyclopedia* (hereafter referred to as *WBE*), eds. Charles F. Pfeiffer, Howard F. Vos, John Rea, 2 vols. (Chicago: Moody, 1975) 2:1686.

24. Merrill F. Unger and William White eds., "Covenant," *Nelson's Expository Dictionary of the Old Testament* 82–83.

25. J. Gordon McConville, "אֲמָנָה," *NIDOTTE* 1:434.

26. J. Gordon McConville, "חָזָה," *NIDOTTE* 2:61–62.

27. Philo *De specialibus legibus* 2:10–12.

28. Philo *De decalogo* 86.

29. *BDB* 46.

30. See Gen 24:41; 26:28; Lev 5:1; Deut 29:12, 14, 18–20; 1 Kgs 8:31; 2 Chr 6:22; 34:24; Neh 10:29; Jer 23:10; Ezek 16:59; 17:13–19; Dan 9:11; Zech 5:3.

31. Robert P. Gordon, "אָלָה," *NIDOTTE* 1:403–4.

32. Deuteronomy 29:12 reads, "that you may enter into the covenant with the LORD your God, and into His oath (לְעָבְרְךָ בִּבְרִית יהוה אֱלֹהֶיךָ וּבְאָלָתוֹ)."

33. Deuteronomy 29:14 reads, "making this covenant and this oath (הַזֹּאת וְאֶת־הָאָלָה הַזֹּאת כֹּרֵת אֶת־הַבְּרִית)." The LXX translates both terms with διαθήκη.

34. Don Garlington, "Oath-taking in the Community of the New Age (Matthew 5:33–37)," *Trinity Journal* (hereafter referred to as *TJ*) 16, no. 2 (Fall 1995): 139–70. In this interesting article, Garlington advocates the position that Jesus did not prohibit all oaths. Rather, he sees Matt 5:33–37 as prohibiting the hypocritical oaths with loop-holes that the Pharisees were found of making.

35. T. W. Cartledge, "שָׁבַע," *NIDOTTE* 4:32–34. See also *BDB* 989.

36. Timothy Friberg, Barbra Friberg, Neva F. Miller, *Analytical Lexicon of the Greek New Testament* (hereafter referred to as *ALGNT*) (Grand Rapids, MI, Baker, 20004) 73. See also *BDAG* 127.

37. Gen 24:41; 26:28; Num 5:21, 23, 27; Deut 29:11, 13, 18–20; 30:7; 1 Kgs 8:31; Neh 10:30; Job 31:30; Ps 10:7; 59:12; Isa 24:6; Jer 42:18; Ezek 17:13, 16; Zech 5:3.

38. Deuteronomy 21:22, 23, and Gal 3:13 cite the principal that everyone who is hanged on a tree is cursed. This was actually carried out in Gen 40:19 and Josh 8:29. Although these passages use עֵץ, there is a possible pun between אֵלָה *ʾēlāh* ("oak") and

אָלָה ʾālāh ("curse"): In 2 Sam 18:9–14 is Absalom caught by his hair in "a great oak" (אֵלָה ʾēlāh) or "a great curse" (אָלָה ʾālāh)? Was King Baasha's son's name "Oak" (אֵלָה ʾēlāh) or "Curse" (אָלָה ʾālāh) (1 Kgs 16:1–6)?

39.   *BDAG* 128.
40.   *ALGNT* 221. See also *BDAG* 525.
41.   ALGNT 285. See also *BDAG* 723.
42.   Henry George Liddell, Robert Scott, *A Greek-English Lexicon* (hereafter referred to as *LSJ*), rev. by Sir Henry Stuart Jones, 9th ed. (Oxford: Clarendon, 1996) 1252.
43.   *ALGNT* 285. See also *BDAG* 723.
44.   *ALGNT* 281. See also *BDAG* 705–6.
45.   Gen 21:23, 24, 31; 22:16; 24:7, 9; 25:33; 26:3, 31; 31:53; 47:31; 50:24; Exod 13:5, 11; 32:13; 33:1; Lev 5:4, 22, 24; 19:12; Num 11:12; 14:16, 23; 30:3; 32:10, 11; Deut 1:8, 34, 35; 2:14; 4:21, 31; 6:10, 13, 18, 23; 7:8, 12, 13; 8:1, 18; 9:5; 10:11, 20; 11:9, 21; 13:18; 19:8; 26:3, 15; 28:9, 11; 29:12; 30:20; 31:7, 20, 21, 23; 34:4; Josh 1:6; 2:12; 5:6; 9:15, 18, 19, 20; 14:9; 21:43, 44; Judg 2:1, 15; 15:12; 21:1, 7, 18, 1 Sam 3:14; 19:6; 20:17, 42; 24:21, 22; 28:10; 30:15; 2 Sam 3:9, 35; 19:7, 23; 21:2, 17, 1 Kgs 1:13, 17, 29–30, 51; 2:8, 23; 2 Kgs 25:24; 2 Chr 15:14, 15; Ezra 10:5; Ps 15:4; 24:4; 63:11; 89:3, 35, 49; 95:11; 102:8; 110:4; 119:106; 132:2, 11; Eccl 9:2; Isa 19:18; 45:23; 48:1; 54:9; 62:8; 65:16; Jer 4:2; 5:2, 7; 7:9; 11:5; 12:16; 22:5; 32:22; 38:16; 40:9; 44:26; 49:13; 51:14; Ezek 16:8; Dan 12:7; Hos 4:15; Amos 4:2; 6:8; 8:7, 14; Mic 7:20; Zeph 1:5; Zech 5:4; Mal 3:5.
46.   Gen 24:9, 37; 50:5, 6, 25; Exod 13:19; Num 5:19, 21; Josh 6:26; 1 Sam 14:27, 28 (twice); 1 Kgs 2:42; 22:16; 2 Kgs 11:4; 2 Chr 18:15; 36:13; Ezra 10:5; Neh 5:12; 13:25; Song 2:7; 3:5; 5:8, 9; 8:4.
47.   *ALGNT* 285. See also *BDAG* 723.
48.   *ALGNT* 151. See also *BDAG* 351.
49.   *ALGNT* 166 See also *BDAG* 376.
50.   Gen 21:31 (Brenton's English Translation of the LXX).
51.   Gen 24:8; Exod 13:19; 22:11; Lev 5:4; Num 5:21; 30:3, 10, 14; Deut 7:8; Josh 2:17, 20; 9:20; Judg 21:5; 1 Sam 14:26; 2 Sam 21:7; 1 Kgs 2:43; 1 Chr 16:16; 2 Chr 15:15; Neh 10:29; Ps 105:9; Eccl 8:2; 9:2; Jer 11:5; Dan 9:11; Zech 8:17.
52.   *LSJ* 572.
53.   *ALGNT* 317. See also *BDAG* 830.
54.   Walter C. Kaiser, Jr., "The Promise Theme and the Theology of Rest," *Bibliotheca Sacra* (hereafter referred to as *BSac*) 130, no. 518 (April–June 1973): 135–50. See also Rolf Rendtorff, *The Covenant Formula: An Exegetical and Theological Investigation*, trans. Margaret Kohl (Edinburgh: T&T Clark, 1998).
55.   *BDAG* 408–9.
56.   *BDAG* 355–56.
57.   *BDB* 730.
58.   Carl Schultz, "עֵדוּת (ʿēdût)," *Theological Wordbook of the Old Testament* (hereafter

referred to as *TWOT*), eds. R. Laird Harris, Gleason L. Archer, Jr., Bruce K. Waltke, 2 vols. (Chicago: Moody, 1980) 2:649–50.

59. Peter Enns, "עֵדוּת," *NIDOTTE* 3:328–29.

60. Exod 16:34; 25:16, 21, 22; 26:33, 34; 27:21; 30:6, 26, 36; 31:7, 18; 32:15; 34:29; 38:21; 39:35; 40:3, 5, 20, 21; Lev 16:13; 24:3; Num 1:50, 53; 4:5; 7:89; 9:15; 10:11; 17:4, 7, 8, 10; 18:2; Josh 4:16; 1 Kgs 2:3; 2 Kgs 11:12; 17:15; 23:3; 1 Chr 29:19; 2 Chr 23:11; 24:6; 34:31; Neh 9:34; Ps 19:7; 78:5; 81:5; 119:14, 31, 36, 88, 99, 111, 129, 144, 157; 122:4; Jer 44:23.

61. Kline has a good discussion of this in *Structure* 113–24.

62. *ALGNT* 254.

63. L. Coenen and A. A. Trites, "Witness," *The New International Dictionary of New Testament Theology: Translated, with additions and revisions, from the German Theologishes Begriffslexikon zum Neuen Testament* (hereafter referred to as *NIDNTT*), ed. Collin Brown, 4 vols. (Grand Rapids, MI: Zondervan, 1986) 3:1038–50.

64. *BDB* 435–36.

65. John E. Hartley, "יָרָה (*yārâ*)," *TWOT* 1:403–5.

66. G. Liedke and C. Petersen, "תּוֹרָה *tôrâ* instruction," *TLOT* 3:1415–22.

67. Liedke and Peterson, *TLOT* 3:1417.

68. Peter Enns, "Law of God," *NIDOTTE* 4:893.

69. R. A. Cole, "Law in the Old Testament," *The Zondervan Pictorial Encyclopedia of the Bible* (hereafter referred to as *ZPEB*), 5 vols., gen. ed. Merrill C. Tenney (Grand Rapids, MI: Zondervan, 1975) 3:883–94.

70. J. A. Motyer, "Law, Biblical Concept of," *EvDT* 674–76.

71. Num 18:19; Josh 24:25; 2 Kgs 17:15; 1 Chr 16:17; 2 Chr 34:31; Ps 50:16; 105:10; Isa 24:5.

72. Jack P. Lewis, "חֹק (*ḥōq*)," *TWOT* 1:316–18.

73. G. Liedke, "חקק *ḥqq* to inscribe, prescribe," *TLOT* 2:468–72.

74. H. Ringgren, "חָקַק *ḥāqaq*," *TDOT* 5:139–47.

75. H. Ringgren, *TDOT* 5:142–43.

76. Peter Enns, "חק," *NIDOTTE* 2:250–51.

77. *ALGNT* 117. See also *BDAG* 249–50.

78. *BDAG* 884.

79. *BDAG* 677–78.

80. *LSJ* 1724–25.

81. *BDAG* 340.

82. *LSJ* 594.

83. *BDAG* 339.

84. *BDAG* 152.

85. *BDB* 1048–49.

86. B. Johnson, "מִשְׁפָּט *mišpāṭ*," *TDOT* 9:86–98.

87.   Peter Enns, "מִשְׁפָּט," *NIDOTTE* 2:1142–44.
88.   G. Liedke, "שׁפט *špṭ* to judge," *TLOT* 3:1392–99.
89.   Robert D. Culver, "מִשְׁפָּט *mishpāṭ*," *TWOT* 2:947–49.
90.   *BDAG* 567.
91.   *BDAG* 569.
92.   *BDAG* 246–47.
93.   *LSJ* 1667.
94.   *ALGNT* 210.
95.   *LSJ* 414.
96.   *BDAG* 137–39.
97.   *LSJ* 479–80.
98.   *BDAG* 250.
99.   *BDB* 845–46.
100.   G. Liedke, "צוה *ṣwh* pi. to command," *TLOT* 2:1062–66.
101.   *BDAG* 339.
102.   *BDAG* 884–85.
103.   *LSJ* 795.
104.   *BDB* 824.
105.   Victor P. Hamilton, "פִּקּוּדִים (*piqqûdîm*)," *TWOT* 2:731–33.
106.   Peter Enns, "פָּקוּד," *NIDOTTE* 3:665.
107.   Beckman, *Hittite Diplomatic Texts* 7:23, 3.1.
108.   Ibid., 7:30–32, no. 4.

CHAPTER FOUR

✦ Covenant as Structure

The Covenantal Structure of the Bible

The Bible is preeminently a book of covenants. This is reflected in the very terms that we use to describe the Scriptures: Old Testament (or Covenant) and New Testament (or Covenant). Kline observes, concerning the OT, that

> the several major kinds of literature—history, law and wisdom, prophecy and praise—as they are employed in the Old Testament all function as extensions (free and creative to be sure) of some main section or feature of the foundational treaties. The functional extension may be by way of didactic or confessional elaboration. But in each case a special relationship can be traced between the function and a particular element of the treaty documents, and thus a literary dimension is added to the functional in our identification of the Old Testament in all its parts as a covenantal corpus.[1]

Concerning the NT, Kline states:

> In the case of the New Testament as in that of the Old Testament, acceptance of its own claims as to its primary divine authorship leads to recognition of its pervasively covenantal nature and purpose. For the New Testament so received will be understood as the word of the ascended Lord of the new covenant, by which he structures the community of the new covenant and orders the faith and life of his servant people in their consecrated relationship to him. And then the human authors of the New Testament books, authorized by their Lord to speak his word, will be seen to function as his "ministers of the new covenant" (cf. 2 Cor. 3:6). With respect to immediate as well as ultimate provenance, the *Sitz im Leben* of the New Testament books is fundamentally covenantal. They all arise out of a covenantal source of authority and all address themselves to the covenant community.[2]

This underlying covenantal structure can be seen by surveying the broad literary classifications of the Old and New Testaments.

The Law

In the Law the covenantal structure of the Bible is most clearly discerned. Kline notes that the weaving together of historical narrative and legislative material is characteristic of the covenant form. The historical portions of the Torah serve the purpose of the covenantal historical prologue in that they trace the historical background of Yahweh's past covenant relationships.[3] Thomas L. Thompson comments that the genre of historiography is so important for Israel that Israel's faith is best understood as a historical faith.[4] The historical sections of the Law (and the rest of Scripture) trace the dealings of the Lord of the covenant and His vassals. This is one reason for the history of the other covenants in the Torah. As historical prologue, it was necessary to recount the covenants that had gone before.

The stipulations of the various covenants, especially the Mosaic covenant, constitute the laws of the Torah. Kline observes that the legal material in the Torah outside of the obvious treaty stipulations are also in a covenantal context. He suggests that the other Pentateuchal laws are presented as elaborations of the original covenant obligations as God continued to speak through Moses, the covenant mediator.[5] The language of the OT law is thoroughly covenantal. It will become apparent in considering the Mosaic law that the form is also thoroughly covenantal. That legal foundation sheds light on the role of the Hebrew prophets.

The Prophets

The stipulations of the Mosaic covenant (Deut 18:15–22; cf. Exod 4:16; 7:1) established the prophetic office. The prophet is the appointed spokesman for the suzerain, in this case, God. The Hebrew for prophet is נָבִיא ("spokesman, speaker, prophet"[6]). Kline explains the prophet as spokesman similar to the covenant emissaries of Great Kings. He points out that the message of the prophets was often cast in the language and categories of international treaty administration.[7] When Hezekiah broke his covenant with the king of Assyria, that king sent his spokesman, Rab-shakeh, to Jerusalem to warn of the consequences (2 Kgs 18:17–35). In the same way, God sent His servants the prophets to warn Israel of the consequences of their sin.

The prophets, acting as God's spokespersons, brought charges against Israel for breaking the stipulations of the covenant. Their admonitions and predictions are firmly grounded in the blessings and curses of the covenant.

Kline explains that "the formulary for the prosecution of treaty violators can be reconstructed, largely from ancient royal letters, and it has been found that the prophetic indictment of Israel repeatedly follows this pattern of the covenant lawsuit."[8] Fee and Stuart explain the covenant background of the prophets:

> God announced the enforcement (positive or negative) of his law through them, so that the events of blessing or curse would be clearly understood by his people. Moses was the mediator for God's law when God first announced it, and thus is a paradigm (model) for the prophets. They are God's mediators, or spokespersons, for the covenant. Through them God reminds people in the generations after Moses that if the Law is kept, blessing will result; but if not, punishment will ensue....
>
> Therefore, one must always bear in mind that the prophets did not invent the blessings or curses they announced. They may have worded these blessings and curses in novel, captivating ways, as they were inspired to do so. But they reproduced *God's* word, not their own. Through them God announced his intention to enforce the covenant, for benefit or for harm depending on the faithfulness of Israel, but always on the basis of and in accordance with the categories of blessing and curse already contained in Leviticus 26, Deuteronomy 4, and Deuteronomy 28–32.[9]

Therefore, the prophets of Israel ministered within a covenantal framework. They communicated God's message of blessing or curse according to the covenant and pointed Israel toward a future promised by God in covenant.[10]

The Writings

The Writings consist of both praise and wisdom. The basis for both is the covenant. As previously indicated, the purpose for the historical prologue in a covenant is to elicit gratitude on the part of the vassal. The Psalms are an expression of that gratitude and make abundant use of covenant terminology. Psalm 118, with its constant refrain, "His lovingkindness is everlasting!" is an example. Psalm 119, with its extensive use of synonyms for the law, would be a prime example. As the worshipper responds in gratitude and praise to God, he or she affirms the covenant relationship. Kline comments, "The Psalter's function in covenantal confession suggests that it may be regarded as an extension of the vassal's ratification response, which is found in certain biblical as well as extrabiblical covenants as part of the treaty text."[11] Therefore, praise honors our Great God and King for Who He is and what He has done. In gratitude then we reaffirm our covenant relationship.

Moses explained to the Israelis that they were to "keep and do" the "statutes and judgments" that he had taught them because "that is your wisdom and your understanding" (Deut 4:5,6). Therefore, the covenant stipulations are preeminent examples of wisdom literature. Kline notes that the OT wisdom literature converts the covenant stipulations into maxims and instructions that regulate conduct in life situations.[12] Murphy notes that wisdom literature expands on the law and has character as its goal:

> While there is often a certain overlap with the Decalogue (e.g., the frequent warnings against adultery), most of the sayings deal with the grey area of forming character and integrity of action. The approach of wisdom to morality is much broader than that of the Decalogue in that it aims at character formation. It is also deeper in terms of the motivation it supplies. Whereas the Decalogue simply invoked divine authority (thou shalt not!), the sages develop specific motivations, and anticipate temptations.... It aims to anticipate a stressful situation, and to strengthen resolve. If one may designate the codes in the OT as "law," the wisdom rules are better described as "catechesis," or moral formation.[13]

Wisdom seeks to apply the covenants to all of life and develop integrity based on adherence to their stipulations. Wisdom's concepts of reward and folly echo the blessings and curses of the covenant.

The Gospels and Acts

The gospels and Acts serve as historical introductions and preambles to the new covenant. Kline states that "the gospels and Acts also perform the function of the treaty preambles by introducing the Messianic Lord of the covenant and identifying him through various witnesses as the divine King of Israel, son of David, and eternal Word."[14] Indeed, "gospel" or εὐαγγέλιον ("good news") is found "in the striking calendar inscr[iption] from Priene of date about BC 9 with reference to the birthday of the Emperor Augustus...."[15] Broyles, although skeptical concerning this "Roman usage," does note that "*euangelion* was used in the Roman imperial cult and applied to the emperor, who was thought to be divine, in the oral proclamations of his birth, his coming of age and especially of his accession to the throne...."[16] The early Christians preached "the good news about the kingdom of God and the name of Jesus Christ" (Acts 8:12). Jesus, as the One Who fulfills the Abrahamic and Davidic covenants and the One Who establishes the new covenant, is an important theme in the Gospels and Acts (Matt 26:28; Mark 14:24; Luke 1:72; 22:20; Acts 3:25; 7:8).

The Letters

The NT letters have similarities not only with OT wisdom literature (e.g., James) and worship (e.g., Col 1:15–20), but also the prophets. Kline sees judgment sections of Paul's letters in particular as reminiscent of the covenant lawsuits of the prophets.[17] Thus, the letters give wise counsel on living in keeping with the stipulations of the new covenant and call to account those who are not so living. The letters show us practically what it means to have the stipulations of the new covenant written on our hearts.

The Revelation

The Revelation, with its seal, trumpet, and bowl judgments, is structured around the concepts of blessing and curse. These concepts are intensely covenantal, as Kline observes that, in Revelation,

> the lines can be traced through the Old Testament prophets to the eschatological curses and blessings of the sanctions section of the treaties. The Book of Revelation is replete with treaty analogues from its opening preamble-like identification of the awesome Lord Christ; through the letters to the churches, administering Christ's covenantal lordship after the manner of the ancient lawsuit; on through the elaborately expounded prophetic sanctions which constitute the major part of the book; and down to the closing documentary clause and canonical curse.[18]

Both the letters (Rev 2–3) and the seven-sealed scroll (Rev 5) call to mind a covenant lawsuit. Beagley explains that

> the image is of a typical first-century document written on a scroll made of sheets of papyrus or (less often) parchment or leather sewn together. Letters, legal documents and the Scriptures themselves were written on such scrolls. Wax seals were often affixed to a document to conceal its contents or (with the impression of the writer's or signatory's mark in the wax) to confirm its authenticity....
>
> But what kind of document was this scroll? It could be "the Lamb's book of life" (Rev 13:8; 20:15; 21:27), but the seals suggest that it is a legal document, perhaps a testament, a document of divorce or a book of destiny....[19]

This scroll is no ordinary legal document; it bears the seal and authority of God Himself, "Seal is also an image of authority itself. A king's signet seal on a document gives it the authority of the king himself; anyone illegally opening a letter sealed by the king is defying his authority."[20] Revelation is the consummation of all of the promises, blessings and curses of the biblical covenants.

A Critique of Covenant Theology and Dispensationalism

The Problem of Understanding

Semantics. I note, at the first, that the issue of covenant theology vs. dispensationalism is a disagreement between brothers. Neither side is denying the fundamentals of the historic Christian faith. Indeed, there exist points of broad agreement between the two parties. Roy L. Aldrich notes six of these points: (1) All agree that dispensations exist. (2) History since Moses is divided into dispensations of law and grace. History from Adam to Moses must consist of at least two dispensations to take into account humankind's condition before and after the fall. Therefore, there are at least four dispensations. (3) There is only one way of salvation since the fall. (4) The new birth is common to all dispensations since the fall. (5) God's moral law is eternal. (6) The saints of all dispensations have more in common than they differ.[21] Gordon R. Lewis, while appreciating the irenic spirit of Aldrich's approach, notes that we are not yet unified. He observes that, despite having the same basis for salvation, Israel and the Church have distinct temporal goals.[22] Thus, in spite of these commonalties, real differences exist.

In the debate between covenant theology and dispensationalism, many of the same terms are used. This gives the illusion that both sides are talking about the same things when they are not. Aldrich notes that "the current debate over dispensationalism suffers for lack of clarity and agreement in the area of basic definitions."[23] For instance, covenant theologians use the term "covenant" in a broader sense than the biblical covenants. Some would include theological constructs such as a covenant of redemption made in eternity between the persons of the Godhead. Louis Berkhof admits that "the Scriptural character of the name [Covenant of Redemption] cannot be maintained." However, he proceeds to state, "But this, of course, does not detract from the reality of the counsel of peace [another term for the Covenant of Redemption]."[24] However, other covenant theologians have recently disagreed with the eternal aspect of the covenant of redemption. Robertson, a covenant theologian, critiques the traditional position as exceeding the bounds of Scriptural evidence and being based on a faulty view of covenant as defined as a mutual contract rather than a sovereignly administered bond.[25] Although Robertson also uses the term, he does so as a category for all the covenants other than the Edenic. He seems to be arguing that the relationship of these covenants to the covenant of redemption is similar to the Abrahamic covenant and its sub-covenants (Palestinian or Land, Davidic, and new):

> It is rather difficult to understand why the dispensationalist would quarrel with the covenant theologian in his desire to see a single "covenant of redemption" overarching history from God's first promise to Adam to the consummation of the ages if he himself affirms that the conditions established under the "Adamic covenant" were to prevail until the arrival of the kingdom age.[26]

Of course, just as the number of dispensations is not part of the *sine qua non*, neither is the manufacture of theological covenants apart from biblical evidence.

Others have questioned the legitimacy of covenant theology's theological covenants. P. R. Williamson contends that covenant theology lacks an adequate exegetical basis. He criticizes the tendency to introduce non-biblical terminology and ideas, while praising covenant theology for correctly emphasizing the importance of the covenant concept. He is critical of the covenant of redemption, seeing it as a theological construct without historical basis that is difficult to reconcile with the Trinity. He is also critical of the covenant of grace as an introduction of non-biblical and misleading terminology. He notes that Eph 2:12, often used as a proof-text, actually reads "covenants [plural] of promise" not one overarching covenant.[27] Lewis Sperry Chafer comments concerning the artificiality of the covenant of redemption that "this covenant rests upon but slight revelation. It is rather sustained largely by the fact that it seems both reasonable and inevitable."[28] He also states that "the phrase Covenant of Grace is not found in the Bible and, as often presented by human teachers, is far from a Scriptural conception."[29] Covenant theology is guilty of creating covenants for which there is no solid biblical basis.

On the other hand, dispensationalists tend to slight the covenants. To be sure, dispensationalists do not deny the biblical covenants. Nevertheless, they do tend to ignore them. Article V of the doctrinal statement of Dallas Theological Seminary reads:

> We believe that the dispensations are not ways of salvation nor different methods of administering the so-called Covenant of Grace. *They are not in themselves dependent on covenant relationships* but are ways of life and responsibility to God which test the submission of man to His revealed will during a particular time... (emphasis mine).[30]

Lewis writes concerning covenant theologians that "the major unifying concept of Scripture, according to covenant theology, is not divine dispensations,
but divine covenants. And the covenants stressed are two: the covenant of
works and the covenant of grace (sometimes differently named)."[31] Obvi-
ously, the basis for these statements is concern about the covenant of works
and the covenant of grace. However, I would note that, in their opposition to
the theological covenants, they blur the distinction between them and the biblical covenants. The statement that dispensations "are not in themselves dependent on covenant relationships but are ways of life and responsibility to
God which test the submission of man to His revealed will during a particular
time ..." seems to deny that *any* covenants can form a basis for the dispensations. Lewis creates a false dichotomy when he states that "the major unifying concept of Scripture, according to covenant theology, is not divine
dispensations, but divine covenants." This sort of thinking shows that there is
certain ambivalence in dispensational circles toward the concept of covenant.
This is doubtless an overreaction to the concept of theological covenants, but
it is, nonetheless, extremely unfortunate.

This dispensational slighting of the divine covenants leads to misunderstandings. Couch gives two examples:

> For example, often dispensationalists may be heard to say "the dispensation of
> Promise continues on into the Old Testament period of the Law because the nation
> of Israel is built on the promises of the Abrahamic covenant." This is a perfect illus-
> tration of confusing and mixing the purposes and functions of the covenants with the
> dispensations.
>
> For example, in his book *Dispensationalism*, chapter three, under the paragraph
> heading The Matter of "Carryovers", Ryrie seems to confuse the Noahic Covenant
> with the Dispensation of Human Government, when he writes, "The rainbow as a
> sign that God will never again bring a worldwide flood on the earth has assured, and
> continues to assure, mankind." Ryrie is trying to say that certain elements of a dis-
> pensation may carry over into other dispensations coming later in the Bible. But the
> rainbow is not a sign of the Human Government dispensation, it is a sign of the
> Noahic Covenant![32]

Tim LaHaye and Thomas Ice, although they do mention the three varieties of
covenants (royal grant, suzerain-vassal, and parity), incorrectly claim that suzerainty treaties are unconditional. They also see covenants as "a contract between two or more individuals," instead of noting the unilateral nature of
covenants as demonstrated above.[33] These errors and others like them show
that there is a need for dispensationalists today to study the covenants in a

deeper way.

Both parties use the terms "dispensation," "administration," and "economy." Vern Sheridan Poythress, a covenant theologian, notes that "belief in dispensation ... as such has very little to do with the distinctiveness of the characteristic forms of dispensational theologians."[34] However, they use the terms in differing ways that lead to misunderstandings. Charles Caldwell Ryrie defines a dispensation as "*a distinguishable economy in the outworking of God's purpose*" (emphasis his).[35] He attempts to distance himself, as many contemporary dispensationalists would, from Scofield's definition, which confuses dispensations and ages.[36] Covenant theologians seem to fixate on the old Scofield definition but they also add a feature that dispensationalists generally do not notice.

The covenant theologian sees a dispensation as the administration of a particular covenant.[37] This leads the covenant theologian to see the dispensationalist as glaringly inconsistent. Berkhof notes that "the second dispensation is called the dispensation of conscience, but according to Paul conscience was still the monitor of the Gentiles in his day, Rom. 2:14, 15."[38]

Of course, the answer is that the Adamic covenant is still in effect but the dispensation of conscience has ceased. Since the Adamic covenant is still in effect, conscience, although not the distinguishing feature of this dispensation, is still a factor in God's dealings with man. Ryrie presents five principles in this matter: (1) Promises are not always fulfilled in the same dispensation in which they are given. (2) Some things start in one dispensation and continue through subsequent dispensations. (3) Something began in one dispensation may be changed in subsequent dispensations. (4) Commands from a dispensation that has ended may be included in subsequent dispensations. (5) Some things completely change from one dispensation to another.[39] This is essentially a correct statement of the solution. The only correction that I would make is that the terms "code of conduct" and "specific revelation" are not the same as "dispensation." Ryrie seems to conflate these terms, "As a code of conduct and a specific revelation from God complete for its time, a dispensation ends."[40] I think it better to see a dispensation as passive description not an active prescription. As Couch states, "I understand the dispensations to be *passive* in nature" (emphasis his).[41] It seems clear to me that the revelation from God and the code of conduct during a dispensation consists of the aggregate of the covenantal stipulations in effect at that time. Therefore, rather than a dispensation being the administration of *a par-*

ticular covenant, as the covenant theologian would say, a dispensation is an administration of *all of the covenantal stipulations in force* at the time.

There is a need for clarity in our terminology concerning covenants and dispensations. A covenant is *established* at a given point in time. Individual stipulations within that covenant are *instituted* at different times. A dispensation *passively describes* the distinguishable manner in which God is *administering* the stipulations of the *all of the covenants in force*. As an administration, the dispensation is *inaugurated*. A dispensation has duration that *corresponds* to a period or age.

The government of the United States of America can illustrate this. If we take the U.S. Constitution as if it were a covenant that, as the preamble to the U.S. Constitution reads, "We the people ... do ordain and *establish*" (emphasis mine). The Constitution superseded the earlier Articles of Confederation. Some stipulations, such as article one, section two, providing for a census every ten years to begin three years after the Constitution was adopted, were not immediately *instituted* but were reserved for a later date. The U.S. Constitution provides for the office of President in article two, section one. The President *administers* the stipulations of the Constitution for a *term* of four years. Therefore, we can speak of the Bush or Clinton *administration* (*dispensation*) and President Clinton's term in office as the Clinton *era* (or *age*). The administration does not define the Constitution, rather ideally it defends and applies the Constitution. This is, to be sure, an imperfect analogy since God did not establish the U.S. Constitution and it is administered by mere men.

Ryrie seems loath to use covenant terminology preferring instead to speak of the "governing arrangement."[42] This leads covenant theologians to believe that dispensationalists are ending covenants prematurely. Therefore, there is, on all sides, confusion of the terms covenant, dispensation, age, and economy. This confusion of terms leads to many of the difficulties in mutual understanding between dispensationalists and covenant theologians. However, a factor of even greater importance exists.

Presuppositions. It is a valid hermeneutical principle that we must interpret unclear passages by clear passages. From this has grown the concept of the analogy of faith. Bernard Ramm notes that one of the controlling principles of Augustine's hermeneutics is that "we must consult the *analogy of faith*, the true orthodox creed, when we interpret. If orthodoxy represents

Scripture, then no expositor can make Scripture go contrary to orthodoxy."[43] The problem is that, if left unchecked, the interpreter's presuppositions can inundate the plain sense of the text in a flood of circular logic. Dillow comments that

> the Protestant doctrine of the analogy of faith has, in practice, sometimes become what might be called "theological exegesis." What started as a valid attempt to allow other Scriptures to help interpret the meaning of obscure passages has gradually become a method of interpreting obviously clear passages in a way that will harmonize with a particular theological tradition. Instead of permitting each text to speak for itself, the theological system determines the meaning....
>
> The analogy of faith, therefore, should only be viewed as one element of the exegetical process. It should not dictate our exegesis, substitute for exegesis, or simply be subsequent to exegesis. Rather, it is part of valid exegetical procedure, but its use should be postponed until a very late stage.[44]

Recently, the hermeneutical spiral approach, where one's presuppositions are constantly checked against the biblical data, shows an awareness of this problem.[45] It is no surprise, therefore, that presuppositions assume a fundamental role in this debate.

The Sine Qua Non

The Distinction Between Israel and the Church. The dispensational *sine qua non* ("that without which *it is* not") illustrates perfectly that the root of this debate is semantic and presuppositional. According to Ryrie, the first aspect of the *sine qua non* of dispensationalism is that *"a dispensationalist keeps Israel and the church distinct"* (emphasis his).[46] Chafer distinguished between an "earthly people," the Jews, and "heavenly people," the Christians.[47] Robertson criticizes dispensationalism's presuppositions at this precise point as being permeated with Platonic dualism.[48] Although an interesting suggestion, it is hard to see merit in this critique. It is difficult to see where, if this were indeed a fundamental presupposition, dispensationalists apply this thinking in the OT. Rather than a Platonic dichotomy, one sees the biblical doctrine of the remnant.

The covenant theologian's position itself is open to a presuppositional critique. Paul S. Karleen points out that Poythress in his *Understanding Dispensationalists*[49] has an unquestioned presupposition that governs his interpretation. He notes that Poythress' real objection seems to be to physical millennialism of which dispensationalism is the most consistent variety.

Poythress sees a distinct millennial future for ethnic Israel as undermining the concept of salvation only in union with Christ.[50] Poythress believes that there can only be one people of God because there is only one representative Head.[51] Karleen explains that Poythress' theology concerning the covenant of grace dictates his interpretation of prophecy. Therefore, covenant theology is not a question of literal vs. spiritual interpretation. Rather it is a question of the relationship between the OT and the NT determined by the covenant of grace. Karleen notes that this unquestioned basis for Poythress' interpretation is not found in Scripture.[52] Because of Poythress' presuppositions, he cannot see the biblical evidence for the distinction between Israel and the Church. He would apply the analogy of faith to obliterate such inconsistencies with his theological system.

Karleen's critique was not only accurate; it was effective. Poythress' response to Karleen's article shows movement toward the dispensationalist position on several points, even attempting to reconcile premillennialism and amillennialism and asserting a belief in a physical kingdom on earth for Israel.[53] Poythress has refined his position on Israel and the Church and now acknowledges diversity in the millennial kingdom.[54] Poythress' main concern seems to be for the unity of the people of God in salvation. He is unsure that all dispensationalists hold to the unity of all believers in salvation. However, dispensationalists affirm this also! Ryrie puts it succinctly, "The basis of salvation in every age is the death of Christ; the *requirement* for salvation in every age is faith; the *object* of faith in every age is God; the *content* of faith changes in the various dispensations" (emphasis his).[55] However, he sees no basic problem with dispensationalists who do hold to a common means of salvation.[56] Once the presuppositions are challenged and the Bible is allowed to speak for itself, the parties began to come together on the distinction between Israel and the Church.

Literal Hermeneutic. The presuppositions of covenant theologians have a similar impact on their hermeneutics. The second point of the *sine qua non* of dispensationalism is, according to Ryrie, that "*this distinction between Israel and the church is born out of a system of hermeneutics that is usually called literal interpretation*" (emphasis his).[57] Both sides, in principle, believe in the literal-grammatical-historical hermeneutic. As has often been noted, covenant theologians are not inclined to allegorize didactic passages dealing with Soteriology. Both sides would say, "If the plain sense makes sense, seek no other sense." However, because of the hermeneutic principle of the analogy of faith, they would disagree as to when the plain sense no longer made sense.

Karleen explains the presuppositional impact on Poythress' hermeneutics resulting in circular reasoning by pointing out that, when Poythress encounters the term "Israel," his presupposition that salvific unity means eschatological unity leads to circular reasoning:

> In other words, when forced to deal with the actual usage of "Israel," he brings the covenant back in again. There cannot be two peoples, even though the terms might seem to suggest it, because there is only one people, or stated negatively, there are not two peoples. The circularity is clearer when we put it this way: there are not two peoples because there are not two peoples.

Karleen points out that salvific unity does not imply prophetic unity, as Poythress assumes:

> Instead of actually looking at the data, Poythress simply brings back the covenant. What is so obviously missing in this is any proof for a connection between the salvatory unity of the elect and the economic/historic/prophetic unity. The economic unity is for Poythress a subhypothesis of the salvatory unity. But whenever he gets face to face with texts that would disprove the economic unity, he simply repeats the main hypothesis and its subhypothesis: There is a salvatory unity and therefore an economic unity. There is an economic unity because there is a salvatory unity.[58]

As Karleen has shown, this logic is entirely circular, but that may be expected when the analogy of faith is used to beg the hermeneutical question.

Since the unchallenged presuppositions of the covenant theologians give them a justification, based on the analogy of faith, not to accept the plain sense of some passages, they will not see themselves as being less literal than the dispensationalists.[59] This is doubtless the reason that covenant theologians dispute dispensationalist claims to be more literal. As Karleen has observed:

> If this rephrasing on my part is correct, then it is easy to see why questions of interpreting this or that passage "literally" will not get us very far in comparing covenant theology and dispensationalism. We are on the surface with that kind of approach. We have to get at the roots of the systems.[60]

The danger is that, if we do not examine our presuppositions, we will fail to communicate with each other concerning the second point of the *sine qua non*.

The Purpose of God. The third aspect of the *sine qua non* of dispensationalism is that the "underlying purpose of God in the world ... [is] the glory of God."[61] The thought is that the covenant theologian has one purpose, i.e., salvation. The dispensationalist claims to have a broader purpose, that of God's glory or a doxological purpose. However, Ryrie notes that "covenant theologians strongly emphasize the glory of God in their theology."[62] Couch states, "I see the covenants as prophetic and redemptive in nature...."[63] As Aldrich noted and Ryrie so ably defends, dispensationalists do believe in only one way of salvation. This seems to be precisely the preeminent concern of the covenant theologian.[64] It is possible that we are not that far apart when we examine our semantics.

Conclusion

I have shown that the concept of covenant determines the very structure of the Bible. Dispensationalism has tended to slight the concept of covenant. However, covenant theology has gone in an unbiblical direction with the creation *ex nihilo* of the theological covenants. Covenant theology has largely misunderstood the dispensationalist position. In the debate between covenant theology and dispensationalism semantics and presuppositions are at the core. Without understanding our terminology and basic assumptions there is little chance that meaningful communication will take place. Indeed, even the *sine qua non* will be misunderstood. If we are to understand the biblical concept of covenant, we must all examine our presuppositions and theology in the light of God's revelation.

NOTES

1. Kline, *Structure* 47.
2. Ibid. 71.
3. Ibid. 53.
4. Thomas L. Thompson, "Historiography (Israelite)," *ABD* 3:206–12.
5. Kline, *Structure* 48.
6. *BDB* 611–12.
7. Kline, *Structure* 61.
8. Ibid. 60.
9. Gordon D. Fee and Douglas Stuart, *How to Read the Bible for All It's Worth: A Guide to Understanding the Bible*, 2nd ed. (Grand Rapids, MI: Zondervan, 1993) 168.
10. See also J. Carl Laney, "The Role of the Prophets in God's Case Against Israel," *BSac* 138, no. 552 (October–December 1981): 313–25; David B. Wyrtzen, "The Theological Center of the Book of Hosea," *BSac* 141, no. 564 (October–December 1984): 315–29.
11. Kline, *Structure* 63.
12. Ibid. 64–65.
13. Roland E. Murphy, "Wisdom in the OT," *ABD* 6:920–31.
14. Kline, *Structure* 71–72.
15. *MM* 259.
16. C. C. Broyles, "Gospel (Good News)," *Dictionary of Jesus and the Gospels* (hereafter referred to as *DJG*), eds. Joel B. Green, Scot McKnight (Downers Grove, IL: InterVarsity, 1992) 282–86.
17. Kline, *Structure* 72–73.
18. Ibid. 73–74.
19. A. J. Beagley, "Scrolls, Seals," *Dictionary of the Later New Testament & Its Developments* (hereafter referred to as *DLNT*), eds. Ralph P. Martin, Peter H. Davids (Downers Grove, IL: InterVarsity, 1997) 1084–86.
20. Gen. eds. Leland Ryken, James C. Wilhoit, Tremper Longman III, "Seal," *Dictionary of Biblical Imagery* (hereafter referred to as *DBI*) (Downers Grove, IL: InterVarsity, 1998) 766.
21. Roy L. Aldrich, "A New Look at Dispensationalism," *BSac* 120, no. 477 (January–March 1963): 42–49.
22. Gordon R. Lewis, "Theological Antecedents of Pretribulationism," *BSac* 125, no. 498 (April–June 1968): 129–38.
23. Aldrich, "A New Look" 42.
24. L. Berkhof, *Systematic Theology*, 4th ed. (Grand Rapids, MI: Eerdmans, 1977) 266.
25. O. Palmer Robertson, *The Christ of the Covenants* 54.
26. Ibid. 208–9.

27. P. R. Williamson, "Covenant," *New Dictionary of Biblical Theology* (hereafter referred to as *NDBT*), eds. T. Desmond Alexander, Brian S. Rosner (Downers Grove, IL: InterVarsity, 2000) 419–29.

28. Lewis Sperry Chafer, *Systematic Theology*, 8 vols. (Dallas, TX: Dallas Seminary Press, 1947) 1:42.

29. Ibid. See also Pentecost, *Things to Come* 65–66.

30. Quoted in Roy L. Aldrich, "An Apologetic for Dispensationalism," *BSac* 112, no. 445 (January–March 1955): 46–54.

31. Lewis, "Theological Antecedents" 130.

32. Couch, "The Relationship Between the Dispensations and Covenants" 405.

33. Tim LaHaye, Thomas Ice, *Charting the End Times* (Eugene, OR: Harvest House, 2001) 78.

34. Vern Sheridan Poythress, *Understanding Dispensationalists*, 2nd ed. (Phillipsburg, NJ: Presbyterian and Reformed, 1995) 11.

35. Charles Caldwell Ryrie, *Dispensationalism* (Chicago: Moody, 1995) 28.

36. Ibid. 23 ff.

37. Robertson, *Christ of the Covenants* 92.

38. Berkhof, *Systematic Theology* 290.

39. Ryrie, *Dispensationalism* 57–58.

40. Ibid. 58.

41. Couch, "The Relationship Between the Dispensations and Covenants" 406.

42. Ryrie, *Dispensationalism* 49. Also, note on page 48 where Ryrie lists all of the details of the Noahic covenant without once using the term covenant! He is perhaps concerned that he not encourage covenant theologians, but clearly this is extreme.

43. Bernard Ramm, *Protestant Biblical Interpretation: A Textbook of Hermeneutics*, 3rd rev. ed. (Grand Rapids, MI: Baker, 1970) 36.

44. Joseph C. Dillow, *The Reign of the Servant Kings: A Study of Eternal Security and the Final Significance of Man* (Hayesville, NC: Schoettle, 1992) 28–29.

45. Ryrie, *Dispensationalism* 80.

46. Ibid. 39.

47. Ibid.

48. Robertson, *Christ of the Covenants* 213–14.

49. Vern Sheridan Poythress, *Understanding Dispensationalists*, 2nd ed. (Phillipburg, NJ: Presbyterian and Reformed, 1995).

50. Ibid. 129.

51. Ibid. 48.

52. Paul S. Karleen, "Understanding Covenant Theologians: A Study in Presuppositions," *Grace Theological Journal* (hereafter referred to as *GTJ*) 10, no. 2 (Fall 1989): 125–38.

53. Vern Sheridan Poythress, "Response to Paul S. Karleen's Paper 'Understanding Covenant Theologians'," *GTJ* 10, no. 2 (Fall 1989): 147–55.

54.   Ibid. 150–53.
55.   Ryrie, *Dispensationalism* 115.
56.   Poythress, "Response" 148.
57.   Ryrie, *Dispensationalism* 40.
58.   Karleen, "Understanding Covenant Theologians" 134–35.
59.   See Ryrie's discussion in Ryrie, *Dispensationalism* 85–88.
60.   Karleen, "Understanding Covenant Theologians" 133.
61.   Ryrie, *Dispensationalism* 40.
62.   Ibid.
63.   Couch, "The Relationship Between the Dispensations and Covenants" 406.
64.   See above and Poythress, "Response" 150–53.

PART TWO

The Divine Covenants

CHAPTER FIVE

The Edenic Covenant

Covenant Type

Is There an Edenic Covenant?

Not all would agree that there really is an Edenic covenant. Williamson is skeptical that Gen 1–2 are consistent with a covenantal framework. He does concede that W. J. Dumbrell's covenant with creation appears to have some exegetical foundation. Williamson agrees that the Noahic covenant alludes to material in Gen 1–3. However, he does not think that Gen 1–3 need to be understood covenantly. Moreover, he dismisses the reference to a covenant of day and night in Jer 33:20, 25 as an allusion to the Noahic covenant and the reference to a covenant with Adam in Hos 6:7 as capable of other interpretations. Williamson is also unpersuaded by Jefferey J. Niehaus' form-critical arguments.[1] Ryrie in both his study Bible[2] and his *Basic Theology*[3] avoids referring to the Edenic and Adamic covenants. This reluctance to see a covenant in Gen 2:5–25 is doubtless due to the lack of an explicit reference to covenant in the passage. However, in this case form-critical evidence is compelling and should not be dismissed cavalierly.

The covenant theologians, of course, see the covenant of works in this passage. M. E. Osterhaven explains:

> Having created man in his own image as a free creature with knowledge, righteousness, and holiness, God entered into covenant with Adam that he might bestow upon him further blessing. Called variously the Edenic covenant, the covenant of nature, the covenant of life, or preferably the covenant of works, this pact consisted of (1) a promise of eternal life upon the condition of perfect obedience throughout a probationary period; (2) the threat of death upon disobedience; and (3) the sacrament of the tree of life, or, in addition, the sacraments of paradise and the tree of the knowledge of good and evil.[4]

Perhaps the aversion expressed by some dispensationalists to a covenant in Gen 2 is due to the fact that most covenant theologians hold to it.

Wayne Grudem has answered the exegetical criticism of Hos 6:7. Although there is a geographical location called Adam (Josh 3:16), it does not fit this context. Grudem asserts that, although the term "covenant" is not used in Gen 1–2, the essential elements of a covenant are present. He also notes that Rom 5:12–21 is consistent with both Adam and Christ being the mediators of a covenant. He answers the criticism of the covenant interpretation of Hos 6:7:

> The RSV text translates, "But *at Adam* they transgressed the covenant," but the marginal note admits that this is a conjectural emendation and that the Hebrew text actually reads "like Adam" (Heb. *ke'ādām*). The Hebrew preposition *ke* means "like," not "at." The word translated "Adam" (Heb. *'ādām*) can also be translated "man," but the statement would make little sense: there is no single well-known transgression of a covenant by *man* to which it could refer. Moreover, it would do little good to compare the Israelites to what they already are (that is, men) and say that they "like man" broke the covenant. Such a sentence would almost imply that the Israelites were not men, but some other kind of creature. For these reasons, the translation "like Adam" is to be preferred. (The identical Hebrew expression translated "like Adam" in Job 31:33 in the NASB, RSV margin, and the NIV margin.)[5]

Rabbinical exegesis understood Hos 6:7 in the same way:

> R. Abbahu [ca. late 3rd century AD] said in the name of R. Jose b. R. Hanina [ca. 3rd century AD]: It is written, *But they are like a man (Adam), they have transgressed the covenant* (Hos. VI, 7) . 'They are *like a man* (Adam)' means like Adam: just as I led Adam into the garden of Eden and commanded him, and he transgressed My commandment, whereupon I punished him by dismissal and expulsion, and bewailed him with *ekah* (how)! (I led him into the garden of Eden, as it is written, *And the Lord God took the man, and put him into the garden of Eden* (Gen. II, 15) ; and I commanded him: *And the Lord God commanded the man* (ib. 17) ; and he transgressed My commandment: *Hast thou eaten of the tree, whereof I commanded thee that thou shouldest not eat* (ib. III, 11)? and I punished him by dismissal: *Therefore the Lord God sent him forth from the garden of Eden* (ib. 23); and I punished him by expulsion: *So he drove out the man* (ib. 24); I bewailed him with *ekah* (how)! And said unto him: *ayyekah: ekah* is written): so also did I bring his descendants into Eretz Israel and command them, and they transgressed My commandment, and I punished them by sending them away and expelling them, and I bewailed them with *ekah*![6]

Therefore, the Hos 6:7 reference to the Edenic covenant stands.

Paul states that "death reigned from Adam until Moses, even over those who had not sinned in the likeness of the offense of Adam" (Rom 5:14). Since Moses mediated the Mosaic covenant, this seems to indicate that Adam is connected with another covenant. In order for a transgression to exist there would have had to be covenant stipulations (i.e., laws). As Paul said, "For until the Law sin was in the world, but sin is not imputed when there is no law" (Rom 5:12). Therefore, Rom 5:14 indicates the existence of the Edenic covenant.

Genesis 2:5–25 contains the elements of a covenant. The fact that we have a record of a covenant not a covenant document *per se* explains the lack of an oath. The oath would be assumed, since the sovereign lord imposed a suzerainty covenant on his vassal. Osterhaven comments that "although the term 'covenant' is not mentioned in the first chapters of Genesis, it is held that all the elements of a covenant are present...."[7] Leland Ryken considers Gen 2:5–25 to be covenantal in structure:

> We catch the first hints of the covenant motif in Genesis 2, where God establishes what is sometimes called a "covenant of works" with Adam and Eve. It is a covenant that establishes the obligations of the creature toward God, as well as an outline of the consequences for disobeying. God's part of the covenant is to establish Adam and Eve in a perfect world where all their needs are met by divine provision. Adam and Eve's debt of gratitude can be paid by obeying God's injunction not to eat from the forbidden tree upon penalty of death (Gen 2:16–17). This language of command will be an important part of the imagery of the covenant throughout the Bible.[8]

Although not explicit, there seems to be a biblical basis to consider that Gen 2:5–25 does in fact report a covenant relationship.

Many dispensationalists are quite sure that a covenant is implied in Gen 2. Scofield, in his reference Bible, referred to the Edenic covenant.[9] E. Schuyler English distinguishes eight covenants that included the Edenic covenant, "The Edenic Covenant was made with Adam and required certain responsibilities on his part relating to the Garden of Eden."[10] Some confusion is discernible in Chafer's position. In *Major Bible Themes* Chafer sees an Edenic covenant in Gen 2.[11] In his *Systematic Theology* he is critical of the concept of the covenant of works as a matter of inference alone without sufficient ground in Scripture.[12] However, elsewhere in his *Systematic Theology*, Chafer states, "Before the fall, Adam was related to God by a covenant of works."[13] The question remains, "Did Adam, or did Adam not, have works as a means of salvation under the Edenic covenant?"

The resolution of this tension is in the fact that Adam, before he fell, needed no salvation. Therefore, obedience or works was not set forth as a means of salvation. Robert P. Lightner explains that God promised Adam death for disobedience not eternal life for obedience. He notes that, as a perfect creation, Adam needed no salvation before the Fall. He observes that covenant theology teaches a different way of salvation before the Fall. Lightner comments that is a strange doctrine for those who wrongly claim that dispensationalists teach more than one way of salvation.[14] Walvoord notes that a promise of life to Adam and Eve, if they were obedient, is totally without Scriptural basis.[15] The covenant theologian's reasoning seems to be:

If Adam eats the fruit, then he will die	$(a \supset d)$.
Adam does not eat the fruit	$(\sim a)$.
Therefore, Adam will not die	$(\therefore \sim d)$.

The covenant theologian's position commits the logical fallacy of denying the antecedent.[16] Interestingly enough, Caspar Olevianus, the father of covenant theology, did not teach the covenant of works. Lyle D. Bierma writes:

> It would seem, then, that past studies of Olevianus' covenant theology have claimed for his *foedus creationis* either too little or too much.... Not only does Olevianus never use the term *foedus operum* but there are several major features of that doctrine in its more developed (Cocceian) form that are missing in his *foedus creationis*.... He nowhere speaks of the promise of eternal life as the reward of Adam's obedience. He refers to obedience as an obligation *iure creationis*, a testimony of love to God, and a condition for bearing the divine image, but never as the stepping-stone to eternal life.[17]

Although both dispensationalists and covenant theologians see a covenant in Gen 2, the difference is that dispensationalists do not see works as ever having been a means of salvation. Adam was not promised life, Adam had life. It remains to be determined what form of covenant the Edenic covenant is.

What Sort of Covenant Is the Edenic Covenant?

We have already seen that all parties acknowledge that Adam related to God on a conditional basis. Only parity covenants and suzerainty covenants are conditional in nature. Man is never God's peer. Therefore, the Edenic covenant must be a suzerainty covenant. We should expect it, upon examination, to contain the major elements of a suzerainty covenant.

Preamble. While there is no explicit preamble in the form "I am *x*" or "These are the words of *x*," Gen 2:4 does introduce God's personal name, Yahweh (יהוה). H. C. Leupold notes that "the title 'Yahweh Elohim' suggests, as it does throughout the chapter, that this was a work of God that significantly displayed the faithful mercy of Yahweh as well as His awe-inspiring power."[18] C. F. Keil and F. Delitzsch note concerning the name, *Yahweh*, that it is the personal covenant name of God in His historical manifestation.[19] Kline also sees the introduction of the name, *Yahweh ʾᵉlōhîm*, as having covenant significance:

> *The Lord God* (Heb. *yhwh ʾᵉlōhîm*). The combination of the generic *ʾᵉlōhîm*, 'God', and the proper name, *Yahweh*, is found repeatedly in Gn. 2 and 3. *ʾᵉlōhîm* is used in Gn. 1 for God as Creator; it denotes God as He is known through His revelation in creation and general providence, including man's inward and intuitive knowledge of God. *Yahweh* is used alone beginning with Gn. 4; it is God's personal name describing Him as revealed through His historical-covenantal revelation as the Lord of eschatological purpose and sovereign fulfillment. The transitional combination, 'Yahweh God', in Gn. 2 and 3 serves to identify Yahweh, the covenant Lord, as God, the Creator.[20]

The phrase "the LORD God commanded" (Gen 2:16) is similar to covenant terminology in that the Great King is the narrator. There are instances among the Hittite treaties where the preamble is merged with the historical introduction (e.g., the treaty between Suppiluliuma I of Hatti and Niqmaddu II of Ugarit).[21] Therefore, the lack of an explicit preamble is not fatal to considering Gen 2:5–25 covenantal in its structure.

Historical Introduction. The historical prologue functions to provide a motivation for gratitude on the part of the vassal. Genesis 1:1–2:25 forms the historical prologue of this section. Genesis 1:1–2:4 reveals God as the Creator of heaven and earth. Genesis 2:5–7 reveals God as the Creator of man.[22] Genesis 2:8–15 points out that God is the One Who forms Eden and places man in charge of it. Genesis 2:18–25 reveals God as the Creator of all life and the One Who made Eve for Adam. In short, Adam and Eve have every motivation for grateful obedience to God.

Stipulations. The covenant stipulations are contained in Gen 2:8–17. They will be discussed later in more detail. It is sufficient to note at this point that covenant stipulations are in evidence, as would be expected in a suzerainty covenant.

Deposition. In keeping with the nature of the record as primeval history, there are no formalized societal structures for storing and reading covenant documents. However, Gen 3:2–3 indicates indirectly that Adam had rehearsed the details of the covenant with Eve, although she did embellish them. Therefore, we know that Adam, as a vassal, did teach the details of the covenant to the one person under his authority.

Divine Witness. God Himself is present as the Witness and enforces the curse when humankind rebels.

Curses and Blessings. This section contains both blessings and curses. The prevailing conditions in Eden constitute the blessing. Genesis 1:10, 12, 18, 21, 25, 31 repeatedly confirms that God's creation is good. Genesis 2:25 relates that "the man and his wife were both naked and were not ashamed." Genesis 2:17 contains the curse, "For in the day that you eat from it you will surely die." Genesis 3 details the outworking of that curse upon the occasion of man's fall. The complementary concepts of blessing and curse are prominent in this passage. This is what would be expected in a suzerainty covenant.

Beneficiaries

Clearly, the recipients of this covenant are the human race. God had created man and man's realm (Gen 1:1–2:14). God placed man in his proper domain (Gen 2:15) and "the LORD God commanded the man" (Gen 2:16). God sovereignly fashions woman from man according to His wisdom. John H. Sailhamer notes that in Genesis the recipient of God's covenant provision is asleep while God acts. He mentions Abraham (Gen 15:12) and Jacob (Gen 28:11) as examples in addition to Adam. Man is seen as passively accepting the covenant imposed upon him.[23]

Stipulations

The stipulations of Gen 2:8–17 are reminiscent of Hittite suzerainty covenants. God installs Adam as a vassal to rule creation and defines his role, boundaries, and responsibilities.[24] Genesis 2:8–15 establishes the boundaries of his vassal kingdom. This prefigures the land promises of the Abrahamic and Land covenants. Dumbrell comments that "Man, moreover, is defined in Ps. 8:5 (with obvious reference to Gen. 1:26) in terms of his relationship to God, and in kingship language.... By creation, man is then the visible representative in the created world of the invisible God."[25] Adam was placed in the garden of Eden "to work it and take care of it (לְעָבְדָהּ וּלְשָׁמְרָהּ)" (Gen 2:15 NIV). The Hebrew עָבַד is used of vassal relationships (Gen 14:4; 2 Sam 10:19; 1 Chr 18:2, 6, 13). Adam was a vassal king under his Lord, the Great King, Yahweh. However, he was more than that.

Adam can also be viewed as a priest. The Hebrew עָבַד is also used of worship (Exod 20:5), perhaps because worship is seen as a vassal relationship to Yahweh (Lev 25:55). The word שָׁמַר is used in Lev 19:30 for worship. Kline observes that, in verse 15, "*Keep* it is perhaps a cultic charge, i.e. to guard the sanctity of God's dwelling; *cf.* the use of the same verb *šāmar* in 3:24; Ne. 13:22; Zc. 3:7."[26] Sailhamer notes that there is a similarity between the appearance and role of the Garden of Eden in Gen 2 and the tabernacle in Exod 25–27 in that both show the glory of God by means of the beauty of the physical setting. He finds also a similarity between God placing man in the garden and establishing the priesthood for the tabernacle.[27] He explains that God's purpose for placing man in the garden has been misunderstood:

> In most EVs man is "put" in the garden "to work it and take care of it" (*l^{ec}obdah ûl^{e}šomrāh*). Although that translation was as early as the LXX (2d cent. B.C.), there are serious objections to it. For one, the suffixed pronoun in the Hebrew text rendered "it" in English is feminine, whereas the noun "garden," which the pronoun refers to in English, is a masculine noun in Hebrew. Only by changing the pronoun to a masculine singular, as the LXX has done, can it have the sense of the EVs, namely "to work" and "to keep." Moreover, later in this same narrative (3:23) "to work the ground" (*la^{c}abod*) is said to be a result of the Fall, and the narrative suggests that the author had intended such a punishment to be seen as an ironic reversal of man's original purpose.... If such was the case, then "working" and "keeping" the garden would not provide a contrast to "working the ground."
>
> In light of these objections, which cannot easily be overlooked, a more suitable translation of the Hebrew *l^{ec}obdah ûl^{e}šomrāh* would be "to worship and to obey" (Cassuto). Man is put in the garden to worship God and to obey him. Man's life in the garden was to be characterized by worship and obedience; he was a priest, not merely a worker and keeper of the garden.[28]

This is in keeping with rabbinical thought. In *Genesis Rabbah* (R. Berekiah, ca. 4th century AD) we find:

> LE-' ABEDAH (TO TILL IT): as you read, *Six days shalt thou labour*-ta-'abod (*ib.*

9). ULE-SHAMERAH (AND TO KEEP IT): Keep (shamor) the Sabbath day (*Deut. V, 12*). Another interpretation: LE-'ABEDAH ULE-SHAMERAH (TO TILL IT AND TO KEEP IT) is an allusion to sacrifices: thus it is written, *Ye shall serve* (ta-'abdun) *God upon this mountain* (*Ex. III, 12*); and, *Ye shall observe* (tishmeru) *to offer unto Me* (*Num. XXVIII, 2*).[29]

Adam had a role that included kingly and priestly functions. This close relationship with God prefigures the blessing aspect of the Abrahamic and new covenants. However, another role can be attributed to Adam under this first covenant.

Adam can also be viewed as a prophet. Kline sees a hint of this role in the naming of the animals.[30] Adam also fellowshipped with God, and mediated God's word to his wife. As has been previously indicated, the mediatorial role is central to the prophetic office. Thus, the first Adam was prophet, priest, and king, as was the last Adam (Rom 5:14; 1 Cor 15:22, 45; Heb 1:1–3, 8; 4:14–15; Rev 19:16).

Genesis 2:16–17 contains the main stipulation upon which all was conditioned. Employing covenant terminology Adam is commanded (עַל־הָאָדָם וַיְצַו יְהוָה אֱלֹהִים) not to eat from the tree of the knowledge of good and evil. The Hebrew וַיְצַו is a *waw* consecutive construction with the *pi'el* imperfect of the verb צוה. Brown, Driver, and Briggs define the *pi'el* of צָוָה as "lay charge (upon), give charge (to), charge, command, order...."[31] Young partly catches the sense when he translates the passage, "And Jehovah God layeth a charge on the man" (Gen 2:16 YLT). I would translate this, "And Yahweh God laid a charge on the man" in keeping with the *waw* consecutive.

Cast in apodictic terms, the stipulation begins with a permission, "From any tree of the garden you may eat freely ..." (Gen 2:16). "Eat freely" is תֹאכֵל אָכֹל, the *qal* infinitive followed by the imperfect of אָכַל. Young translates this phrase, "Eating thou dost eat ..." (Gen 2:16 YLT). Driver takes this construction in Gen 2:16 to be concessive. However, he sees the usage in Gen 2:17 of the same construction (מוֹת תָּמוּת) to express a command, "You will surely die...."[32] The one exception provides the occasion of exercising true moral choice.

The prohibition "from the tree of the knowledge of good and evil you shall not eat, for in the day that you eat from it you will surely die" (Gen 2:17) continues the apodictic form. Graciously, God did not immediately carry out the sentence. However, this has taxed the ingenuity of many expositors who would have expected the immediate demise of Adam and

Eve. Perhaps the cleverest is Justin Martyr (AD 100–165):

> For as Adam was told that in the day he ate of the tree he would die, we know that he did not complete a thousand years. We have perceived, moreover, that the expression, 'The day of the Lord is as a thousand years,' is connected with this subject. And further, there was a certain man with us, whose name was John, one of the apostles of Christ, who prophesied, by a revelation that was made to him, that those who believed in our Christ would dwell a thousand years in Jerusalem; and that thereafter the general, and, in short, the eternal resurrection and judgment of all men would likewise take place.[33]

However, Sailhamer is probably correct when he notes that in the Pentateuch מוֹת תָּמוּת means that one is under a verdict of death (e.g., Gen 20:7; Exod 31:14; Lev 24:16). He believes that the verdict was executed by expelling Adam and Eve from Eden and the tree of life (Gen 3:22–24).[34] David H. Lane notes that Adam died spiritually immediately and began to die physically. He also takes the meaning to be "you shall be doomed to death."[35] Following this sort of analysis, the Jerusalem Bible translates this phrase, "You are doomed to die" (Gen 2:17 JB). Spiritual death was the immediate penalty and humankind was doomed to die physically.

Establishment

The covenant was established with the issuance of God's command to Adam in Gen 2:16–17. It appears to have begun before Eve was fashioned from Adam (Gen 2:18–22). However, there can be little doubt that Adam taught Eve concerning the covenant at an early date (Gen 3:2). Therefore, the Edenic covenant begins, for all practical purposes, with the creation of humankind. In the case of this covenant, all of the stipulations were instituted at the same time that the covenant was established (see table 3). As we shall see later, this is not always the case.

Duration

The Edenic covenant was broken when Adam and Eve sinned (Gen 3:1–13). When the covenant is broken, the curse was implemented (Gen 3:14–24) and remains in force. As Chafer states, "Much that is in this covenant is perpetual throughout all generations until the curse is lifted from creation (Rom. 8:19–23)."[36] With the Edenic covenant broken, God instituted His next covenant with humankind, the Adamic covenant (see figure 2).

HAL HARLESS

Type of Covenant	Stipulation of Covenant	Beneficiaries	Established	End
Suzerainty	Do not eat from the tree of the knowledge of good and evil.	Humankind as represented by Adam and Eve	At the Creation of man (Gen 2:16, 17)	At the Fall of man (Gen 3:7)

Table 3. Edenic Covenant

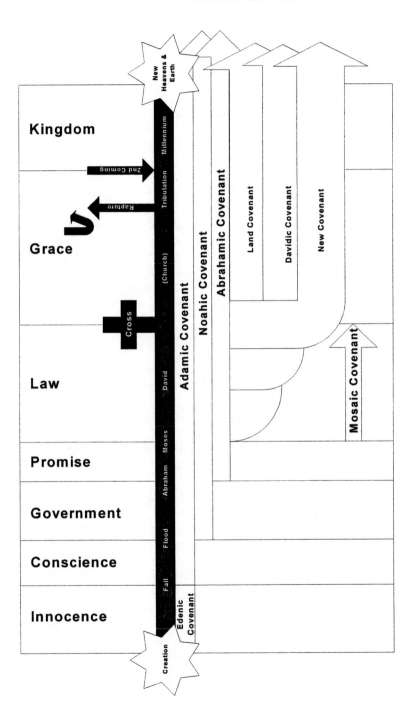

Figure 2. Covenants and Dispensations

NOTES

1. Williamson, "Covenant," *NDBT* 421.

2. Charles C. Ryrie, *The Ryrie Study Bible: New American Standard* (hereafter referred to as *RSB*) (Chicago, Moody, 1976).

3. Charles C. Ryrie, *Basic Theology: A Popular Systematic Guide to understanding Biblical Truth* (Chicago: Moody, 1986).

4. M. E. Osterhaven, "Covenant Theology," *EvDT* 301–3.

5. Wayne Grudem, *Systematic Theology: An Introduction to Biblical Doctrine* (Grand Rapids, MI: Zondervan, 1994) 516. McComiskey agrees with Grudem's analysis. However, he contends that the evidence is inconclusive. His main concern seems to be that, if Gen 1–2 is covenantal, it not be confused with the covenants of promise (Thomas Edward McComiskey, *The Covenants of Promise: A Theology of the Old Testament Covenants* [Grand Rapids, MI: Baker, 1985] 213–21).

6. *Midr. Gen. Rab.* 19:9, *The Soncino Midrash Rabbah*, trans. H. Freedman, Simon Maurice, 10 vols., Judaic Classics Library, ver. 2.1 [CD-ROM] (Brooklyn, NY: Judaica,1991) 1:154–55.

7. Osterhaven, "Covenant Theology," *EvDT* 302.

8. Leland Ryken, "Covenant," *DBI* 176–78.

9. C. I. Scofield, *The New Scofield Reference Bible* (hereafter referred to as *NSRB*), ed. E. Schuyler English (New York: Oxford University Press, 1969) 5, footnote on Gen 2:16.

10. E. Schuyler English, *A Companion to The New Scofield Reference Bible* (New York: Oxford University Press, 1972) 55.

11. Lewis Sperry Chafer, *Major Bible Themes: 5? Vital Doctrines of the Scripture Simplified and Explained*, rev. John F. Walvoord (Grand Rapids, MI: Zondervan, 1974) 142.

12. Ibid. 140. See also Chafer, *Systematic Theology* 4:156–57.

13. Chafer, *Systematic Theology* 1:42.

14. Robert P. Lightner, "Perspectives on Theonomy: Part 3: A Dispensational Response to Theonomy," *BSac* 143, no. 571 (July–September 1986): 228–45. See also McComiskey, *The Covenants of Promise* 218–19.

15. John F. Walvoord, "Millennial Series: Part 7: Amillennial Soteriology," *BSac* 107, no. 427 (July–September 1950): 281–90.

16. The form ($p \supset q$, ~p, $\therefore$ ~q) is invalid and is often confused with *modus tollens* ($p \supset q$, ~q, $\therefore$~p). See Norman L. Geisler, Ronald M. Brooks, *Come, Let Us Reason: An Introduction to Logical Thinking* (Grand Rapids, MI: Baker, 1990) 83–84.

17. Lyle D. Bierma, *German Calvinism in the Confessional Age: The Covenant Theology of Caspar Olevianus* (Grand Rapids, MI: Baker, 1996) 117–18.

18. H. C. Leupold, *Exposition of Genesis*, 2 vols. (Grand Rapids, MI: Baker, 1942),

1:115.

19. C. F. Keil, F. Delitzsch, *Pentateuch*, vol. 1 of Commentary on the Old Testament (hereafter referred to as COT), trans. James Martin, 10 vols. (Edinburgh: T. & T. Clark, 1866-91; reprint, Peabody, Mass.: Hendrickson, 1996) 1:47.

20. Meredith G. Kline, "Genesis," *The New Bible Commentary: Revised* (hereafter referred to as *NBC)*, eds. D. Guthrie, J. A. Motyer, 3rd ed. (Grand Rapids, MI: Eerdmans, 1970) 83.

21. Beckman, *Hittite Diplomatic Texts* 30–31, 4.1–2.

22. "Adam" (אדם) is Hebrew for "man."

23. John H. Sailhamer, "Genesis," in *Genesis–Numbers*, vol. 2 of The Expositor's Bible Commentary (hereafter referred to as EBC), gen. ed. Frank E. Gaebelein, 12 vols. (Grand Rapids, MI: Zondervan, 1990) 2:46.

24. Olevianus uses vassal terminology also, "Tota vita nostra debetur Deo iure creationis, ut eius gloriae serviat, & nulla pars diabolo aut vitiis. Haec est una obligatio ius creationis, quo nos tanquam vasalli Deo" (*Comm. on Rom. 8:12–13*, 341; quoted in Bierma, *German Calvinism* 115).

25. W. J. Dumbrell, *Covenant and Creation: A Theology of the Old Testament Covenants* (Chatham, Kent: Paternoster, 1984; reprint, 2000) 33–34. While accepting Dumbrell's point about the passage's kingship language, I agree with Couch that Ps 8 is Messianic (Mal Couch, "Progressive Dispensationalism: Is Christ Now on the Throne of David?—Part II," *CTJ* 2, no. 5 [June 1998]: 142–56).

26. Kline, "Genesis," *NBC* 84.

27. Sailhamer, "Genesis," EBC 2:43.

28. Ibid. 2:45.

29. *Midr. Gen. Rab.* 16:5, *The Soncino Midrash Rabbah* 1:129.

30. Kline, "Genesis," *NBC* 84.

31. BDB 845–46.

32. S. R. Driver, *A Treatise on the Use of the Tenses in Hebrew and Some Other Syntactical Questions* (Grand Rapids, MI: Eerdmans, 1874; reprint, 1998) 42–43.

33. Justin Martyr, *Dialogue of Justin* 81, in *The Ante-Nicene Fathers*, 10 vols., eds. Alexander Roberts, James Donaldson, in The Master Christian Library ver. 8.0 [CD-ROM] (Albany, OR: AGES Software, 1997) 1:461.

34. Sailhamer, "Genesis," EBC 2:48.

35. David H. Lane, "Theological Problems with Theistic Evolution," *BSac* 151, no. 602 (April–June 1994): 155–74.

36. Lewis Sperry Chafer, *Systematic Theology* 1:42.

CHAPTER SIX

The Adamic Covenant

Covenant Type

In many respects the Adamic covenant is a continuation of the Edenic covenant. Walvoord observes that

> in place of the covenant of works as such, premillenarians often offer the Edenic covenant in its place. This covenant though not expressly called a covenant in Scripture includes all the aspects of man's responsibility before the fall, including the prohibition of the forbidden fruit. As understood by the premillenarians, this covenant ceased to exist when the fall occurred and was succeeded by the Adamic covenant providing the basic conditions for man's life on the earth after the fall, some of which conditions continue until the end of the present world order.[1]

In fact, among covenant theologians, the Edenic covenant is often referred to as the Adamic covenant. The nature of the Adamic covenant is largely determined by the curses invoked upon the failure of the Edenic covenant. It is, therefore, a suzerainty covenant in form although abbreviated. The arguments for the form of the Edenic covenant also apply to the Adamic covenant.

The Adamic covenant begins with God's theophany in judgment on the covenant breakers. Niehaus notes this usage in the Scriptures and the ancient Near East:

> The idea that God judged his people for their covenant trespasses in the Old Testament does not need elaboration. But the role of theophany in God's covenantal arrangements is another matter.... God appeared in theophanic glory as part of his covenant administration primarily in four ways. He appeared to initiate a covenant.... He appeared to instruct, encourage, or correct his covenant vassal.... He appeared to commission or encourage a prophet in covenant lawsuit.... He appeared to bring covenantal judgment on rebellious vassals (e.g., to the fallen man and woman, Ge 3:8–19.... Data from the ancient world in general are more scattered and uneven

than those of the Old Testament. But there are points of contact between the Old Testament and the ancient Near East.[2]

Genesis 3:8–24 fits the form of the covenant lawsuit.[3] As God comes in judgment to the covenant-breaking Adam and Eve, He establishes the conditions under which they are henceforth to live.

Beneficiaries

As in the Edenic covenant, our first parents, and through them the entire human race, are the main recipients of the Adamic covenant. Chafer notes that

> this is an unconditional covenant in which God declares to man what his lot in life will be because of his sin. There is no appeal allowed, nor is any human responsibility involved.
>
> The covenant as a whole provides important features which condition human life from this point on…. To a large extent, man continues from this point on to operate under the Adamic covenant.[4]

The serpent is, of course, included in the curse. However, the serpent stands for Satan whose activity and eventual defeat are of paramount importance to humankind.

Establishment

The Adamic covenant is established at the fall of humankind in Gen 3:1–7. God appears as Judge and conducts an interrogation in Gen 3:8–13. His appearance was not as quiet as we would assume from the English translations, "And they heard the sound of the LORD God (וַיִּשְׁמְעוּ אֶת־קוֹל יְהוָה אֱלֹהִים) walking in the garden in the cool of the day (לְרוּחַ הַיּוֹם)" (Gen 3:8). Sailhamer explains that Gen 3:8 is mistranslated. He notes that similar terminology in Deut 5:25 ("hear the voice of the LORD our God" לִשְׁמֹעַ אֶת־קוֹל יְהוָה אֱלֹהֵינוּ) and 18:16 ("hear again the voice of the LORD my God" אֶת־קוֹל יְהוָה אֱלֹהָי לִשְׁמֹעַ) resulted in the Israelis fearing that they would die (Exod 20:19). He also suggests that the "wind (רוּחַ)" may be similar to the "wind" in 1 Kgs 19:11.[5] This passage records a theophanic judgment not a quiet conversation. Niehaus remarks concerning the biblical and ancient Near Eastern parallels:

> God thundered through the Garden of Eden after his man and woman sinned, he thundered atop Mount Sinai, he thundered before Elijah and Ezekiel, and he thundered from Mount Zion in eschatological glory. But God is not the only god

who thundered. It was thought throughout the ancient Near East that thunder was a holy utterance of some god or other. Sumerian, Hittite, Akkadian, Egyptian (Amarna), and Ugaritic evidence makes this clear. What also becomes apparent as we survey the evidence is that theophany or theophanic language in the ancient Near East often happened because a god was said to appear as a part of covenant administration—namely, to thunder against covenant breakers.[6]

Yahweh delivers three curses, each introduced with, "And Yahweh Elohim said.... He said.... He said (אָמַר... אָמַר ... אֱלֹהִים יְהוָה וַיֹּאמֶר)": to the serpent (Gen 3:14–15), to the woman (Gen 3:16), and to the man (Gen 3:17–19). The stipulation of these curses forms the basis for the Adamic covenant.

Stipulations

Adam and Eve had possessed life and blessing in a perfect land. With the fall the covenant curses institute a reversal of their condition. Sailhamer notes that Adam and Eve were created for worship (לְעָבְדָהּ) (Gen 2:15), but after the fall were cursed to "to cultivate the ground (הָאֲדָמָה אֶת־לַעֲבֹד)" (Gen 3:23). They were created for obedience (וּלְשָׁמְרָהּ) (Gen 2:15), however, after the fall were kept (לִשְׁמֹר) from "the tree of life" (Gen 3:24).[7] In three speeches, Yahweh elaborated the curse. Yet, in the midst of the curse is a hint of future blessing.

First, God addressed the serpent (Gen 3:14–15). This passage is referred to as the *protoevangelium* in that, while predicting the defeat of the serpent, it is the first hint of victory and redemption for humankind. The curse on the serpent is twofold: (1) The serpent is condemned to eat dust as his curse for tempting Adam and Eve to eat the forbidden fruit. (2) Hostility is predicted between the serpent's seed and Eve's seed. An individual is predicted from Eve's seed who will crush the serpent's head although the serpent will wound his heel. Sailhamer explains that this is a prediction of the total defeat of the serpent. He notes that eating dust means total defeat (Isa 65:25; Mic 7:17). He explains that both Eve and the serpent are identified with their seeds and that Moses intends this battle of seeds to point beyond Eve and the serpent. Although the woman's seed is wounded, nevertheless, He is ultimately victorious. Sailhamer observes that this passage is ambiguous. It raises the question, "Who is the seed of the woman?" It does not answer it.[8] Charles L. Feinberg concludes that a definite reference to the virgin birth is in view.[9] Thus, the serpent stands for Satan. Paul probably has Gen 3:14–15 in view in Rom 16:10 in predicting the defeat of Satan by the Christians, no doubt, because of Christ's victory on the cross. Ryrie explains that

> the animosity between Satan and Christ was first predicted after the sin of Adam and Eve (Gen. 3:15). The enmity between spiritual descendants of Satan and the family of God was predicted here. Also an individual (Christ) from among the woman's seed would deal a fatal blow to Satan's head, while Satan would bruise Christ's heel (a nonfatal blow, but one that caused Him great suffering). This exchange of blows took place at the cross.[10]

Therefore, God's curse on the serpent, giving him the bad news of his total defeat, becomes to us the first hint of the good news, the Protoevangelium. This stipulation, of course, is not instituted until the cross.

Next, God addresses the woman (Gen 3:16). Her curse is also twofold: (1) She is cursed with added pain in childbirth. (2) Her relationship with her husband will be distorted. Kline comments that "travail would now characterize man's genealogical development and the reinstituted marriage relationship would be disturbed by sinful inclinations towards the abuse of its authority structure (cf. 4:7 for the idiom)."[11] Sailhamer notes concerning these curses that the woman and her husband were originally intended to enjoy a harmonious relationship (Gen 2:18, 21–25) and the blessing of children (Gen 1:28). He points out that it is precisely those blessings that are now tainted by the fall. Nevertheless, Sailhamer notes that every birth pain is also a reminder of the coming victory of the seed of the woman. Sailhamer explains the dire impact of the Fall on human relationships:

> The word תְּשׁוּקָה (t'šûqāh "longing"; NIV, "desire") is "unusual and striking" (BDB, p. 1003). Apart from 3:16, it occurs only in Gen 4:7 and Song of Songs 7:10. Its use in Song of Songs shows that the "longing" can refer to physical attraction, but in Gen 4:7 the "longing" carries the sense of a desire to overcome or defeat another. It is unwise to read too much into the word itself. The way that the whole of this section of the curse— וְאֶל־אִישֵׁךְ תְּשׁוּקָתֵךְ וְהוּא יִמְשָׁל־בָּךְ: (w'el-ʾîšēk t'šûqātēk w'hûʾ yimšol-bāk "Your desire will be for your husband, and he will rule over you")— foreshadows the Lord's words to Cain in 4:7— וְאֵלֶיךָ תְּשׁוּקָתוֹ וְאַתָּה תִּמְשָׁל־בּוֹ: (w'ēleykā t'šûqāṭô w'attāh timšol-bô "it desires to have you but you must master it")— suggests that the author intended the two passages to be read together. If so, the sense of "desiring" in 3:16 should be understood as the wife's desire to overcome or gain the upper hand over her husband. In the same way, the sense of yimšol-bāk is as in the NIV: "he will rule over you." Within the context of the Creation account in chapters 2 and 3, this last statement stands in sharp contrast to the picture of the man and the woman as "one flesh" (l'bāśār ʾehād 2:24) and the picture of the woman as a "helper suitable for him" (ʿēzer k'negkô 2:18). The Fall has had its effect on the rela-

tionship of the husband and wife.[12]

Susan T. Foh contends that "desire (תְּשׁוּקָה)" means "desire to control" (cf. Gen 4:7) and that "rule (מָשַׁל)" suggests suppression and dominance.[13] The reversal was dramatic. Into Eve's family relations, both with her children and her husband, sin had introduced pain and distortion.

Finally, God addresses the man (Gen 3:17–19). Adam's curse is also twofold: (1) difficulty obtaining food from the ground and (2) returning to the ground through death and decay. The progress of the fall is presented by means of the theme of eating in Genesis 2–3. The verb אָכַל ("to eat") occurs seventeen times in the twenty-two verses of Genesis 3. Originally, man could freely eat from any tree of the garden except one (Gen 2:16). Eve was tempted to eat from the tree of the knowledge of good and evil (Gen 3:1–5). When Adam and Eve sinned it was by eating from that tree (Gen 3:6). God's question to the fallen couple was, "Have you eaten from the tree of which I commanded you not to eat?" (Gen 3:11). Therefore, the curse is that "because you have listened to the voice of your wife, and have eaten from the tree about which I commanded you, saying, 'You shall not eat from it'; cursed is the ground because of you; in toil you will eat of it all the days of your life" (Gen 3:17).[14] Allen P. Ross notes that "painful toil translates the same word used in v. 16 for the woman's pain. This word occurs only three times in the OT, in vv. 16–17 and 5:29."[15] The land will produce weeds as well as the plants that Adam is to eat (Gen 3:18). Adam will have to toil to obtain his bread (Gen 3:19). Kline remarks concerning the second curse:

> To dust you shall return. Because the ground entered into the composition of man (cf. 2:7), the curse on the ground became a power unto death working in his very members (cf. Nu. 5:16ff.). Death, formerly present in nature in subservience to man, would now terrorize man the covenant-breaker as the wages of his sin.[16]

In Gen 3:18 the ground is cursed. Moreover, Adam, who is made from the ground (Gen 2:7), is cursed to return to the ground (Gen 3:19) and barred from the tree of life (Gen 3:22). A reminder of this is the relationship that Moses draws between Adam (אָדָם) and the ground (אֲדָמָה) in Gen 2:7 and 3:19.[17] By his rebellion, Adam abdicated his position as Yahweh's vassal on the Earth. No longer was he serving and worshipping God in the land. Instead he is giving hard service to the land and, being kept from the tree of life, he and all of his descendants are under a sentence of death until they return to the dust from whence they came.

Taken as a whole these stipulations define a world that is a reversal of the Edenic condition. God's retribution had turned, with poetic justice, each blessing into a curse. Ross remarks that "these punishments represent retaliatory justice. Adam and Eve sinned by eating; they would suffer in order to eat. She manipulated her husband; she would be mastered by her husband. The serpent destroyed the human race; he will be destroyed."[18] Nevertheless, in the destruction of the serpent is the hint of future redemption. Perhaps also the "garments of skin" that Yahweh God made for them, because they entailed a sacrifice, provides another hint of redemption. We know, in any case, by Gen 4:3–5 there is a sacrificial worship of God. Hebrews 11:4 indicates that faith was involved in the proper offering of those sacrifices. There seems then to have been some rudimentary knowledge of atoning sacrifice. Beyond this, we cannot safely speculate (see table 4).

Duration

The Adamic covenant endures from the moment of that first human sin (Gen 3:1–19) to the point where "there shall be no longer any curse" (Rev 22:3). Chafer notes that "to a large extent, man continues from this point on to operate under the Adamic covenant."[19] G. R. Beasley-Murray comments on Rev 22:3:

> *There shall no more be anything accursed* may simply mean that nothing unclean or abominable shall find entrance into the holy city (21:27). But it is more likely that we have here a deliberate contrast to the curse pronounced in the original paradise that brought woe on all creation (Gn. 3:14–19). The effects of that curse have been completely overcome in the new Jerusalem.[20]

Craig S. Keener confidently asserts that "the removal of the curse is from Zechariah 14:11, and in this context it refers to the reversal of the curse in Eden (Gen 3:16–19)."[21] Although some lifting of the curse begins in the millennial kingdom, the full revocation of the Adamic covenant awaits the new heavens and the new earth spoken of in Rev 21:1. Walvoord comments on Rev 22:3:

> To emphasize the blessedness of the new situation, verse 3 states that there is no more curse. In the millennial scene, there is a lifting of the curse upon the earth, but not a total deliverance from the world's travail brought in by sin, for in the millennium, it is still possible for a "sinner" to be "accursed" (Isa. 65:20) with resulting physical death. In the new heaven and the new earth, there will be no curse at all and

no possibility or need of such divine punishment.[22]

Paul writes in Rom 8:18–23 that all of creation will one day be set free when the sons of God are revealed. Surely, this refers to the same event. Therefore, the Adamic covenant endures from the fall to the new heavens and new earth with the effects being partially lifted during the millennium (see figure 2).

Type of Covenant	Stipulations of Covenant	Beneficiaries	Established	End
Suzerainty (Curses)	To Serpent: • Eat dust entire life • Total defeat by the woman's seed To Woman: • Pain in birth • Distorted relationship with husband To Man: • Pain in work • Death • Hope/Sacrifice	• Humankind as represented by Adam and Eve • Satan as represented by the Serpent	At the Fall of man (Gen 3:1–19)	At the new heavens and the new earth (Rev 21:1; 22:3) though lessened during the millennium

Table 4. Adamic Covenant

NOTES

1. John F. Walvoord, *Millennial Kingdom* (Grand Rapids, MI: Zondervan, 1959) 78. See also Eugene H. Merrill, "A Theology of the Pentateuch," *A Biblical Theology of the Old Testament*, ed. Roy B. Zuck (Chicago: Moody, 1991) 18–23.
2. Jefferey J. Niehaus, *God at Sinai: Covenant and Theophany in the Bible and Ancient Near East* (Grand Rapids, MI: Zondervan, 1995) 108–9.
3. Ibid. 30–42.
4. Chafer, *Major Bible Themes* 142.
5. Sailhamer, "Genesis," EBC 2:52. See also Niehaus, *God at Sinai* 155–59. Walton, Matthews, and Chavalas explain that "Akkadian terminology has demonstrated that the word translated 'day' also has the meaning 'storm.' This meaning can be seen also for the Hebrew word in Zeph 2:2. It is often connected to the deity coming in a storm of judgment. If this is the correct rendering of the word in this passage, they heard the thunder (the word translated 'sound' is often connected to thunder) of the Lord moving about in the garden in the wind of the storm. In this case it is quite understandable why they are hiding (John H. Walton, Victor H. Matthews, Mark W. Chavalas, *The IVP Bible Background Commentary: Old Testament* [hereafter referred to as *BBCOT*] [Downers Grove, IL: InterVarsity, 2000] 33).
6. Niehaus, *God at Sinai* 125–36.
7. Sailhamer, "Genesis," EBC 2:48; 2:59.
8. Sailhamer, "Genesis," EBC 2:55–56.
9. Charles L. Feinberg, "The Virgin Birth in the Old Testament," *BSac* 117, no. 468 (October–December 1960): 313–24.
10. Ryrie, *Basic Theology* 166.
11. Kline, "Genesis," *NBC* 85.
12. Sailhamer, "Genesis," EBC 2:56–58.
13. Susan T. Foh, "What is the Woman's Desire," *Westminister Theological Journal* (hereafter referred to as *WTJ*) 37, no. 3 (Spring 1975): 376–83. See also Grudem, *Systematic Theology* 464–65.
14. Sailhamer, "Genesis," EBC 2:56–57.
15. Allen P. Ross, "Genesis," *The Bible Knowledge Commentary: An Exposition of the Scriptures by Dallas Seminary Faculty: Old Testament* (hereafter referred to as *BKCOT*), eds. John Walvoord, Roy B. Zuck (n.p.: Victor, 1985) 33.
16. Kline, "Genesis," *NBC* 85.
17. Sailhamer, "Genesis," EBC 2:57.
18. Ross, "Genesis," *BKCOT* 33.
19. Chafer, *Major Bible Themes* 142.
20. G. R. Beasley-Murray, "The Revelation," *NBC* 1308.
21. Craig S. Keener, *The IVP Bible Background Commentary: New Testament* (hereafter referred to as *BBCNT*) (Downers Grove, IL: InterVarsity, 1993) 819.

22.   John F. Walvoord, *The Revelation of Jesus Christ* (Chicago: Moody, 1966) 331. See
Pentecost, *Things to Come* 563–80 for a differing view.

CHAPTER SEVEN

The Noahic Covenant

Covenant Type

Genesis 6:18 is the first explicit reference to covenants in the Bible. While there is virtually no debate as to the covenantal nature of Gen 6:18; 8:20–9:17, there is a debate as to the nature of the covenant. God told Noah, "I will establish My covenant with you (וַהֲקִמֹתִי אֶת־בְּרִיתִי אִתְּךָ)" (Gen 6:18). The phrase "I will establish" translates the Hebrew וַהֲקִמֹתִי which is the first person common *hip̔il* perfect of קוּם ("to stand") with a *waw* consecutive. It could be translated, "I will cause to stand." Dumbrell, noting other instances of בְּרִית הֵקִם, sees this as implying the reestablishment or continuation of an existing covenant.[1] Williamson, however, is skeptical and claims that הֵקִם בְּרִית does not demand this interpretation.[2] Actually, the *hip̔il* of קוּם, in conjunction with בְּרִית is used fourteen times in the OT (Gen 6:18; 9:9, 11, 17; 17:7, 19, 21; Exod 6:4; Lev 26:9; Deut 8:18; 2 Kgs 23:3; Jer 34:18; Ezek 16:60, 62). Dumbrell is correct in that all of these occurrences, with the possible exception of Jer 34:18, refer to confirming an existing covenant. Jeremiah 34:18 speaks of confirming the covenant by action. However, this is not contradictory in that a covenant must exist before one can fulfill its stipulations. Within the Torah, the *hip̔il* of קוּם is also used in establishing oaths. Genesis 26:3 has, "Establish the oath (וַהֲקִמֹתִי אֶת־הַשְּׁבֻעָה)" and Deut 9:5 has, "To confirm the oath (הָקִים אֶת־הַדָּבָר)." Numbers 30:13, 14 speaks of a husband's right to confirm or annul the oaths that his wife has made, "Every binding oath to humble herself, her husband may confirm it (שְׁבֻעַת אִסָּר לְעַנֹּת נָפֶשׁ אִישָׁהּ יְקִימֶנּוּ וְאִישָׁהּ)" (Num 30:13). The evidence does seem to be conclusive that the *hip̔il* of קוּם with covenant or oath terminology possesses the sense of "confirm" or "reestablish."

This raises the question of the identity of the covenant that is being reestablished or confirmed. Sailhamer notes language reminiscent of Gen 1–2 in Gen 8:15–19 and that "the restoration of God's Creation was founded on the establishment of a covenant."³ Dumbrell posits a covenant with creation based on Jer 33:20 and allusions to themes from Gen 1–3 in the Noahic covenant.⁴ Dumbrell rejects the Edenic covenant as the covenant being confirmed here because he does not hold to its existence. As I have demonstrated, there is ample evidence for the existence of the Edenic covenant. However, since that covenant ended with the Fall and the establishment of the Adamic covenant, it cannot be the covenant in question. Moreover, one need not see a creation covenant in Jer 33:20. Williamson objects that the covenant with day and night of Jer 33:20; 25 may well be the Noahic covenant itself.⁵ By process of elimination, if we have ruled out the Edenic covenant and the hypothetical covenant of creation, what remains is the Adamic covenant. Scofield observes that "the Noahic Covenant reaffirms the conditions of life of fallen man as announced by the Adamic Covenant, and institutes the principle of human government to curb the outbreak of sin, since the threat of divine judgment in the form of another flood has been removed."⁶ Murphy agrees and comments:

> *My covenant.* The word *my* points to its original establishment with Adam. My primeval covenant, which I am resolved not to abandon. *Will I establish.* Though Adam has failed, yet will I find means of maintaining my covenant of life with the seed of the woman.⁷

Therefore, it is best to see the Noahic covenant as a continuation and expansion of the conditions established under the Adamic covenant in response to humankind's fall and not a reestablishment of the hypothetical covenant of creation or the original Edenic covenant.⁸

In form, the Noahic covenant is a grant covenant. As such, it is unilateral and unconditional. The superior swears, binding Himself for the benefit of the vassal. Kidner comments, "Any idea that a covenant is basically a bargain is forestalled by such an opening to the series."⁹ Hillers notes that the obligation is all God's:

> This is a covenant, unmistakably, because the same Hebrew word used for the Sinai pact, *bᵉrit*, occurs repeatedly here. It is also between God and man, involves an obligation that is binding "for all ages," and God takes the initiative. Beyond these generalities, there is not much resemblance to the Sinai covenant; on the contrary, it contrasts both formally and, more important, in intention. There is no history as a basis for the covenant. There is no obligation whatever laid on Noah and his descen-

dants, expressed or implied. This is simply a unilateral promise of God, and it makes no difference what Noah does. Even human corruption will not change it.... God will not destroy the world by flood again, "for the thoughts of a man's mind are evil from little up".... Even if man is hopelessly corrupt, God will not again destroy him. The obligation is on God. It is he who will have to "remember" the covenant, and the "sign" is for God to see so that he does not forget.[10]

While agreeing that the Noahic covenant is "simply a unilateral promise of God," I would disagree with Hillers' assertion that "there is no history." Hillers' devotion to the documentary hypothesis blinds him to the existence of the historical prologue in the flood narrative itself which he assigns to a different source. In this history the focus is in part on the virtue of the vassal, Noah. Noah was favored by God (Gen 6:8); righteous (Gen 6:9; 7:1) in contrast with the general wickedness of the time (Gen 6:1–7); and obedient (Gen 6:22; 7:5). This is very similar to the grant treaty between Suppiluliuma I of Hatti and Niqmaddu II of Ugarit.[11] In addition, as is normal for a grant covenant, the blessings are in the stipulations so there is no separate blessing section. There is a curse on those who violate the grant. God has granted life and therefore His curse (i.e., the death penalty) is on murderers (Gen 9:5, 6). The Noahic covenant contains a blessing that grants title to the earth (Gen 9:1) and repeatedly affirms God's gift ("I have given" Gen 9:2, 3). Therefore, by form and content we see that the Noahic covenant is a grant covenant.

Beneficiaries

The Noahic covenant does primarily benefit humankind (Gen 9:9–12; 15–17) as it was extended to Noah, his sons, and their wives. All of their descendants, the human race, are explicitly included in the Noahic covenant after them (Gen 9:9). Moreover, the covenant was also extended to all other living creatures (Gen 9:10) and even the earth itself (Gen 9:13). The Noahic covenant extends to all life on planet Earth.

Stipulations

Robertson refers to the Noahic covenant as "the covenant of preservation."[12] Indeed, all of the stipulations of the Noahic covenant deal with the preservation of the human race and are physical rather than spiritual in nature. Grudem observes that the covenant that God made with Noah after the flood (Gen. 9:8–17) was not a covenant that promised all the blessings of eternal life or spiritual fellowship with God, but simply one in which God promised all mankind and the animal creation that the earth would no longer be destroyed by a flood. In this sense the covenant with Noah, although it certainly does depend on God's grace or unmerited favor, appears to be quite different in the parties involved (God and all mankind, not just the redeemed), the condition named (no faith or obedience is required of man), and the blessing that is promised (that the earth will not be destroyed again by flood, certainly a different promise from that of eternal life). The sign of the covenant (the rainbow) is also different in that it requires no active or voluntary participation on man's part.[13]

However, this does not mean that the Noahic covenant has no implications for the plan of salvation. Couch states, "I consider it [the Noahic covenant] redemptive in a physical sense because it will spare all flesh a death by drowning in a universal flood."[14] In the Noahic covenant God moved to protect human beings to so that they can be the recipients of His mercy.

The divine grant to humankind was fourfold. First, God granted humankind the entire earth (Gen 9:1, 7) to rule as His vassals. This was a reaffirmation of the Adamic covenant. Although humankind fell, they still are to rule over the earth (Gen 1:28). That position was not revoked by the Adamic covenant. Therefore, the first stipulation of the Noahic covenant reestablished humankind as God's vassal on the earth.

Second, all flesh was given to humankind for food (Gen 9:2–4). Aside from providing an additional food source, this provision had the effect of protecting humankind from wild animals now that the previous harmony of nature had broken down (Gen 9:2). Presumably, up to this point in time, humankind had been herbivores. God now expanded His earlier provision (Gen 1:29; 9:3) with the sole exception that consuming blood is forbidden (Gen 9:4). The reason for this prohibition is that the blood is equated with life and life belongs to God alone. Much later we find this thought in the Jerusalem council's requirements of Gentile converts (Acts 15:20). This respect for life set the stage for the next stipulation.

Third, because man bears the divine image, God ordained the death penalty for murder (Gen. 9:5, 6). Ryrie comments that "Homicide (which in a sense is always fratricide, v. 5) demands a punishment that matches the crime. The justification for capital punishment, here established, is the nobility of human life, which is made *in the image of God*."[15] This penalty was to be enforced by humans acting as God's vassals in His place. God swears, "I will require the life of man" (Gen 9:5). But God's method of enforcement is that "whoever sheds man's blood, by men his blood shall be shed" (Gen 9:6).

This is the basis for human government. Chafer notes, "Most important was the establishment of the essence of government in which man was given the right to kill murderers (Gen. 9:5–6)."[16] Keil and Delitzsch also see this command as the foundation of all human government.[17] God ordained the death penalty as a means of restraining human violence to preserve the human race. Thus, as Leupold notes, "Government, then, being grounded on this word, is not by human contract, or by surrender of certain powers, or by encroachment of priestcraft. It is a divine institution."[18] As Paul writes to the Romans, "There is no authority except from God, and those which exist are established by God" (Rom 13:1). Today, as then, "if you do what is evil, be afraid; for it [the government] does not bear the sword [the power of death] for nothing; for it is a minister of God, an avenger who brings wrath upon the one who practices evil" (Rom 13:4).

Lastly, there will be no more universal floods and the rainbow was given as a sign (Gen 9:9–17). In preserving humankind God reassured Noah that He will never again send a universal flood to destroy all humankind. The flood was doubtless necessary at that time to prevent the spread of wickedness, but God is making it clear that it is not going to be His normal *modus operandi*. God is not relinquishing His right to judge and will do so repeatedly in local instances (e.g., Sodom and Gomorrah, Gen 18:16–19:29). As Peter notes (2 Pet 3:5–9) this does not indicate laxity on God's part but patience, since He is "not wishing for any to perish but for all to come to repentance" (2 Pet 3:9).[19]

God expresses this promise in the strongest of terms by employing a sign, the rainbow. Von Rad notes that "the Hebrew word that we translate 'rainbow' usually means in the OT 'the bow of war.' The beauty of the ancient conception thus becomes apparent: God shows the world that he has put aside his bow."[20] Kline explains that "*My bow* translates qešeṯ, the usual meaning of which is the weapon. Thus, the recurring rainbow imposed on the retreating storm by the shining again of the sun is God's battle bow laid aside, a token of grace staying the lightning-shafts of wrath."[21] Ross also notes that

> the rainbow arcs like a battle bow hung against the clouds. (The Heb. word for rainbow, qešeṯ, is also the word for a battle bow.) Elsewhere in the Old Testament, God referred to judgment storms by using terms for bows and arrows.

> The bow is now "put away," hung in place by the clouds, suggesting that the "battle," the storm, is over. Thus the rainbow speaks of peace. In the ancient Near East, covenant treaties were made after wars as a step toward embarking on peace. Similarly God, after judging sin, made a covenant of peace.[22]

Dumbrell notes that there is a broad consensus among Bible expositors concerning the nature of this sign as "a divine declaration of peace."[23] Kidner, however, is somewhat more cautious and would like a more explicit reference.[24] Since the bow is pointed toward heaven, some even see in the rainbow sign the acting out of a self-maledictory curse by God.[25] In language reminiscent of covenant deposition instructions, Gen 9:16 explains that the sign of the rainbow serves to remind God of the covenant. Dumbrell explains:

> Of course, we must not think that something additional to and outside of the divine nature is necessary to stimulate God to provide for the obligation to which he has committed himself, for one would hesitate to ascribe memory lapses to the Creator of the universe! For the use of 'remember' in the Old Testament is hardly ever, as it invariably is with us, simply a reference to the power of the psychological recall of the past. Biblically, when the past is 'remembered', what is often meant is that what is done in present experience is logically dependent upon some past event. This is what is meant in Genesis 9.[26]

God committed Himself in the strongest of terms to the preservation of the human race (see table 5).

Establishment

God proclaims to Noah, "I will establish My covenant with you (אֶת־בְּרִיתִי אִתָּךְ וַהֲקִמֹתִי)" (Gen 6:18). Therefore, Gen 6:18 seems to be a prediction of the covenant to come in Gen 9:1–17. Kline disagrees:

> *My covenant.* Rather than taking this verse as an anticipation of 9:9ff., this covenant should be understood as the relationship within which the Flood-salvation was effected; see on 8:1. Like the new covenant, it was confirmed not by an oath symbolizing judgment (*cf.* Gn. 15:17–21) but by a real passage through an actual divine judgment.[27]

However, that would deny the future sense of the *waw* consecutive וַהֲקִמֹתִי ("I will establish").[28] Although Noah and his family did indeed pass through an actual divine judgment, sacrifices and a symbolic oath do also seem to exist here. Therefore, the conclusion that Gen 6:18 is anticipatory stands.

Noah's sacrifice (Gen 8:20) forms the occasion for the Noahic covenant. Williamson notes that the sacrifice was anticipated (cf. Gen 7:2–3) and critical for the making of the covenant.[29] Sailhamer notes parallels with Moses' altar at Sinai. He concludes that

> these observations suggest is that the author is intentionally drawing out the similarities between God's covenant with Noah and the covenant at Sinai. Why? The answer that best fits with the author's purposes is that he wants to show that God's covenant at Sinai is not a new act of God. The covenant is rather a return to God's original promises. Once again at Sinai, as he had done in the past, God is at work restoring his fellowship with man and bringing man back to himself.[30]

Murphy perceives reconciliation as the purpose of these offerings.[31] However, Walton, Matthews, and Chavalas are more cautious and note that

> the purpose of Noah's sacrifice is not stated. The text calls them "burnt offerings," which served a broad function in the sacrificial system. It may be more important to note what the text does not call the sacrifice. It is not a sin offering, nor specifically designated a thank offering. The burnt offerings are usually associated with petitions or entreaties set before God.[32]

The sense of an offering that accompanies a request makes good sense in this context. Noah, having just survived the Flood, would entreat God that such a cataclysm might never occur again. God heard Noah's prayer and accepted his sacrifice. We have God's divinely revealed thought process in Gen 8:21, 22.

Duration

The first indicator of the duration of the Noahic covenant is contained in the revelation of divine thought in Gen 8:22:

> While the earth remains,
> > Seedtime and harvest,
> > And cold and heat,
> > And summer and winter,
> > And day and night
> Shall not cease.

God reestablished the normal pattern of life on earth and promised that it would continue "while the earth remains (עֹד כָּל־יְמֵי הָאָרֶץ)" (Gen 8:22). Young translates this, "During all days of the earth" (Gen 8:22 YLT). Rabbinical midrash views the Noahic covenant as enduring as long as the earth but not eternally:

> WHILE THE EARTH REMAINETH, SEED TIME AND HARVEST, AND COLD
> AND HEAT, AND SUMMER AND WINTER, AND DAY AND NIGHT SHALL
> NOT CEASE (VIII, 22). R. Judan [ca. 3rd century AD] said in R. Aha's name [ca.
> 2nd century AD]: What did the children of Noah think: that the covenant made with
> them would endure to all eternity? That is not so, but only as long as the heaven and
> earth endure will their covenant endure. But when that day cometh, of which it is
> written, For the heavens shall vanish away like smoke, and the earth shall be worn
> out like a garment (Isa. LI, 6), then [shall the verse be fulfilled], And it [sc. the
> covenant] will be broken on that day (Zech. XI, 11).[33]

Williamson seems to agree, "Significantly, this covenant is described as 'everlasting', a term which, in the context, appears to signify at least 'as long as the earth endures' (8:22)."[34] Please note that in context this time span applies only to the promise of regular seasons.

The next indicator of the duration of the Noahic covenant is Gen 9:12. God tells Noah that the covenant is to be "for all successive generations (עוֹלָם לְדֹרֹת)" (Gen 9:12). The ASV is more literal with its translation, "for perpetual generations" (Gen 9:12 ASV). Keil and Delitzsch agree, "An 'everlasting covenant' is a *covenant 'for perpetual generations,'* i.e., one which shall extend to all ages, even to the end of the world."[35] Chafer notes that "the Noahic Covenant (Gen. 8:20–9:17) ... discloses the divine intent respecting human government and posterity in all succeeding generations beginning with Noah."[36] In context, this refers to the promise that there will never be another universal flood. From Noah's time and forever, there will never be a generation without the Noahic covenant's promise.

Finally, the Noahic covenant is called an "everlasting covenant (עוֹלָם בְּרִית)" (Gen 9:16). In context this refers also to the promise that there will be no more universal floods. However, the promise is extended to "every living creature" (Gen 9:16) both humankind and the animal kingdom. Neither man nor animal need ever fear another universal flood.

Therefore, I draw two conclusions about the duration of the Noahic covenant. First, we can expect that the regularity of the seasons will continue only so long as this present earth. They need not continue under a "new heaven and new earth" (Rev 21:1, cp. Rev 21:22–25). Second, both humankind and all other living creatures are promised that there will never be another universal flood. In this respect the Noahic covenant will never end (see figure 2). Some details, such as the eating of meat (1 Cor 6:13) and the prohibition of murder (Rev 21:8, 27) will over time be rendered superfluous. However, humankind will be God's vassal ruling over even the "new earth" (Rev 21:7). Then will the word of Christ Jesus truly be fulfilled, "Blessed are the gentle for they shall inherit the earth" (Matt 5:5) (see figure 2).

Type of Covenant	Stipulations of Covenant	Beneficiaries	Established	End
Grant	To Humankind: • Title to the earth • Permission to eat meat without blood • Death penalty for murder To Humankind, All Creatures, and the Earth: • No more universal floods	Humankind as represented by Noah's family The earth All living creatures	After the Flood and Noah's offering (Gen 8:20)	"Eternal covenant"

Table 5. Noahic Covenant

NOTES

1. Dumbrell, *Covenant and Creation* 26.
2. Williamson, "Covenant," *NDBT* 420–21.
3. Sailhamer, "Genesis," EBC 2:91.
4. Dumbrell, *Covenant and Creation* 43.
5. Williamson, "Covenant," *NDBT* 421.
6. Scofield, *NSRB* 15.
7. James G. Murphy, *Genesis*, Barnes' Notes, vol. 1 of 14 vols. (Boston: Estes and Lauriate, 1873; reprint, Grand Rapids, MI: Baker, 1998) 1:188–89.
8. Merrill, "A Theology of the Pentateuch," *A Biblical Theology of the Old Testament* 23–24.
9. Derek Kidner, *Genesis: An Introduction & Commentary*, vol. 1 of Tyndale Old Testament Commentaries, gen. ed. D. J. Wiseman (Downers Grove, IL: InterVarsity, 1967) 101.
10. Hillers, *Covenant* 101–2.
11. Beckman, *Hittite Diplomatic Texts* 30–32, 4.1–7. Hillers, *Covenant* 105–6, notes that the other examples of grant covenants lack an explicit oath and are therefore in contrast with the Noahic and Abrahamic covenants. However, lack of evidence is not evidence of lack. It is impossible, based on our knowledge of ancient Near Eastern covenants to imagine a covenant without an oath. The resolution comes in realizing that our documents do not record every detail of the covenant ceremony. Indeed, in the case of grant covenants, they take on the nature of title deeds. The Bible, because of its emphasis on God's covenant dealings with mankind, adds more detail concerning the oath than other ancient Near Eastern covenant documents.
12. Robertson, *Christ of the Covenants* 109–25.
13. Grudem, *Systematic Theology* 520.
14. Couch, "The Relationship Between the Dispensations and Covenants" 416.
15. Ryrie, *RSB* 19.
16. Chafer, *Major Bible Themes* 130.
17. Keil and Delitzsch, *Pentateuch*, COT 1:96–97.
18. Leupold, *Genesis* 1:333.
19. I realize that God's patience is "toward you," (i.e., the elect). However, had God obliterated the entirety of mankind, His purposes for the elect would have been frustrated also.
20. Gerhard von Rad, *Genesis: A Commentary*, rev. ed., trans. John H. Marks, The Old Testament Library, gen. eds. G. Ernest Wright, John Bright, James Barr, Peter Ackroyd (Philadelphia: Westminister, 1972) 134.
21. Kline, "Genesis," *NBC* 90.
22. Ross, "Genesis," *BKCOT* 40.
23. Dumbrell, *Covenant and Creation* 29.

24. Kidner, *Genesis* 102.
25. Hillers, *Covenant* 102.
26. Dumbrell, *Covenant and Creation* 31.
27. Kline, "Genesis," *NBC* 88.
28. See Driver, *Treatise* 125–26.
29. Williamson, "Covenant," *NDBT* 421.
30. Sailhamer, "Genesis," EBC 2:93.
31. Murphy, *Genesis*, Barnes' Notes 1:199.
32. Walton, Matthews, and Chavalas , *BBCOT* 39.
33. *Midr. Gen. Rab.* 34:11, *The Soncino Midrash Rabbah* 1:274–75.
34. Williamson, "Covenant," *NDBT* 421.
35. Keil and Delitzsch, *Pentateuch*, COT 1:97.
36. Chafer, *Systematic Theology* 1:42.

CHAPTER EIGHT

The Abrahamic Covenant

Covenant Type

The Abrahamic covenant is revealed progressively in five main passages: Gen 12:1–3, 7; 13:14–17; 15:1–21; 17:1–21; and 22:16–18.[1] An analysis of these sections of Genesis will provide us with the clues to determine the covenant type of the Abrahamic covenant. Then I will compare the Abrahamic covenant with other ancient Near Eastern covenant forms.

Genesis 12:1–3, 7

Prominent in this passage is the sole condition, "Go forth from your country, and from your relatives and from your father's house, to the land which I will show you" (Gen 12:1). Abraham was commanded by God to "Go forth (לֶךְ־לְךָ)," literally "for yourself (לְךָ)." It is in Abraham's best interest to obey. The verb לֵךְ is a *qal* imperative of הָלַךְ ("go, come, walk"[2]). Ryrie sees this as a statement of God's intention to bless Abraham:

> The imperative, "Go forth from your country," expresses a condition that would have invalidated the covenant if Abraham had not obeyed. However, grammatically this imperative, followed by two imperfects and a series of cohortative imperfects in verses 2–3, expresses an intention, namely what God intended to do for Abraham. Other examples of this use are found in 30:18 and 45:18.[3]

Pentecost holds that this was a condition for the establishment of the Abrahamic covenant but that the nature of the covenant is unconditional:

> Whether God would institute a covenant program with Abraham or not depended upon Abraham's act of obedience in leaving the land. When once this act was accomplished, and Abraham did obey God, God instituted an irrevocable, unconditional program....
>
> The *fact* of the covenant depended upon obedience; the *kind* of covenant inaugurated

was totally unrelated to the continuing obedience of either Abraham or his seed.[4]

Abraham's initial obedience was partial in that he brought along his nephew, Lot, and yet the covenant was still reaffirmed (Gen 12:7). However, he did eventually obey this command totally. In that sense Abraham fulfilled the condition historically.

It should be noted that Ross, Leupold, et al. see an additional condition in verse 2 with the command to be a blessing, "And so you shall be a blessing (וֶהְיֵה בְּרָכָה)" (Gen 12:2b).[5] The Hebrew is somewhat difficult to translate. There appear to be four ways of taking this construction. First, the phrase can be taken as a *qal* infinitive absolute and therefore a statement of certainty. Second, it can be taken to be a *qal* imperative but having the force of a statement of consequence. Third, it can be taken as a *qal* imperative, and as such, as a command. Fourth, it can be taken as a cohortative imperfect with the force of an intention.

Many translations seem to take the position that הֱיֵה is a *qal* infinitive absolute. For an infinitive absolute one would normally expect a second form of the same verb. This is lacking in this verse. Apparently, some think that an additional הָיָה can be supplied. While it is true that הָיָה is often understood, in this instance, it would seem to be unwarranted to supply it. This tradition goes back to the LXX which translates וֶהְיֵה בְּרָכָה, as ἔση εὐλογητός. The Greek word ἔση is a second person singular future passive indicative of εἰμί ("to be"). There is no imperative in this translation. The passive voice also would rule out a command where we would expect the active or imperative voice. The Greek εὐλογητός is an adjectival form of εὐλογέω ("to bless"). The LXX in this instance could be translated, "And you will be blessed" (my translation). The New Berkeley Version, the Lamsa Version, and the Amplified Bible also translate this, "And you shall be a blessing." The KJV is similar, "And thou shalt be a blessing." The JB and the NEB, although they take Abraham's name to be the subject, "It will be used as a blessing," and "It shall be used in blessings," still follow essentially the same translation.

The second option sees וֶהְיֵה בְּרָכָה as a *qal* imperative but taken as a statement of consequence. This approach is followed by the NASB, "So you shall be a blessing," and the RSV, "So that you will be a blessing." Kline sees this as a creative benediction.[6] Kyle M. Yates takes a similar position, "Be thou a blessing (bᵉrākâ). The imperative form actually expresses a consequence— 'so that thou shalt be a blessing.'"[7] This view is preferable to the first in that it does acknowledge the imperative force of the verb. However, it initially accepts the imperative only to weaken it later.

The third option, taking וֶהְיֵה בְּרָכָה as a *qal* imperative with the force of a command, is followed by Young, "be thou a blessing" (Gen 12:26 YLT). Leupold sees a moral responsibility in this phrase:

> The fourth: "And be thou a blessing." The form in which this item of the promise appears differs materially from that of all the rest. Instead of being an imperfect horative, it is the imperative, "and be thou" (*wehyeh*). Now it is true enough that an imperative may be joined to a hortative (K. S. 364 n), but it cannot be denied that this is "strange" (K. S. 203) in this case. Merely to make this imperative just one more promise strips it too utterly of its peculiar character, as does A. V.: "and thou shalt be a blessing." The fact of the matter is that it, indeed, expresses something that God does: God is the One, who in the last analysis makes Abram to be a true blessing unto others. But at the same time, a moral responsibility of Abram's is involved: he should do his part that he may become a blessing to others. Consequently the imperative, "be thou a blessing." He personally should aim to live such a life the others are blessed by it.[8]

Ross carries the idea further and makes this a second condition:

> The call had two imperatives, each with subsequent promises. The first imperative was to get out (Leave your country ... go to the land, v. 1), and the second imperative was to be a blessing. (The second imperative, in v. 2, is imprecisely rendered in many versions, including the NIV, as a prediction, you will be a blessing. But lit., it is, "Be a blessing.") His leaving started a chain of reactions. If Abram would get out of Ur, God would do three things for him, so that he could then be a blessing in the land (the second imperative); and he had to be that blessing so that God would do three more things for him. This symmetry should not be missed, for it strengthens the meaning. Abram's calling had a purpose: his obedience would bring great blessing.[9]

If this is indeed a second condition, the same approach as to the first condition holds here also. Abraham's obedience affected the fact of the covenant not the kind of covenant, i.e., unconditional.

The fourth option, taking וֶהְיֵה בְּרָכָה as a cohortative imperfect, is the better supported grammatically. The other three verbs in Gen 12:2 (אֲבָרֶכְךָ, אֶעֶשְׂךָ, and אֲגַדְּלָה) are acknowledged to be cohortative. However, only the verb אֲגַדְּלָה is unambiguously cohortative in form. It is reasonable to also take הְיֵה as an imperfect cohortative. Driver, before citing Gen 12:2, explains that "the cohortative, then, marks the presence of a strongly-felt inclination or impulse: in cases where this is accompanied by the ability to carry the wished-for action into execution, we may, if we please, employ *I, we will...* in translating...."[10] Ryrie appeals to this grammatical principle:

> The phrase "be a blessing" is seen by some to be a condition for fulfillment of the covenant. However, grammatically this expresses a consequence that is expected to occur with certainty or an intention. The Gesenius, Kautzsch, Cowley Hebrew grammar cites this passage as an example of intention.[11]

Indeed, Driver strongly denies that the cohortative can ever have the sense of a command.[12] Thus it seems that, rather than a command, Gen 12:2 expresses God's firm intention to make Abraham a blessing.

Also prominent in this section is the divine pronouncement, "I will." The phrase "I will" occurs six times in these four verses. These cohortative imperfects express God's firm intention. This clearly reveals the sovereign unilateral nature of this covenant. God is binding Himself alone. The only obligation placed on Abraham has been fulfilled. None other remains. Arnold G. Fruchtenbaum explains the concept of unconditional covenant as a sovereign divine act where God unconditionally obligates Himself to bring to pass promises that He has made to the covenanted people. He notes that such covenants are unilateral, since they are dependent on God alone. Such covenants are typified by the formula "I will."[13] As Gen 26:4–5 indicates, there is no remaining obligation for the descendants of Abraham. This passage reveals that the Abrahamic covenant is unilateral and unconditional.

Genesis 13:14–17

In this passage God unconditionally grants title to the land and promises descendants to Abraham. Here as in Gen 12:1–3, 7 the emphasis is on the "I will" of God. The verb "I will give (אֶתְּנֶנָּה)" (Gen 13:15) is either a cohortative *qal* imperfect form or it has a third person feminine suffix which would refer to "land" (אֶרֶץ). There is no indication of human conditions for the continuance of the Abrahamic covenant once it is established. So far, every indication is that the Abrahamic covenant is an unconditional covenant.

Genesis 15:1–21

God began with a covenant preamble, "I am the LORD who brought you out of Ur of the Chaldeans to give you this land to possess it" (Gen 15:7). Abraham immediately seeks assurance concerning the land promise, "O Lord

God, how may I know that I shall possess it?" (Gen 15:8). Kidner explains
that

> God's regular provision for such a need is 'signs' and 'seals' (*cf.* Rom. 4:3,11a) to
> confirm the spoken word. Here His full answer is a formal covenant (verse 18), exe-
> cuted in two stages. The first is in this chapter, an inauguration of a particularly
> vivid kind. The second stage, in chapter 17, was the giving of the covenant sign, cir-
> cumcision....
>
> The covenant ritual resembles that of Jeremiah 34:18. In its full form, probably
> both parties would pass between the dismembered animals to invoke a like fate on
> themselves should they break their pledge. Here, however, Abram's part is only to
> set the scene and guard it from violation (11)....[14]

Leupold has additional detail about the covenant ritual:

> A covenant is to be established. God condescends to let it be made after the
> fashion of covenants made in those days, particularly among the Chaldeans. K. C.
> points to the historical evidence of the use of the same ceremony when the North
> Syrian Mati'lu is put under obligation to Aschschurnirari. The covenanting parties
> would pass between the halves of the beasts, and this may have implied that a simi-
> lar lot, viz., being killed, was to befall their own cattle in the event of their violating
> the covenant. But a modification of the procedure is involved in this case: neither do
> both parties pass between the halves, nor is the threat implied.[15]

Instead of both parties walking between the halves of the sacrifice, God alone
performed the ritual (Gen 15:12, 17). This signifies that God alone is obligat-
ing Himself to fulfill this covenant.[16] Thus, God confirmed His covenant in
the most solemn and sure manner that Abraham could understand.[17]

This passage ends with a description of the land that Abraham and his
descendants are to inherit. God states, "To your descendants I have given this
land (לְזַרְעֲךָ נָתַתִּי אֶת־הָאָרֶץ הַזֹּאת)" (Gen 15:18). The Hebrew נָתַתִּי is the *qal* perfect form of נָתַן ("to give"). Driver explains that

> the perfect is employed to indicate actions the accomplishment of which lies indeed
> in the future, but is regarded as dependent upon such an unalterable determination of
> the will that it may be spoken of as having actually taken place: thus a resolution,
> promise, or decree, especially a Divine one, is frequently announced in the perfect
> tense.[18]

Driver explains that this idiom expresses the certainty of the future event:

> But the most special and remarkable use of the tense, though little more than an
> extension of the last idiom, is as the *prophetic perfect*: its abrupt appearance in this
> capacity imparts to descriptions of the future a forcible and expressive touch of real-

ity, and reproduces vividly the certainty with which the occurrence of a yet future
event is contemplated by the speaker.[19]

So, this passage is also a grant of an absolutely certain and unconditional nature.

Genesis 17:1–21

At ninety-nine years of age, God appeared to Abraham again. Thirteen years
have passed since the birth of Ishmael. Ishmael would have been considered
to be on the threshold of manhood. God reaffirmed the covenant in a passage
that deals primarily with the "seed" aspect of the covenant establishing Isaac
as the heir to the covenant. God identified Himself to Abraham in a covenant
preamble as "God Almighty." Yates comments on that

> the divine name *El Shadday*, with its message that, "Nothing is impossible with
> God, who is all-powerful and all-sufficient," must have brought unusual encourage-
> ment to Abram. The word *El Shadday* evidently calls attention to both of these at-
> tributes of God. Early Jewish scholars claimed that it was derived from *sh-da*,
> meaning, "He who is sufficient." Some scholars derive it from the root *shadad*, "to
> destroy." Others relate it to the Assyrian word *shadu*, "mountain." The LXX gives
> us *hikanos*, "sufficient." Perhaps the translator should stay as near the meaning of
> "all-powerful" as possible, especially since the word *El* speaks of power. The One
> who has all power also has all resources to supply every need of his people.[20]

Leupold strongly supports the derivation of El Shadday from the verb שָׁדַד:

> The divine name *El Shadday* here demands attention. "God Almighty," or
> "Almighty God," (A. V.), is a very satisfactory translation. So other versions: Luther
> — *der allmaechtige Gott*; Vulgate usually, *omnipotens*. It would appear that this
> name *Shadday* comes from the root *shadad*, which may mean, "deal violently," but
> would in reference to God signify "to display power." This derivation is so natural
> and the sense so satisfactory that efforts to lay inferior and unworthy meanings to
> this divine name should not have been made.[21]

Whatever the derivation it would seem that the ideas of power and suffi-
ciency are found in this divine name. The sense is that God is completely
able to fulfill His covenant commitments.

Abraham is then commanded to "walk before Me and be blameless"
(Gen 17:1). This is maturity not sinless perfection. If one were inclined to see
here a condition, it would be a condition for the establishment of the covenant and not its continued existence. Since the covenant was established, one

can assume that Abraham met the condition. Therefore, at present, the covenant is unconditional for Abraham's descendants. However, Ryrie notes that
the grammar is the same as I have already explained concerning Gen 12:1
and expresses God's intention not a command.[22] Abraham's blameless condition would have to be according to the stipulations of the Abrahamic covenant, since the Mosaic covenant was not yet established.

Verses 1 and 2 are in the form of epic or didactic poetry employing cli-
mactic parallelism. The promise builds from God's self-revelation, to Abraham's obligation, to a reaffirmation of the covenant and the promise of many
descendants:

> I am God Almighty;
>> Walk before Me, and be blameless.
> And I will establish My covenant between Me and you,
>> And I will multiply you exceedingly (Gen 17:1–2).

Note also the emphasis on the divine "I will" (cohortative imperfects) that we
see so often repeated in the Abrahamic covenant. The emphasis is on God's
initiative. The phrase "I will establish" (וְאֶתְּנָה) is the *qal* imperfect cohortative
first person singular form of נָתַן ("*to give... to grant, permit, suffer*,"[23] or
"give, put, set"[24]). This covenant is a gift or a grant from God. The word "ex-
ceedingly" translates the Hebrew phrase בִּמְאֹד מְאֹד, literally, "in greatly
greatly" (my translation). The repetition is a means of emphasizing the de-
gree. Abraham is not merely told that he will be "multiplied" or that he will
be "multiplied greatly." No, Abraham is to be "greatly multiplied greatly!" In
true covenant form, God established Who the maker of the covenant is and
its purpose. Abraham responded by falling on his face before God as a ges-
ture of submission and reverence.

Some have seen the sign of circumcision as introducing an element of
conditionality into the Abrahamic covenant. Does the addition of the condition of circumcision change the unconditional nature of the Abrahamic covenant? We must be clear about what is and is not conditional in this text.
Fruchtenbaum explains that

> it is, of course, true that circumcision was required by the Abrahamic Covenant, but
> it was not a condition for God to fulfill His promises. Although the Jews failed to
> practice circumcision during the forty years of wilderness wanderings, God, in ful-
> fillment of the Abrahamic Covenant, brought the Jews into the land anyway. Cir-
> cumcision was finally resumed only after the Jews were inside the Promised Land.
> The penalty for failure was to be *cut off from his people*.... however, the phrase

normally means execution. Failure to obey would result in the death penalty. Again,
the requirement of circumcision did not render the covenant itself as conditional, but
provided a command within the covenant. Yet God always fulfilled His part, even
when the command and the penalty were disobeyed.[25]

In other words, the covenant is unconditional, but there is a condition to take
part in the covenant. It has been previously noted that there is but one condition for the establishment of the Abrahamic covenant (i.e., for Abraham to
leave land and relatives) and one condition to establish that one is a partaker
in the Abrahamic covenant (i.e., circumcision). Abraham met the first condition. The last one is met by every Jew in the world today.

Genesis 22:16–18

In response to Abraham's willingness to obey God's command to sacrifice
Isaac, God reiterated the seed and blessing aspects of the Abrahamic covenant. Ryrie notes that, since the Abrahamic covenant was firmly established
prior to the events of Gen 22:16–18, it would be inconsistent this passage as
suddenly adding conditions to an unconditional covenant.[26] This passage
does not import the concept of conditionality into the Abrahamic covenant.
However, even if one were inclined to see a condition here, it would have
been met historically by Abraham.

Additionally, God promised Abraham that his descendants will "possess
the gate of their enemies" (Gen 22:17). Brown, Driver, and Briggs note that
the Hebrew שַׁעַר ("gate") bears the meaning of "space inside gate, as public
meeting-place, market ... place of public well ... where elders, judges, king,
sat officially...."[27] Gesenius notes that "at the gates of cities there was the fo-
rum... where trials were held, and the citizens assembled, some of them for
business, and some to sit at leisure, to look on and converse...."[28] This is
equivalent to promising Israel that they would possess the headquarters, capital, the seat of their enemies' power, and the hub of their strength. Thus, Israel is promised ultimate victory over her enemies.

Conclusions from the Biblical Evidence

The form of the Abrahamic covenant is characteristic of the grant covenant.
Bright notes the differences between the patriarchal covenants and suzerainty
covenants, "It will be noted that this conception of covenant [suzerainty

covenant] is markedly different in emphasis from that found in the patriarchal narratives. Their covenant consists in unconditional promises for the future, in which the recipient was obligated only to trust."[29] Livingston attempts
to fit the Abrahamic covenant into the suzerainty covenant form. However, in
so doing he ignores the grant covenant form and resorts to statements such
as, "In some cases the curses and blessings are *implicit rather than listed.*
Genesis 17:12–14 states that the circumcised will be in the covenant and the
uncircumcised will not, and 18:19 *suggests* that the fulfillment of God's
promises was related to man's performance of justice" (emphasis mine).[30]
This is eisegesis not exegesis! Pentecost, in responding to Allis' similar
claim that conditions may be implied, writes, "In reply to this argument it
will readily be observed that Allis begins with a most damaging admission—
there are no stated conditions in Scripture to which the amillennialist may
turn for confirmation of his position. His whole case rests on silence, on implied and unstated conditions."[31] As I have demonstrated previously, the ancient Near Eastern covenants relied on explicit rather than implicit
conditions. Therefore, as a grant covenant, the Abrahamic covenant is both
unconditional and unilateral.[32]

In true grant covenant form, the grant is given to the faithful vassal without any conditions attached. The conditions actually precede the covenant
rather than being a part of it. This is the order of events mentioned in Nehemiah, "Thou art the LORD God, who chose Abram ... and Thou didst find
his heart faithful before Thee, and didst make a covenant with him to give
him the land" (Neh 9:7–8). After the grant was made the performance was
based solely on the faithfulness of God. Nehemiah writes, "Thou hast fulfilled Thy promise, for Thou art righteous" (Neh 9:8). The implication is that
it would have been unrighteous for God not to have fulfilled the covenant.
When God confirms the covenant to Isaac, the reason that he gave was "because Abraham obeyed Me and kept My charge, My commandments, My
statutes, and My laws" (Gen 26:5). As previously indicated, terms such as
"commandments," "statutes," and "laws" are relative to the covenantal setting and are not to be assumed to point to the Mosaic covenant. Sailhamer
explains

> that blessing is tied to Israel's faith, not their obedience to the law. How else can you
> explain Gen 26:5 which tells us, very clearly I believe, that Abraham's *faith*
> amounted to (not resulted in, but amounted to) his keeping God's statutes, com-
> mandments, and laws? Abraham could not have "kept the Sinai Law," which had

not been given till the time of Moses. Abraham lived a life of faith and that *was* his "keeping the law."[33]

The Abrahamic covenant then is marked by the divine statement "I will." God alone cut this covenant (Gen 15:17–18) and the obligation is His alone.

The only proper response to a promise like this is faith. When God compared Abraham's descendants to the stars of the night sky, "Then he [Abraham] believed in the LORD, and He reckoned it as righteousness" (Gen 15:6).[34] Levy estimates that approximately three thousand stars are visible to the naked eye at a dark country site.[35] This would be too few to represent Abraham's descendants were this saying not metaphorical. The point is that both the stars and the descendants are so many as to be uncountable by Abraham. Leupold comments on the nature of Abraham's faith:

> The biggest word in the chapter, one of the greatest in the Old Testament! Here is the first instance of the use of the word "believe" in the Scriptures. *He°emîn*, Hifil of *aman* , "to confirm" and "support," means "trust," "believe," implying *fiducia*, rather than *assensus*. It is construed with *be*, as here, or with *le*. The form is unusual, perfect with *waw*, not as one would expect, imperfect with *waw conversive*. Apparently, by this device the author would indicate that the permanence of this attitude is to be stressed: not only: Abram believed just this once, but: Abram proved constant in his faith, *er bewaehrte sich als Glaeubiger* (K. S. 367 i).[36]

The content of Abraham's faith was the promise of descendants that God had just given him. Kidner comments that "Abram's trust was both personal (*in the Lord*, AV, RV) and propositional (the context is the specific *word of the Lord* in verses 4,5)."[37] Fruchtenbaum comments concerning the content of Abraham's faith:

> Cox insists that "Abraham was saved through faith in that same gospel." As evidence he quotes Galatians 3:6–9 which, in turn, quotes Genesis 15:6; but all Paul is saying is that Abraham's faith was the means of salvation. Paul does not say that the content of Abraham's faith was the substitutionary death of Christ. Furthermore, Genesis 15:6 states that Abraham was reckoned righteous because *he believed in Jehovah*. Obviously, the means of salvation was faith; but what is it that Abraham believed? Neither in the immediate context nor in the wider context of the story of Abraham in Genesis is it ever said that Abraham believed that the Messiah would come and die for Abraham's sin; but it does say that Abraham believed the promises of God which primarily had to do with the land and the seed. In the majority of the cases, the *seed* referred to an immediate son: Isaac. The content of Abraham's faith was the promises of God. These promises were many, but not one of them was that the Messiah would die for his sins.[38]

Thus, Abraham was saved by grace alone through faith alone just as we are. However, the content of his faith was different due to progressive revelation.

Ancient Near Eastern Parallels

As we would expect, the Abrahamic covenant has affinities with other ancient Near Eastern grant covenants.[39] The historic prologue material in these passages record Abraham's fulfillment of the condition for the covenant. This is similar to the historic prologue to the covenant between Suppiluliuma I of Hatti and Niqmaddu II of Ugarit which notes the honor that Niqmaddu II had shown to the Hittite princes and noblemen and the loyalty that Suppiluliuma had witnessed in Niqmaddu II.[40] In addition, as is normal for a grant covenant, the blessings are in the stipulations (Gen 12:2–3) so there is no separate blessing section in these passages. God delineates the boundaries of Abraham's grant in language reminiscent of the above-mentioned covenant:

> To your descendants I have given this land,
>   From the river of Egypt as far as the great river, the river Euphrates:
> the Kenite and the Kenizzite and the Kadmonite
>   and the Hittite and the Perizzite and the Rephaim
> and the Amorite and the Canaanite and the Girgashite and the Jebusite (Gen 15:18–21).

The covenant between Suppiluliuma I of Hatti and Niqmaddu II of Ugarit reads:

> all of the land of Ugarit, together with its border districts ...
>   [Now] Suppiluliuma, Great King, King of Hatti, Hero, has deeded by means of a sealed document these [border districts], cities, and mountains to Niqmaddu, [king] of the land of Ugarit, and to his sons and grandsons forever.[41]

Indeed, similar terminology is used to describe the relationship established by these covenants. God told Abraham that "I will bless those who bless you, and the one who curses you I will curse" (Gen 12:3). Suppiluliuma I declares that Niqmaddu "is hostile to my enemy and at peace with my friend."[42] The only curse is on the one who would set aside the grant. As God told Abraham, "The one who curses you I will curse," Suppiluliuma I declares that "whoever alters the words of this treaty tablet will transgress the oath. The Thousand Gods shall be aware (of the perpetrator....)"[43] These similarities reinforce the conclusion that the Abrahamic covenant is in the grant covenant form.

The grant covenant in the ancient Near East was considered irrevocable. When Niqmepa (ca. 1350 BC), the son of Niqmaddu II of Ugarit, brought a border dispute to the attention of Mursili II, the son of Suppiluliuma I of Hatti, Mursili referred to the grant covenant that his father had made to settle the issue.[44] In the treaty between Tudhaliya IV of Hatti and Kurunta (ca. 1250 BC) of Tarhuntassa, we see that even the Great King was not able to overturn a grant covenant.[45] In this treaty it was not even permitted for the recipient of the grant to relinquish it. Thus, as a grant covenant, we would expect the Abrahamic covenant to remain inviolate and irrevocable.

Beneficiaries

There is a progressive narrowing of the focus of this promise. In Gen 12:1–3, 7 the promise is to Abraham. In Gen 13:14–17 the promise is to Abraham in distinction from his family. In Gen 15:1–21 the promise is to Abraham's descendants not "Eliezer of Damascus." In Gen 17:1–21 God clearly promises that the covenant will be confirmed with Sarah's child. So the covenant promise is focused on a single point, "But my covenant I will establish with Isaac" (Gen 17:21). After the offering of Isaac, God confirmed the seed and blessing promises to Abraham (Gen 22:16–18).

In subsequent revelation God continues, as the Great King, to choose the successors to his vassal Abraham. In Gen 26:2–4, 24 God appears to Isaac and confirms the Abrahamic covenant to him. The land (Gen 26:3), blessing (Gen 26:3–4, 24), and seed (Gen 26:4, 24) aspects of the covenant are all confirmed. In Gen 28:10–17 God appears to Jacob in a dream at Bethel and confirms the Abrahamic covenant to him. God again confirms the land (Gen 28:13, 15), seed (Gen 28:14), and blessing (Gen 28:14) aspects of the covenant. Finally, in Gen 35:9–15 (see also Gen 49) we have God's confirmation of the Abrahamic covenant with all of the descendants of Jacob (Israel). As with the other confirmations, all three aspects of the Abrahamic covenant are mentioned: the blessing (Gen 35:9–10), the seed (Gen 35:11), and the land (Gen 35:12). The covenant begins with Abraham, is confirmed to Isaac, then Jacob (Israel), and finally to the tribes of Israel.

Although it is not revealed in detail at that time, there is a hint of the Abrahamic covenant affecting the entire world. Abraham was promised that "in you all the families of the earth shall be blessed (בְּךָ כֹּל מִשְׁפְּחֹת הָאֲדָמָה וְנִבְרְכוּ)" (Gen 12:3). It was reaffirmed to Isaac that "by your descendants all the nations of the earth shall be blessed (וְהִתְבָּרֲכוּ בְזַרְעֲךָ כֹּל גּוֹיֵי הָאָרֶץ)" (Gen 26:4). God reconfirmed to Jacob that "in thee and in thy seed shall all the families of the earth be blessed (וְנִבְרֲכוּ בְךָ כָּל־מִשְׁפְּחֹת הָאֲדָמָה וּבְזַרְעֶךָ:)" (Gen 28:14). Paul saw this being fulfilled by justification by faith alone in Christ alone (Gal 3:6–9).[46]

Paul illustrated the extension of the blessings of the Abrahamic covenant to the Gentiles in Rom 11:17–24 by employing the image of grafting wild olive branches (Gentiles) into a domestic olive tree. Ryrie comments that "the root of the tree is the Abrahamic covenant which promised blessing to both Jew and Gentile through Christ."[47] Fruchtenbaum explains that

> the natural branches are the Jews (Israel) and the wild olive branches are the Gen-
> tiles (v. 17). The Olive Tree in this passage does not represent Israel or the Church,
> but it represents the place of spiritual blessing. The root of this place of blessing is
> the Abrahamic Covenant. The point that Paul makes here is the same point that he
> made in Ephesians 2:11–16 and 3:5–6. The Gentiles, by their faith, have now be-
> come partakers of Jewish spiritual blessings. This Olive Tree represents the place of
> blessing, and now Gentiles have been grafted into this place of blessing and partak-
> ing of its sap. Gentiles have been made partakers of Jewish spiritual blessings as
> contained in the Abrahamic Covenant. The Gentiles are not taker-overs, but partak-
> ers of Jewish spiritual blessings.... The point he is making is that God is doing
> something that is unnatural: He is bringing Gentiles into the place of blessing based
> on the Jewish covenants.[48]

This terminology of grafting is seen among the rabbinical sources for inclusion of Gentiles in Israel's blessing:

> R. Eleazar [ca. 1st–2nd century AD] further stated: What is meant by the text,
> And in thee shall the families of the earth be blessed? The Holy One, blessed be He,
> said to Abraham, 'I have two goodly shoots to engraft on you (יֵשׁ לִי לְהַבְרִיךְ בָּךְ
> שְׁתֵּי בְרֵכוֹת טוֹבוֹת): Ruth the Moabitess and Naamah the Ammonitess'.[49]

It is important to note that the other aspects (land and seed) of the Abrahamic covenant are not extended to the Gentiles. Contrary to the thinking of the Crusaders, Gentiles do not inherit the land of Israel. Only the blessings aspect of the Abrahamic covenant extend, not just to Israel, but to the entire world.

Stipulations

There seems to be broad consensus concerning the stipulations of the Abrahamic covenant. In number they total thirteen,[50] fourteen,[51] or fifteen (by my count). They may be divided into three broad categories: (1) personal promises to Abraham, (2) national promises to Israel, and (3) universal promises to Gentiles.[52] The Abrahamic covenant can be viewed as containing three aspects: land, seed, and blessing. Fruchtenbaum notes these aspects and their development in subsequent covenants with Israel:

> At its most elementary level the covenant contains three aspects: the land, the seed, and the blessing. The land aspect is developed in a land covenant that many have called the "Palestinian covenant." The seed aspect is covered in what is usually referred to as the "Davidic covenant." The blessing aspect is presented in a "new covenant."[53]

So the differing promises are given to Abraham, Israel, and the Gentiles concerning the land, the seed, and the blessing. These aspects of land, seed and blessing will be expanded in subsequent covenants.

Abraham. To Abraham personally God stipulated:

1. That he was to be the progenitor of a great nation, i.e., Israel (Gen 12:2; 13:16; 15:5; 17:2; 22:17). This stipulation was instituted over the next four centuries as Israel grew to be a great nation.
2. That he would be the progenitor of other nations, i.e., the Arab states (Gen 17:4–6). This stipulation has been instituted over time through Ishmael's descendants.
3. That kings would come from him (Gen 17:6). This stipulation is instituted when Saul became king over Israel and also has a bearing on the Davidic covenant.
4. That Abraham's descendants would be enslaved in Egypt for 430 years (Gen 15:13–14). This stipulation began with Jacob's migration to Egypt and set the time for the institution of the land promises.
5. That the name of Abram would be changed to Abraham (Gen 17:5). This stipulation was instituted immediately.
6. That Sarai's name would be changed to Sarah (Gen 17:15). This stipulation was immediately instituted.
7. That Sarah would give Abraham an heir (Gen 15:2–4; 17:16–21). This stipulation was instituted with the birth of Isaac.
8. That Abraham's name would be great (Gen 12:2). Perhaps this stipulation was immediately instituted. It is certainly in force today as Muslims, Christians, and Jews all revere Abraham.

9. That he would be blessed (Gen 12:2; 22:17). This stipulation was immediately instituted.
10. That he would bless others (Gen 12:2). This stipulation was immediately instituted.
11. That those who blessed Abraham would themselves be blessed (Gen 12:3). This stipulation was immediately instituted and continues in force today.
12. That those who cursed Abraham would themselves be cursed (Gen 12:3). This stipulation was immediately instituted and continues in force.
13. That the world would be blessed in Abraham (Gen 12:3; 22:18). This stipulation was instituted with the death of Christ (Gal 3:8).
14. That he would possess a land (Gen 12:1, 7; 13:14–15, 17; 15:18–21; 17:8). This stipulation was not instituted until Joshua and has never been completely fulfilled. The Land covenant elaborates on this.
15. That circumcision was to be the sign of the covenant (Gen 17:9–14). This stipulation was instituted immediately and continues in force.

Many of these promises were fulfilled in Abraham's lifetime (e.g., an heir through Sarah). However, Abraham did not see others in his lifetime (e.g., possession of the land).

The author of the letter to the Hebrews makes note of the fact that some promises remained to be fulfilled (Heb 11:13–16). Pentecost explains:

> Again, this covenant has an important bearing on the doctrine of resurrection. The promise entailed in the covenant is the basis of the Lord's refutation of the unbelief of the Sadducees in the fact of the resurrection. To those who denied the possibility of resurrection the Lord affirmed that resurrection was not only possible but necessary. Since God had revealed Himself as the God of Abraham, Isaac, and Jacob (Ex. 3:15), with whom He had entered into covenant relationships, and since these men had died without receiving the fulfillment of the promises (Heb. 11:13), inasmuch as the covenants could not be broken it was necessary for God to raise these men from the dead in order to fulfill His word. Paul, before Agrippa (Acts 26:6–8), unites "the promise to the fathers" with the resurrection of the dead in his defense of the doctrine. Thus the fact of physical resurrection is proved by the Lord and Paul from the necessity laid upon God to fulfill His covenant, even though it entails physical resurrection to do so. Consequently the fact of the believer's resurrection is united to the question of the kind of covenant made with Abraham.[54]

Since God never fails to perform His word, there must be a resurrection and a kingdom in which all of the promises to the patriarchs will find fulfillment.

Israel. To Israel, as Abraham's descendants, God promised:

1. That Israel would become a great nation (Gen 12:2; 17:2). As already noted, this stipulation was instituted over the next four centuries as Israel grew to be a great nation.
2. That Israel would become an innumerable people (Gen 13:16; 15:5; 22:17). As noted, this stipulation was instituted over time.
3. That they would eventually possess all of the land of Canaan (Gen 12:7; 13:14–15; 15:18–21; 17:8). This stipulation has never been fully realized and is expanded in the Land covenant.
4. That they would eventually prevail over their enemies (Gen 22:17). This stipulation has not been instituted yet although Israel has seen some miraculous victories. It awaits the kingdom where Messiah will rule the nations (Psalm 2:5, 6, 8, 9, 12).
5. That they must be circumcised in order to participate in the covenant (Gen 17:9–14). This stipulation was instituted immediately.

Please note that there is considerable overlap between the personal promises to Abraham and the promises to his descendants.

The boundaries of the land are delineated as "from the river of Egypt (מִנְּהַר מִצְרַיִם) as far as the great river, the river Euphrates (וְהַר־פְּרָת)" (Gen 15:18). Ryrie explains the differing views of the territory that Gen 15:18 defines:

> Debate continues on the identity of the river of Egypt. One view equates the river (nahar) of Egypt with the wadi (nahal) of Egypt, the modern wadi el-'Arish, which, during the rainy season, flows from the middle of the Sinai Peninsula into the Mediterranean ninety miles east of the Suez Canal (Num. 34:5; Josh. 15:4, 47; 1 Kings 8:65; 2 Kings 24:7; 2 Chron. 7:8; Isa. 27:12; Ezek. 47:19; 48:28). This is the view of Walter C. Kaiser, Jr. The other view identifies the river of Egypt as the Nile, specifically its eastern channel. The word nahar used in Genesis 15:18 always refers to a continuously flowing river, which the Nile is and the wadi el-'Arish is not. This is the view of Bruce K. Waltke and K. A. Kitchen.[55]

The focus seems to be on the southern border. However, the northern border, about which there seems to be no debate, would encompass a good deal of Syrian territory and all of Lebanon! No matter how troubling this passage may be to the nations of Syria, Lebanon, and Egypt, this territory has been

promised to Abraham and his descendants, Israel. It is also clear that this
stipulation has not yet seen fulfillment.

Gentiles. To the Gentiles, God promised:

1. That those who blessed Israel would be blessed (Gen 12:3). This
   stipulation was immediately instituted and continues in force today.
2. That those who cursed Israel would be cursed (Gen 12:3). This
   stipulation was immediately instituted and continues in force today.
3. That blessing would extend to the Gentiles through Abraham (Gen
   12:3; 22:18). This was instituted at the death of Christ (Gal 3:8).

Certainly the promised blessing and curse of Gen 12:3 has been carried out
repeatedly in human history. From Assyria to Babylon to Rome to Nazi
Germany, the curse has been invoked. Moreover, God has indeed blessed all
of the families of the earth by the gift of His Son (Gal 3:11–18) (see table 6).

Establishment

The establishment of the Abrahamic covenant occurred in stages that parallel
Abraham's spiritual development. In Gen 12:1–3, 7 God states His firm intent toward Abraham. At that point, Abraham's obedience was incomplete in
that he had not yet gone "forth... from your relatives" (Gen 12:1). Lot was
still with him. After Abraham separated from Lot, God reaffirmed His promise (Gen 13:14–17). The actual covenant is recorded in Gen 15 after "he believed in the LORD" (Gen 15:6), and "on that day the LORD made a
covenant with Abram" (Gen 15:18). In Gen 17:2 ("I will establish My cove-
nant" וְאֶתְּנָה בְרִיתִי), 7 ("I will establish My covenant" וַהֲקִמֹתִי אֶת־בְּרִיתִי), and 19
("I will establish My covenant" וַהֲקִמֹתִי אֶת־בְּרִיתִי) the covenant is reconfirmed,
with Isaac being explicitly named as the heir. Therefore, Gen 17 is a reestablishment of the Abrahamic covenant that was necessary to demarcate clearly
the line of succession. Finally, in Gen 22:16–18 God reaffirms His promise
to Abraham.

Duration

The Abrahamic covenant is eternal. It is explicitly so called in Gen 13:15;
17:8, 13, 19 (בְּרִית עוֹלָם); 1 Chr 16:15–18; and Ps 105:8–11. The author of He-

brews calls the Abrahamic covenant "immutable" (Heb 6:13–18). The eternal nature of the Abrahamic covenant flows from its unconditional and unilateral nature.[56] It was not of human invention and no human failures can break it (see figure 2).

The promise of the land was to Abraham's "descendants forever (עוֹלָם־עַד)" (Gen 13:15), "for an everlasting (עוֹלָם) possession" (Gen 17:8). The plain sense of this is that the promise of the land to Abraham and his physical descendants will never be abrogated. They will hold title to the land forever. Abraham himself would had to have taken it that way. The normal rule in hermeneutics is "when the plain sense makes sense seek no other sense."[57] Perhaps because of the clear import of these promises they have come under attack.

There have been three main attempts to deny the eternal import of this passage: (1) Spiritualize the passage to refer to the Church. But then why are all the families of the earth to be blessed through Abraham and his descendants, if they are all his family in the first place? Clearly a distinction is made between Abraham's descendants and those, other than his descendants, who are to be blessed through him. (2) See the passage as being fulfilled historically usually during the reign of David or Solomon. This is a *non sequitur* unless it is coupled with a weakening of the word "forever" (עוֹלָם). The extent of David's kingdom does not matter if the land is "an everlasting (עוֹלָם) possession" (Gen 17:8). This leads to the third attempt to deny the eternal nature of this promise. (3) Redefine "forever" and "everlasting" and see implicit conditions in the covenant. Ryrie notes:

> Please observe the inherent self-contradiction of the amillennial position. If the covenant is conditional, then even the amillennialist does not need to look for a fulfillment in the days of David, Joshua, or Solomon. If the covenant was fulfilled in either of those times, then it was not conditional. If it was fulfilled under Joshua or Solomon, then the church does not fulfill it. If the church fulfills it, then one need not look for a fulfillment in the days of Joshua or Solomon. It would appear that the amillennialist needs to have the spare tires of possible fulfillments under Joshua or Solomon or by the church in case the argument for conditionality goes flat![58]

We have already examined the concept of implicit conditionality at length and will not repeat that analysis at this time. However, the redefinition of "forever" merits examination.

The point of contention in the interpretation of these passages is the word "forever" (עוֹלָם). It is true that עוֹלָם can mean "a long time" and does not always mean "forever." MacRae explains that

> though ʿolām is used more than three hundred times to indicate indefinite continuance into the very distant future, the meaning of the word is not confined to the future....
>
> Jenni holds that its basic meaning "most distant times" can refer to either the remote past or to the future or to both as due to the fact that it does not occur independently (as a subject or as an object) but only in connection with prepositions indicating direction (min "since," ʿad "until," lᵉ "up to") or as an adverbial accusative of direction or finally as the modifying genitive in the construct relationship. In the latter instance ʿolām can express by itself the whole range of meanings denoted by all the prepositions "since, until, to the most distant time"; i.e. it assumes the meaning "(unlimited, incalculable) continuance, eternity." (THAT II. p. 230) J. Barr (Biblical Words for Time (1969), p. 73) says, "We might therefore best state the "basic meaning" as a kind of range between 'remotest time' and 'perpetuity'". But as shown above it is sometimes used of a not-so-remote past. For the meaning of the word in its attributive use we should note the designation of the LORD as ʾel ʿolām, "The Eternal God" (Gen 21:33).[59]

On the basis of this ambiguity, Leupold seeks to take עוֹלָם as a "long time" and to negate the covenant when Israel rejected Jesus as their Messiah:

> Such possession is guaranteed by God as extending ʿadh ʿolam, "for a long time." We have preferred to render this expression thus, because it actually implies nothing more than an indefinitely long season whose end cannot yet be determined, being derived from ʿalam, "to be hidden." Under circumstances the expression may mean actual eternity. On the other hand, it may imply no more than for the rest of a man's lifetime (Exod. 21:6). Now, surely, as commentators of all times have clearly pointed out, especially already Luther and Calvin, this promise to Abram is conditional, requiring faith. God cannot give rich promises of good which materialize even when men have cast off His Savior. History is the best commentary on how this promise is meant. When the Jews definitely cast off Christ, they were definitely as a nation expelled from the land. All who fall back upon this promise as guaranteeing a restoration of Palestine to the Jews before the end of time have laid into it a meaning which the words simply do not convey.[60]

It is interesting that Leupold mentions that under certain circumstances עוֹלָם may actually mean eternity. I am sure that his hope is in a salvation that lasts for an "eternity" not just a "long time!" Actually, judging by MacRae, it appears that עוֹלָם certainly means "eternity" in the future in at least three hundred out of the four hundred and thirty-nine instances in the OT. That being the case we should presume עוֹלָם means "eternity" unless there is a compelling reason to think otherwise. Leupold has greatly overstated his case.

Leupold's understanding of the Abrahamic covenant is conditioned by his presuppositions. Moses affirmed that God would never reject Israel (Lev 26:43–44). Perhaps the prophet Jeremiah has the best commentary of all as to how God considers the "forever" of this covenant:

Thus says the LORD,
Who gives the sun for light by day,
     And the fixed order of the moon and the stars for light by night,
Who stirs up the sea so that its waves roar;
     The LORD of hosts is His name:
"If this fixed order departs
     From before Me," declares the LORD,
"Then the offspring of Israel also shall cease
     From being a nation before Me forever."
Thus says the LORD,
"If the heavens above can be measured,
     And the foundations of the earth searched out below,
Then I also will cast off all the offspring of Israel
     For all that they have done," declares the LORD (Jer 31:35–37).

David also affirms the eternality of the land aspect of the Abrahamic covenant in 1 Chr 16:15–18 and Ps 105:8–11. Leupold assumes without proof that the covenants are conditional. Then, based on that assumption, since Israel has experienced failures, he would invalidate the covenant. Admittedly, Israel was expelled from the land. However, there is no more reason to deny the possibility of a return from this exile than there was to deny a return from the Babylonian exile. There are requirements to participate in the covenant (i.e., circumcision). However, the failure of individuals to participate in the covenant does not invalidate the covenant. As Paul pointed out in Rom 11:1–5, there has always been a believing remnant that is qualified to receive the promises. Leupold makes a strange statement for a Calvinist, "God cannot give rich promises of good which materialize even when men have cast off His Savior." This betrays a weak grasp of God's sovereignty.

The main aspects of the Abrahamic covenant are developed in three later covenants. Just as we saw that the Noahic covenant renewed and expanded on the Adamic covenant, so the Abrahamic covenant's land, seed, and blessing aspects are elaborated on in the Land (or Palestinian), Davidic, and new covenants (see figure 2). Pentecost notes that

further, this covenant has a most important bearing on the doctrines of Eschatology. The eternal aspects of this covenant, which guarantee Israel a permanent national existence, perpetual title to the land of promise, and the certainty of material and spiritual blessing through Christ, and guarantee Gentile nations a share in these blessings, determine the whole eschatological program of the Word of God. This covenant becomes the seed from which are brought forth the later covenants made with Israel. The essential areas of the Abrahamic covenant, the land, the seed, and the blessing, are enlarged in the subsequent covenants made with Israel.... Thus it may be said that the land promises of the Abrahamic covenant are developed in the Palestinian covenant, the seed promises are developed in the Davidic covenant, and the blessing promises are developed in the new covenant. This covenant, then, determines the whole future program for the nation Israel and is a major factor in Biblical Eschatology.[61]

We turn now to those three covenants.

Type of Covenant	Stipulations of Covenant	Beneficiaries	Established	End
Grant	• Father of a great nation • Father of other nations • Father of kings • Descendants enslaved in Egypt • Name changed to Abraham • Name would be great • He would be blessed • He would bless others • Those who blessed him would be blessed • Those who cursed him would be cursed • World blessed in him • He would possess the Land • Circumcision	Abraham	In Gen 15, after the promises of Gen 12 and 13. Confirmed in Gen 17 and 22.	Eternal covenant
	• Become a great nation • Become an innumerable people • Possess the Land • Prevail over enemies • They must be circumcised	Israel		

Continued on the next page

Table 6 (*Continued*)

Type of Covenant	Stipulations of Covenant	Beneficiaries	Estab-lished	End
Grant	To Gentiles: • Those who bless Israel will be blessed • Those who curse Israel will be cursed • The world will be blessed through Abraham Summary: • Land • Seed • Blessing	Gentiles	In Gen 15, after the promises of Gen 12 and 13. Con-firmed in Gen 17 and 22.	Eternal covenant

Table 6. Abrahamic Covenant

NOTES

1. Williamson claims that there are two Abrahamic covenants because of differences that he sees between the passages (Williamson, "Covenant," *NDBT* 422–24). However, if this were the case, which one of the two does Scripture refer to when later the Abrahamic covenant is renewed to Abraham's descendants? Eaton thinks "that the covenant and oath of Gen. 15, 17 and 22 belong together and all make one covenant taken over the course of many years" (Michael Eaton, *No Condemnation: A New Theology of Assurance*, [Downers Grove, IL: InterVarsity, 1995] 65).

2. *BDB* 229–37.

3. Ryrie, *Basic Theology* 528.

4. Pentecost, *Things To Come* 74–75.

5. Ross, "Genesis," *BKCOT* 47; Leupold 412–13.

6. Kline, "Genesis," *NBC* 93.

7. Kyle M. Yates, "Genesis," in *The Wycliffe Bible Commentary* (hereafter referred to as *WBC*), eds. Charles F. Pfeiffer and Everett F. Harrison (Chicago: Moody, 1972) 17.

8. Leupold, *Genesis* 1:412–13.

9. Ross, "Genesis," *BKCOT* 47.

10. Driver, *Treatise* 53.

11. Ryrie, *Basic Theology* 528.

12. Driver, *Treatise* 55–56.

13. Arnold G. Fruchtenbaum, "Where Are We Now? The Prophetic Plan of the Abrahamic Covenant," in *The Fundamentals for the Twenty-First Century: Examining the Crucial Issues of the Christian Faith*, gen. ed. Mal Couch (Grand Rapids, MI: Kregel, 2000) 157.

14. Kidner, *Genesis* 124. See also Robertson, *Christ of the Covenants* 128–46 and Pentecost, *Things To Come* 76–78.

15. Leupold, *Genesis* 1:480.

16. Weinfeld notes that "a similar oath occurs in the Abban-Yarimlim deed, where Abban, the donor, takes the oath by cutting the neck of a lamb (*kišād 1 immeru iṭbuh*), saying '(may I be cursed) if I take back what I gave you'" (Moshe Weinfeld, *The Promise of the Land: The Inheritance of the Land of Canaan by the Israelites* [Berkeley, CA: University of California Press, 1993] 251–52).

17. See chapter 2.

18. Driver, *Treatise* 17.

19. Ibid. 18.

20. Yates, "Genesis," *WBC* 23.

21. Leupold, *Genesis* 1:512.

22. Ryrie, *Basic Theology* 528.

23. Benjamin Davidson, *The Analytical Hebrew and Chaldee Lexicon* (Grand Rapids,

MI: Zondervan, 1973) 568–69.

24.   *BDB* 678–81.

25.   Arnold G. Fruchtenbaum, *Israelology: The Missing Link in Systematic Theology*, 2nd rev. (Tustin, CA: Ariel Ministries, 1994) 145–46.

26.   Ryrie, *Basic Theology* 529.

27.   *BDB* 1044–45.

28.   Gesenius, *Hebrew-Chaldee Lexicon* 843.

29.   John Bright, *A History Of Israel*, 3rd ed. (Philadelphia: Westminister, 1981) 155.

30.   Livingston, *Pentateuch* 154–57.

31.   Pentecost, *Things To Come* 78.

32.   Merrill, "A Theology of the Pentateuch," *A Biblical Theology of the Old Testament* 26–30.

33.   John H. Sailhamer, "The Messiah and the Hebrew Bible," *Journal of the Evangelical Theological Society* (hereafter referred to as *JETS*) 44, no. 1 (March 2001): 20.

34.   Since Gen 15:6 (וְהֶאֱמִן בַּיהוָה וַיַּחְשְׁבֶהָ לּוֹ צְדָקָה) does not contain the word "Abram," it might be better to take the subject to be God. This would make sense also because God is clearly the subject of the other verb, "and He considered (וַיַּחְשְׁבֶהָ)." Also note that the verb (הֶאֱמִן) is in the *hipᶜil* which is causative. Therefore, Gen 15:6 could be translated, "And He [God] had caused him [Abram] to trust in Yahweh, and He [God] considered it [to be] to him [Abram] righteousness" (my translation). This would be in keeping with Paul's statement that saving faith is "not of yourselves, it is the gift of God" (Eph 2:8).

35.   David H. Levy, *The Sky: A User's Guide* (New York: Cambridge University Press, 1991) 2. Mr. Levy is a noted astronomer and the discoverer of 17 comets including comet Shoemaker-Levy 9 that struck Jupiter.

36.   Leupold, *Genesis* 1:476.

37.   Kidner, *Genesis* 124.

38.   Fruchtenbaum, *Israelology* 152.

39.   See also Weinfeld, *The Promise of the Land* 222–64.

40.   Beckman, *Hittite Diplomatic Texts* 30–32, 4.2.

41.   Ibid. 31–32, 4.4–6.

42.   Ibid. 32, 4.6.

43.   Ibid. 32, 4.7.

44.   Ibid. 159–60, 31A.1, 2, 4.

45.   Ibid. 111, 18C.10.

46.   Interestingly, most Bible cross references indicate that Gal 3:8 is a quote of Genesis 12:3. It is not. Galatians 3:8 reads ἐνευλογηθήσονται ἐν σοὶ πάντα τὰ ἔθνη. The LXX of Genesis 12:3 reads ἐνευλογηθήσονται ἐν σοὶ πᾶσαι αἱ φυλαὶ τῆς γῆς. However, the LXX of Genesis 26:4 is much closer (ἐνευλογηθήσονται ἐν τῷ σπέρματί σου πάντα τὰ ἔθνη τῆς γῆς) although Paul seems to combine both quotes.

47.   Ryrie, *RSB* 1718.

48. Fruchtenbaum, *Israelology* 744.

49. *b. Yebam.* 63a, *The Soncino Talmud*, trans. Isidore Epstein, Judaic Classics Library, ver. 2.1 [CD–ROM] (Brooklyn, NY: Judaica, 1991).

50. George N. H. Peters, *The Theocratic Kingdom of Our Lord Jesus, the Christ as Covenanted in the Old Testament*, 3 vols. (New York: Funk & Wagnalls, 1884; reprint, Grand Rapids, MI: Kregel, 1988) 1:293–94. See Pentecost, *Things To Come* 72–73.

51. Fruchtenbaum, "Where Are We Now?" *Fundamentals* 158–59. He counts the change of Abraham's name (Gen 17:5).

52. Ibid. See also Ryrie, *Basic Theology* 526–27 and John F. Walvoord, "Millennial Series: Part 12: The Abrahamic Covenant and Premillennialism" in *Bibliotheca Sacra* 108, no. 432 (October–December 1951): 414–22.

53. Fruchtenbaum, "Where Are We Now?" *Fundamentals* 160.

54. Pentecost, *Things To Come* 70–71.

55. Ryrie, *Basic Theology* 527–31.

56. Pentecost, *Things To Come* 75–82.

57. Pentecost, *Things To Come* 1–64 and Paul Lee Tan, *The Interpretation of Prophecy* (Dallas, TX: Bible Communications, Inc., 1974) 187–92.

58. Ryrie, *Basic Theology* 530.

59. Alan A. MacRae, "עלם (ʿlm)," *TWOT* 2:672–73.

60. Leupold, *Genesis* 1:441.

61. Pentecost, *Things To Come* 71–72.

CHAPTER NINE

The Land Covenant

Covenant Type

The Name of the Covenant

The covenant that we find in Deut 29–30 has traditionally been referred to in dispensational circles as the Palestinian covenant. It delineates the conditions that govern life "in the land."[1] Fruchtenbaum notes that this is a poor choice of terms in today's world:

> The traditional name for this covenant is the Palestinian covenant, a legitimate name at the time it was coined, because this covenant largely concerns the land known for centuries as Palestine. However, this is now an unfortunate term for two reasons. First, it was a name given to the land by the Roman emperor Hadrian after the second Jewish revolt under Bar-Kochba (A.D. 132–135), for the purpose of erasing any Jewish remembrance of the land. Second, due to the historical events in the Middle East in the twentieth century, the name is associated more with Arabs than with Jews. Perhaps a better title would be Land covenant.[2]

I will follow Fruchtenbaum's suggestion and refer to this covenant as the Land covenant. However, please be aware, when others refer to the Palestinian covenant, that these are synonymous terms.

One Covenant or Two?

Deuteronomy 29:1 reads, "These are the words of the covenant which the LORD commanded Moses to make with the sons of Israel in the land of Moab, *besides the covenant* which He had made with them at Horeb" (emphasis mine). On the surface of this text it would appear to be speaking of a second covenant. Williamson speaks of the "Mosaic covenant(s)"[3] Fruchtenbaum remarks that "although this covenant is within the fifth book of Moses, of Moses, Deut 29:1 clearly shows that the Palestinian Covenant is distinct from the Mosaic covenant...."[4] On the other hand, William E. Biederwolf dogmatically asserts that "the Covenant which God here makes with His people is not a new covenant besides the one He made with them in Horeb, but rather a renewed declaration of that same covenant."[5] This would seem to be a flat denial of the text. F. C. Cook makes the assertion that "this and the following chapter contain the address of Moses to the people on the solemn renewal of the covenant."[6] The concept of multiple covenants within the book of Deuteronomy seems to have also caused some confusion in the Talmud. Through some rather convoluted mathematics, the rabbis came up with the interesting suggestion that there were forty-eight covenants behind every commandment![7] Therefore, we must first determine if our text indicates that we are in fact dealing with two covenants.

The dividing lines have been drawn largely on dispensational issues. The covenant theologians, in keeping with their penchant to see one overarching Covenant of Grace, tend to deny that there are separate covenants in view here. Robertson is a prime example:

> The problem of the dispensational understanding of the revelation of law in Scripture surfaces rather obviously when their treatment of the "covenant" of law in distinction from the "dispensation" of law is considered. As a matter of fact, both the Old and the New Scofield Bibles present two covenants associated with the revelation of law to Moses. These two covenants are radically different in their substance. One of these "covenants" administered through Moses is conditional in its very essence, and the other is absolutely unconditional, according to dispensationalism....
>
> A basic misreading of the text of Scripture apparently has led to the introduction of this additional covenant in contradistinction from the Mosaic covenant established at Sinai....
>
> Yet the setting of Deuteronomy 30 requires that it be understood as reporting nothing other than a renewal of the Mosaic covenant of law. The entire book of Deuteronomy presents itself in covenantal form as a renewal of the bond which God established originally with Israel at Sinai.[8]

Dispensationalists, on the other hand, tend to see a second covenant separate from the Mosaic covenant.[9] Ryrie comments, "Moses now details the agreement under which the people would enter the land of Palestine. This Palestinian covenant was in addition to the Mosaic covenant given at Sinai (*Horeb*)."[10] Indeed, Deut 29:12–13 and 30:20 indicate that this covenant is based upon the Abrahamic and not the Mosaic covenant.[11] So, with dispensationalists affirming, and covenant theologians denying the Land covenant, we will examine the text to determine which view is correct.

Deuteronomy 29:1 states that "the covenant which the LORD commanded Moses to make with the sons of Israel in the land of Moab" was "besides the covenant (מִלְּבַד הַבְּרִית) which He had made with them at Horeb." Brown, Driver, and Briggs define בַּד as "separation" and לְבַד as "*in a state of ... separation, alone, by itself.*" They note that, when לְבַד is followed by מִן, it functions as a preposition, "*apart from, besides.*" It appears that מִלְּבַד is simply an inverted form of לְבַד מִן.[12] Louis Goldberg also defines בַּד as "alone, by itself, a part, besides...."[13] This expression is used to describe God's uniqueness, "He is God; there is no other besides Him (הָאֱלֹהִים אֵין עוֹד מִלְבַדּוֹ הוּא)" (Deut 4:35). A literal translation of מִלְּבַד might be "for a separation from." Therefore, this new covenant is "for a separation from the covenant which He had made with them at Horeb (מִלְּבַד הַבְּרִית אֲשֶׁר־כָּרַת אִתָּם בְּחֹרֵב)" (Deut 29:1 my translation). Mendenhall notes that "the exception in Deut. 29:1—H 28:69 is explicitly aware of the fact that what follows is a different covenant tradition."[14] This covenant is at its heart separate and isolated from the Mosaic covenant.

Argument from the Structure of Deuteronomy

As previously indicated, it appears that the mention of an additional covenant apart from the Mosaic covenant in Deuteronomy was confusing to the Talmudic sages.[15] One Talmudic approach was to consider Deut 29:1 as the subscription to Deut 27–28.[16] This solution found its way into the Hebrew Bible's versification, which considers Deut 29:1 to be 28:69, and from there into the debate over the Land covenant.

Not all covenant theologians or dispensationalists have held to the party line on the nature of Deut 29:1–30:20. Surprisingly, Jack Deere, a dispensationalist, seems not to hold to the existence of the Land covenant:

> Some see this verse as an introduction to the fourth address of Moses beginning in verse 2, but probably it concludes the covenant renewal ceremony in Moab. This preference is reflected in the Hebrew text which numbers this verse as 28:69 rather than 29:1. The words, the covenant ... in Moab, in addition to the covenant He had made with them at Horeb, have led some to posit the existence of a separate covenant (i.e., a Palestinian Covenant) in addition to the Mosaic Covenant. The wording, however, was not meant to reflect the making of a new covenant, but the renewing of the Mosaic Covenant made at Horeb. Moses' fourth address introduces no new

covenantal provisions that were not already made explicit in his other speeches. So
Deuteronomy 29:2–30:20 recapitulates the covenant details laid down in the preced-
ing chapters.[17]

I disagree that this address "introduces no new covenantal provisions." The
guarantees of regathering (Deut 30:3–5) and conversion (Deut 30:6) are significant new stipulations. Kline sees Deut 29–30 as part of the larger Curses
and Blessings section of Deuteronomy.[18] However, even Kline regards Deut
29:1 as introducing a new section:

> (Heb. Bible 28:69). Though some, following the Hebrew arrangement, regard
> this as a subscription, and it would indeed be an accurate description of what pre-
> ceded, it is probably to be understood as a superscription. On the relation of verses 1
> and 2 compare the similar sequence from 4:45 to 5:1.[19]

I think that Kline has brought up a major clue as to the nature of Deut 29:1 in
the structure of the Mosaic addresses that make up the book of Deuteronomy.

Deuteronomy consists of seven Mosaic discourses arranged to correspond to the general form of an ancient Near Eastern suzerainty covenant,
and an epilogue that deals with the succession of covenant leadership upon
Moses' death (Deut 34). Each discourse begins with a prologue (Deut 1:1–5;
4:44–49; 27:1; 29:1; 31:1; 31:30; 33:1). Three of these prologues contain
geographical references as well (Deut 1:1–5; 4:44–49; and 29:1), as does the
epilogue (Deut 34:1). The remaining four prologues probably omit geographical references because the location had not changed from the previous
section (Deut 27:1; 31:1; 31:30; 33:1). In each case, the prologue is a super-
scription for the discourse that follows. If Deut 29:1 were a subscript for
Deut 27:1–28:68, it would be the only such instance in Deuteronomy and
would break the structural pattern of the rest of the book.

The language used in Deut 29:1 is very similar to the language of the
other prologues. Deuteronomy 29:1 reads, "These are the words of the covenant which the LORD commanded Moses (אֵלֶּה דִבְרֵי הַבְּרִית אֲשֶׁר־צִוָּה יְהוָה אֶת־מֹשֶׁה)
to make with the sons of Israel in the land of Moab...." Deuteronomy
1:1 is very similar, "These are the words which Moses spoke to all Israel
(אֵלֶּה הַדְּבָרִים אֲשֶׁר דִּבֶּר מֹשֶׁה אֶל־כָּל־יִשְׂרָאֵל) across the Jordan...." Deuteronomy
4:44–46 has, "Now this is the law which Moses set before the sons of Israel
(וְזֹאת הַתּוֹרָה אֲשֶׁר־שָׂם מֹשֶׁה לִפְנֵי בְּנֵי יִשְׂרָאֵל) ... across the Jordan...." Deuteronomy
27:1 reads, "Then Moses and the elders of Israel charged the people, saying
(וַיְצַו מֹשֶׁה וְזִקְנֵי יִשְׂרָאֵל אֶת־הָעָם לֵאמֹר)...." Deuteronomy 31:1 has, "So Moses went

and spoke these words to all Israel (מֹשֶׁה וַיְדַבֵּר אֶת־הַדְּבָרִים הָאֵלֶּה אֶל־כָּל־יִשְׂרָאֵל
וַיֵּלֶךְ).” In Deut 31:30 we read that “Moses spoke in the hearing of all the as-
sembly of Israel the words (וַיְדַבֵּר מֹשֶׁה בְּאָזְנֵי כָּל־קְהַל יִשְׂרָאֵל אֶת־דִּבְרֵי)....” Finally,
in Deut 33:1 we have, “Now this is the blessing with which Moses the man
of God blessed the sons of Israel before his death (אֶת־בְּנֵי יִשְׂרָאֵל לִפְנֵי מוֹתוֹ
וְזֹאת הַבְּרָכָה אֲשֶׁר בֵּרַךְ מֹשֶׁה אִישׁ הָאֱלֹהִים).” The similarity of all of these prologues
is apparent and indicates a similar function as headers introducing the following discourses.

The similarity of language and structure leads to the conclusion that Deut
29:1 is the prologue introducing the speech of Deut 29–30. Keil and Delitzsch state, “28:69 (ch. 29:1) is not the close of the address in ch. 5–28 as
Schultz, Knobel, and others suppose; but the heading to ch. 29–30, which relate to the making of the covenant mentioned in this verse (vid. ch. 29:12,
14).”[20] R. K. Harrison also notes that this “discourse (chs. 29, 30) consists of
a supplementary address, exhorting the people to accept the terms of the new
covenant and promising them forgiveness in case of sin, if attended by
wholehearted repentance.”[21] I have demonstrated that Deuteronomy 29–30 is
a separate covenant from the Mosaic covenant. It remains to be seen what
sort of covenant it is.

Structure of Deuteronomy 29–30

Deuteronomy 29–30 is loosely structured as a covenant. McCarthy observes
that

> with this analysis of chapters 29–30 we can outline the section in terms of the cove-
> nant formula as follows:
> 1) *Mise en scène* (28, 69);
> 2) Historical Prologue (29, 1b–8);
> 3) List of Parties (9–14);
> 4) Stipulation (15–18);
> 5) Curse (19–27);
> 6) Blessing (30, 1–10);
> 7) Exhortation (30, 11–14);
> 8) Curse-blessing (15–19);
> 9) Witnesses (19);
> 10) Exhortation (19b–20).
> Not that these elements appear as such, so as to form a kind of formal covenant
> document.[22]

McCarthy denies here what he has so well proved. What is unclear is the reason for his denial, since these elements do indeed form a kind of covenant document. This should not surprise us since that is the stated purpose that Deut 29:1 announces. Deuteronomy 29–30 contains five of the six acknowledged characteristics of the ancient Near Eastern suzerainty form: preamble, historical introduction, stipulations, witnesses, curses, and blessings.[23] It lacks only deposition instructions, which is certainly understandable, since Deuteronomy as a whole is a covenant document and has its own deposition instructions. Therefore, we must consider the Land covenant to be in the form of a covenant. Moreover, when we examine the content we see that this covenant serves as a grant covenant.

Conclusions from the Biblical Evidence

Although the Deuteronomy 29–30 is in the form of a covenant, the content is different from the Mosaic covenant. Ryken remarks that

> another notable image is the simultaneous affirmation of two covenants that enrich and give nuance to Deuteronomy's theology. The covenant of Horeb (Deut 6–18) emphasizes God's gracious election of Israel and the expected human responsibility for obedience to the laws and will of God. But this covenant of Horeb ends ultimately in curse and exile (Deut 28:45–68) . Deuteronomy 29:1 presents a second covenant of Moab made "in addition to the covenant that [the LORD] made with them at Horeb." The Moab covenant emphasizes much more the judging and saving activity, not of humans but of God, in the face of the failure and limitations of human power and obedience (Deut 29–32, cf. Deut 32:39). The two emphases—on human obedience (the Horeb covenant) and divine promise and power (the Moab covenant)—remain side by side in Deuteronomy, even as God's promise and blessing predominate and overcome the limitations of human failure and rebellion (Deut 33–34).[24]

The content of the Land covenant is in keeping with a grant covenant. In language reminiscent of Gen 15:17–18, this is "a covenant with the LORD your God, a covenant the LORD is making with you this day and sealing with an oath" (Deut 29:12 NIV). This covenant is unilateral. The Mosaic covenant results in the curse (Lev 26:14–45; Deut 28:15–68). However, the Land covenant, while promising divine discipline, never threatens revocation of Israel's title to the land. Williamson observes that

> the covenant in Deuteronomy is likewise a distinct development in God's relationship with Israel (*cf.* Deut. 29:1); the new generation had to commit themselves to

the Mosaic covenant before taking possession of the Promised Land. Although in one sense this was a renewal or remaking of the Sinaitic covenant with a new generation, there are some significant differences in emphasis, which may suggest that this covenant qualifies the conditional nature of Israel's unique relationship with Yahweh, especially in relation to their future tenure of the Promised Land. Yahweh had earlier guaranteed the staged removal of the Canaanites (Exod. 23:30; 34:11). He had also indicated that Israel would likewise be expelled, if she failed to meet her covenant obligations (Lev. 18:24–30). However, now it is disclosed that even exile to the most remote parts of the earth (Deut. 30:4) will not thwart God's ultimate purpose; rather, the promises made to Abraham will find further fulfillment (30:5), and the divine–human relationship will be sustained by an inner change (30:6). Thus the covenant in Deuteronomy is not simply a remaking of the Sinaitic covenant with a new generation. It is a reaffirmation of obligations laid out in the 'covenant of circumcision' (Gen. 17; cf. Deut. 30:6–10) for all future generations (29:14–15), and an anticipation of the 'new covenant' which will guarantee that a divine–human relationship between Yahweh and Abraham's 'seed' will be maintained for ever (*cf. Jer. 31:31–34) by facilitating the fulfillment of the important ethical obligations.[25]

Therefore, although continual enjoyment of the land is conditional, the Land covenant unconditionally promises Israel's eventual possession of the land.

The grant form is appropriate because, as the recipients of God's favor, Israel required instruction as to the behavioral expectations that God had for them. God promised discipline and temporary removal from the land. Nevertheless, He also promised eventual restoration to the land and spiritual renewal. R. Allen Killen and John Rea comment on the Land covenant's dual nature:

> *Palestinian covenant* (Deut 29–30). Though a part of the renewal of the Mosaic covenant, this covenant is considered separately by some. The *parties* are God and Israel. *The conditions* are that God will bless Israel if she remains faithful to Him, and He will curse her if she turns from Him, as expressed in the blessings and the curses promulgated from Mount Gerizim and Mount Ebal (Deut 27:9 ff.). *The results,* after all the blessings and the curses have been experienced by Israel in the course of her history, are that, if and when she repents, God will regather her from the utmost parts of the earth, reestablish her in Israel and bless her. The *security* for the covenant is found in the ordinances of heaven and of earth (Deut 30:19).
>
> This covenant has a unilateral aspect—promises and rewards for keeping the covenant, and curses as the consequence of breaking it. The assurance was given that national repentance of Israel will most surely occur (Deut 30:1–10). Yet there is also a bilateral aspect—Israel must repent. This repentance will come to pass because of God's sovereign grace in the lives of individual Jews when Christ returns

(Zech 12:10–14; 13:6; cf. Isa 66:19–20). God's ordinances take into consideration both what man will do in his freedom, and what God plans to do in His sovereign grace. Both these elements appear in the Palestinian covenant.[26]

Walvoord explains that this is in no way contradictory of the Abrahamic covenant's unconditional guarantees for two reasons. First, the Abrahamic covenant takes precedence over the Land covenant (cf. Gal 3:17). Second, the Land covenant concerns, not the right to title of the land, but the right to enjoyment of the land by any given generation. He notes that Israel is promised dispersions as a punishment for disobedience, but that these dispersions are temporary in nature.[27] Therefore, both the Abrahamic and the Land covenants leave no doubt that Israel has eternal title to the land given to them by God. The particular generation may or may not experience possession by virtue of their obedience (Deut 30:16–20). However, ultimately Israel will possess both the land and a heart to obey God.

Paul quotes Deut 30:11–14 in Rom 10:6–8 and applies it to "the righteousness that is based on faith" (Rom 10:6). If Deut 29–30 were merely a renewal of the Mosaic covenant, Paul would be misapplying Deut 30:11–14, since "the law is not based on faith" (Gal 3:12 NIV). However, since Deut 29–30 is a grant covenant and the right response to a grant is trust in the grantor's word (cf. Gen 15:6; Rom 4:3), Paul's use of Deut 30:11–14 is very appropriate. Also, the immediate context in Deut 30:6-10 speaks of the circumcision of the heart (cf. Rom 2:29) which points to the new covenant's blessings. By giving Israel a circumcised heart, God enables the very obedience that will guarantee her continued enjoyment of the land.

Ancient Near Eastern Parallels

In general, Deut 29–30 is a grant covenant. In particular, Weinfeld sees a close parallel with Assyrian loyalty oaths:

> The change of leadership in the ANE was accompanied by a pledge of loyalty on behalf of the people. The so-called vassal treaties of Esarhaddon (= VTE) which have so much in common with Deuteronomy are none other than fealty oaths imposed by the retiring king on his vassals concerning his successor (Assurbanipal). The covenant in the land of Moab, which is concluded at the time when Moses nominates Joshua as his successor (Deut 3:23–29; 31:1–8), resembles then formally the situation found in VTE. The difference is only that the contents of the Mosaic covenant are divine law and the sworn pledge refers to God whereas VTE is concerned with stipulations of a political nature, referring to the human suzerain. For-

mally, however, the two documents are of similar nature. Especially striking is the covenantal scene in VTE and in Deuteronomy. Both scenes have the entire population gathered: young and old (Deut 29:9–11, cf. 2 Kgs 23:1–3, and VTE 4–5; for the Assyrian covenantal ceremony, see Weinfeld 1976: 392–93). In both scenes the gathered take the pledge not only for themselves but also for the future generations (Deut 29:14, VTE 6–7, cf. Sefire treaty I A 1–5 [Fitzmyer 1967: 12–13])....

Another parallel feature between the Assyrian oath of loyalty and the one of Deuteronomy is the theme of self-condemnation in connection with the violation of the oath. The end of Deuteronomy 29 reads: "And the generations to come... will ask: 'Why did YHWH do thus to this land?' and they will say: 'Because they forsook the covenant of YHWH'" (vv 21–24). The same motif is found in the neo-Assyrian texts concerning the breach of the oath. Thus the annals of Assurbanipal state: "the people of Arabia asked one another saying: 'Why is it that such evil has befallen Arabia?' and they say 'Because we did not observe the obligation sworn to the god of Ashur'"....[28]

Walton, Matthews, and Chavalas note the parallels to other cultures' covenant forms. They observe that "the concept that one who keeps a violation secret will nevertheless be vulnerable to the curses is found in Aramaic (Sefire) and Hittite treaties, where the curse includes the destruction of the violator's name (family)."[29]

A particularly appropriate parallel exists concerning the Hittite covenants between Suppiluliuma I of Hatti and Niqmaddu II of Ugarit.[30] As I have already shown, this treaty was in the form of a grant covenant and was unconditional. The land was given to Niqmaddu and his descendants forever. This grant was appealed to in solving legal disputes.[31] However, upon placing Niqmaddu's son, Niqmepa, on the throne of Ugarit, Mursili II of Hatti imposed a suzerainty covenant on him.[32] The terms reveal the Hittite approach to resolving this tension between an unconditional grant and the need to impose conditions on a vassal. Mursili II mentions that failing to protect the King of Hatti would violate his oath. Mursili II states that, if Niqmepa's life, his wives, his sons, and his land are dear to him, so should the person of the King of Hatti and his sons be dear to him.[33] This is somewhat subtle, but the threat is clear. However, all subtlety vanishes in the curse section. Niqmepa is threatened with destruction by the oath gods of himself, his wives, his sons, his grandsons, his house, his city, his land, and all that he owns.[34] Presumably, the Hittite King would have no compunctions about aiding the gods in assuring that the covenant-breaker got his just deserts! Thus, the Hittite solution is that the grant covenant gave the land to Niqmaddu and his descendants in perpetuity. However, if Niqmepa violates the suzerainty covenant, he and all of his descendants will be killed, thus vacating his claim.

This stands in stark contrast with God's gracious dealings with Israel. Walton, Matthews, and Chavalas note the uniqueness of the Land covenant:

> Unlike the treaties of the ancient Near East, the covenant as represented in Deuteronomy has a forgiveness clause that offers second chances when the covenant has been violated. Repentance and recommitment to the terms of the covenant would result in restoration. Such mercy was not impossible with ancient treaties, but there is no example of such a possibility being explicitly included in the written document.[35]

I note in passing the similarity between Moses calling "heaven and earth to witness" (Deut 30:19) and the Hittite practice of doing the same.[36] The Lord has promised Abraham a seed in an eternal covenant. He cannot destroy Israel in order to vacate their title to the land without breaking His oath. Therefore, God has made the possession of the land conditional but the title to the land is unconditional.

Beneficiaries

Clearly, this covenant concerns Israel and her possession of the land. The Land covenant cannot be made to apply to any other group without doing violence to the normal meaning of language. Since this covenant is with Israel (Deut 29:10–15), there must always be a remnant of Israel to receive the promise of ultimate restoration. Pentecost observes that

> the Palestinian covenant established by God (Deut 30:1–9; Jer 32:36–44; Ezek 11:16–21; 36:21–38) gives the basis on which Israel will occupy the land which was first given Abraham's seed in the Abrahamic covenant. This covenant makes the existence of a remnant imperative to fulfill the promised inheritance of the land.[37]

The beneficiaries of the Land covenant are all Israel; past, present, and future.

Stipulations

The Land covenant sets forth the conditions under which Israel will enjoy the possession of the land, predicting three exiles and a final return. Chafer observes that "this covenant illustrates how a covenant basically unconditional and sure in its fulfillment nonetheless has conditional elements for any particular generation."[38] Walvoord sees the three exiles as Egypt, Assyria/Babylon, and Rome.[39] I would disagree since the sojourn in Egypt was already past from Moses' point of view. Also the Assyrian and Babylonian exiles are not joined together in any historical sense. Therefore, it is unlikely that Moses had the Egyptian sojourn in mind.[40]

Assyrian Exile. Deuteronomy 28:36–68 is an incredibly detailed prediction of the dispersions that Israel was to experience. These were predicted in a more general way in Lev 26:14–45. After delineating the many curses and calamities that would befall Israel for disobedience, Moses began to prophesy of a series of exiles. The first exile is detailed in Deut 28:36–48. Moses writes, "The LORD will bring you and your king, whom you set over you, to a nation which neither you nor your fathers have known" (Deut 28:36). We should note that here Moses predicts a time when Israel will have a king. Therefore, this exile could not have taken place during or before the period of the Judges. The exile is to be "to a nation which neither you nor your fathers have known" (Deut 28:36). Since the patriarchs were from Babylon and visited Egypt often, eventually settling there, neither the Babylonian exile nor the Egyptian bondage can be in view here. Therefore, instead of taking the Assyrian and Babylonian exiles together, Deut 28:36–48 is referring to the Assyrian exile. This passage predicts captivity and depopulation (Deut 28:36, 37, 41), crop failures and famine (Deut 28:38–40, 42, 48; cf. Lev 26:23–26), foreign oppression, political and economic (Deut 28:43–44, 48; cf. Lev 26:14–17), leading to decline and eventual destruction (Deut 28:43, 45, 48). Although a remnant of the kingdom of Israel still exists (Jer 3:18; Luke 2:36; Rev 7:4–8), the lostness of the ten northern tribes is proverbial exactly as predicted (Deut 28:37, 46). The defeat of the Northern kingdom of Israel was completed by Assyria in 721 BC.

Babylonian Exile. The second exile is predicted in Deut 28:49–62. Moses prophesies, "The LORD will bring a nation against you from afar (גּוֹי מֵרָחוֹק), from the end of the earth, as the eagle swoops down, a nation whose language you shall not understand (גּוֹי אֲשֶׁר לֹא־תִשְׁמַע לְשֹׁנוֹ)" (Deut 28:49). The prophet Jeremiah, in predicting the Babylonian exile, writes, "'Behold, I am bringing a nation against you from afar (גּוֹי מִמֶּרְחָק), O house of Israel,' declares the LORD. 'It is an enduring nation, It is an ancient nation, A nation whose language you do not know, Nor can you understand what they say (גּוֹי לֹא־תֵדַע לְשֹׁנוֹ וְלֹא תִשְׁמַע מַה־יְדַבֵּר)'" (Jer 5:15). Although Aramaic became familiar to Israel after seventy years of captivity, it was not initially a language understood by the common people (cf. 2 Kgs 18:26). Moreover, please note that this land of exile is not referred to as a land that was unknown to either Israel or the patriarchs as the first and third exiles are (Deut 28:36, 64). This passage describes siege (Deut 28:51–53) and its horrific effects including cannibalism (Deut 28:54–57; cf. Lev 26:29) and plague (Deut 28:58–61). The Jewish historian, Josephus (AD 37–ca. AD 100), writes:

> Now in the ninth year of the reign of Zedekiah, on the tenth day of the tenth month, the king of Babylon made a second expedition against Jerusalem, and lay before it eighteen months, and besieged it with the utmost application. There came upon them also two of the greatest calamities, at the same time that Jerusalem was besieged, a famine and a pestilential distemper, and made great havoc of them....[41]

The result was great loss of life and severe depopulation (Deut 28:62). The defeat of the Southern kingdom of Judah was completed by Babylon in 587 BC after exiles in 605 BC and 597 BC.

Roman Exile. The third and final exile is prophesied in Deut 28:63–68 and was fulfilled by the Roman dispersion. Israel was to be "torn from the land where you are entering to possess it" (Deut 28:63). This dispersion was different in that "the LORD will scatter you among all peoples, from one end of the earth to the other end of the earth" (Deut 28:64). This was the beginning of the Jewish Diaspora. The Jews' experience of continual persecution culminating in the Holocaust is predicted in chilling terms:

> Among those nations you shall find no rest, and there will be no resting place for the sole of your foot; but there the LORD will give you a trembling heart, failing of eyes, and despair of soul. *So your life shall hang in doubt before you; and you will be in dread night and day, and shall have no assurance of your life.* In the morning you shall say, "Would that it were evening!" And at evening you shall say, "Would that it were morning!" because of the dread of your heart which you dread, and for the sight of your eyes which you will see (Deut 28:65–67) (emphasis mine).

Josephus chronicles the fulfillment of this prediction by the Romans in AD 70:

> Yet could not that garrison resist those that were deserting; for although a great number of them were slain, yet were the deserters many more in number. These

were all received by the Romans, because Titus himself grew negligent as to his former orders for killing them, and because the very soldiers grew weary of killing them, and because they hoped to get some money by sparing them; for they left only the populace, and sold the rest of the multitude, with their wives and children, and *every one of them at a very low price, and that because such as were sold were very many, and the buyers very few* ... (emphasis mine). [42]

Egypt was their destination as predicted in Deut 28:68:

> And now, since his soldiers were already quite tired with killing men, and yet there appeared to be a vast multitude still remaining alive, Caesar gave orders that they should kill none but those that were in arms, and opposed them, but should take the rest alive. But, together with those whom they had orders to slay, they slew the aged and the infirm; but for those that were in their flourishing age, and who might be useful to them, they drove them together into the temple, and shut them up within the walls of the court of the women; over which Caesar set one of his freed men, as also Fronto, one of his own friends; which last was to determine everyone's fate, according to his merits. So this Fronto slew all those that had been seditious and robbers, who were impeached one by another; but of the young men he chose out the tallest and most beautiful, and reserved them for the triumph; and *as for the rest of the multitude that were above seventeen years old, he put them into bonds, and sent them to the Egyptian mines* [emphasis mine]. Titus also sent a great number into the provinces, as a present to them, that they might be destroyed upon their theaters, by the sword and by the wild beasts; but those that were under seventeen years of age were sold for slaves. [43]

In AD 132 the Jewish population of Palestine attempted a revolt against Rome under the leadership of a messianic pretender by the name of Shimon Bar Kokhba. Bar Kokhba even won the support of the venerable Rabbi Akiba.[44] However, in the end, all hope of a Jewish kingdom seemed crushed by the overwhelming Roman response to the Bar Kokhba revolt (AD 132–35). Those of a skeptical mindset who assign a late date to the Pentateuch must explain this detailed prediction of the Roman dispersion written centuries before the fact.

Moses describes the result of this third dispersion in Deut 29:22–28. The land is described as "brimstone and salt, a burning waste, unsown and unproductive, and no grass grows in it" (Deut 29:23; cf. Lev 26:31–33; 43). The NIV translates, "The whole land will be a burning waste of salt and sulfur— nothing planted, nothing sprouting, no vegetation growing on it" (Deut 29:23 NIV). In 1867 Samuel Clemens described the desolation of the Holy Land:

Here there are evidences of cultivation—a rare sight in this country—an acre or two of rich soil studded with last season's dead cornstalks of the thickness of your thumb and very wide apart. But in such a land it was a thrilling spectacle. Close to it was a stream, and on its banks a great herd of curious-looking Syrian goats and sheep were gratefully eating gravel. I do not state this as a petrified fact—I only *suppose* they were eating gravel, because there did not appear to be anything else for them to eat....

We could not stop to rest two or three hours out from our camp, of course, albeit the brook was beside us. So we went on an hour longer. We saw water then, but nowhere in all the waste around was there a foot of shade, and we were scorching to death. "Like unto the shadow of a great rock in a weary land." Nothing in the Bible is more beautiful than that, and surely there is no place we have wandered to that is able to give it such touching expression as this blistering, naked, treeless land....

....There is not a solitary village throughout its whole extent [of the valley near Ain Mellahah]—not for thirteen miles in either direction. There are two or three small clusters of Bedouin tents, but not a single permanent habitation. One may ride ten miles, hereabouts, and not see ten human beings. To this region one of the prophecies is applied:

"I will bring the land into desolation; and your enemies which dwell therein shall be astonished at it. And I will scatter you amoung the heathen, and I will draw out a sword after you; and your land shall be desolate and your cities waste [Lev 26:32–33]."

No man can stand here by deserted Ain Mellahah and say the prophecy has not been fulfilled.[45]

This interim period describes the land as desolate and Israel in the Diaspora.

Deuteronomy 29:24 asks the obvious question, "Why has the LORD done thus to this land? Why this great outburst of anger?" (Deut 29:24). The answer is that Israel had broken the covenant (Deut 29:25–28). Therefore, the land was cursed (Deut 29:27) and the people were dispersed (Deut 29:28).

Restoration. However, God will not leave Israel in this state. God will sovereignly move in the future to restore Israel. Deuteronomy 30:1–5 (cf. Lev 26:42–45) describes this final return. The first phase is Israel recalling the blessings and the curses "to mind in all nations where the LORD your God has banished you" (Deut 30:1).[46] Perhaps the Zionist movement is the beginning of these stirrings.

The second phase is when Israel will "return to the LORD your God and obey Him with all your heart and soul" (Deut 30:2). Deuteronomy 30:6–10 also describes the circumcision of Israel's hearts in national repentance. This event is also described in Zech 12:10–14 and Rom 11:26–27. This also anticipates the new covenant. Pentecost notes that

> this covenant has the guarantee of God that He will effect the necessary conversion which is essential to its fulfillment. Romans 11:26–27; Hosea 2:14–23; Deuteronomy 30:6; Ezekiel 11:16–21 all make this clear. This conversion is viewed in Scripture as a sovereign act of God and must be acknowledged to be certain because of His integrity.[47]

When the promise of restoration is reiterated in the prophets, the promise of a new heart is often in the context. Jeremiah reports God's promise, "Behold, I will gather them out of all the lands to which I have driven them in My anger, in My wrath and in great indignation; and I will bring them back to this place and make them dwell in safety" (Jer 36:37). Immediately, God promises that "I will give them one heart and one way, that they may fear Me always, for their own good and for the good of their children after them. I will make an everlasting covenant with them that I will not turn away from them, to do them good; and I will put the fear of Me in their hearts so that they will not turn away from Me" (Jer 32:39–40). All of this is just forty-one verses after the promise of the new covenant and immediately before Jer 33 which reaffirms the Davidic covenant. Ezekiel records a similar divine promise of restoration, "I will gather you from the peoples and assemble you out of the countries among which you have been scattered, and I will give you the land of Israel" (Ezek 11:17). This promise is also followed by the promise of new heart, "I will give them one heart, and put a new spirit within them. And I will take the heart of stone out of their flesh and give them a heart of flesh, that they may walk in My statutes and keep My ordinances and do them. Then they will be My people, and I shall be their God" (Ezek 11:19–20). Ezekiel 36:19–30 follows the same pattern: restoration from the lands of Israel's dispersion (Ezek 36:19–24), then cleansing and a new heart (Ezek 36:25–27). Because the Land, Davidic, and new covenants are all based in the Abrahamic covenant, they are interrelated in the prophets.

Phase three is described in Deut 30:3–7 as a regathering of Israel to the land from all of the world and the judgment of Israel's enemies (Deut 30:7, cf. Zech 12:7–9; Isa 11:1–12). Ezekiel 37:1–14 also predicts a two stage return, the first physical and political (Ezek 37:1–8, 11–13) and the second spiritual (Ezek 37:9–10, 14).[48] Peters (1823–1909) comments:

Fully admitting the difficulties attached to this point, yet over and against them is *the Word of God*; and *the believer* is at no loss in making his decision when God says: *Jer.* 31 : 35–37. What our eyes now behold in the perhaps now unconscious witness of God (Isa. 43 : 10–13; Isa. 44 : 8, etc.) causes us firmly to hold to the testimony of the future that is yet to be added in the eyes of all nations. In the light of a thousand predictions like Ezek. 39 : 28 ; Deut. 30 : 3, 4 ; Isa. 43 : 5, 6, etc., who, that receives *the Word as given by the Almighty*, can reject such a restoration.[49]

Robert Jamieson, A. R. Fausset, and David Brown comment concerning the promise of a restoration that "the words may be interpreted either wholly in a spiritual sense (John 11:51, 52), or, as many think, in a literal sense also (Rom. 11). They will be recalled from all places of the dispersion to their own land and enjoy the highest prosperity."[50] From Moses' vantagepoint, all of these stipulations were not yet instituted. All three of the predicted dispersions have occurred by now. History is yet awaiting the institution of the final return and national repentance of Israel (see table 7).

Establishment

The establishment of the Land covenant is recorded in Deut 29–30. This passage is not a covenant document *per se*, but rather a partial record of the covenant ceremony that Moses conducted with the Israelis in the land of Moab (Deut 29:1). The ritual element is lacking, but the terms are included in the address Moses gave. Moses concluded with an exhortation to choose life by choosing to love and obey the Lord (Deut 30:19–20) . The Land covenant was one of the last acts of Moses and was given to Israel immediately before they entered the land.

Duration

The Land covenant is an eternal covenant. There are two reasons for this conclusion. First, the Land covenant is derived from the Abrahamic covenant and the Abrahamic covenant is an "eternal covenant." Second, Ezek 16:1–63 indicates that, despite Israel's failure, the Land covenant will endure forever. In Ezek 16:1–59 the prophet writes of Israel's failure by means of the image of an adulterous wife. However, in Ezek 16:60–63 God promises forgiveness, restoration, and the establishment of an "everlasting covenant (בְּרִית עוֹלָם וַהֲקִמוֹתִי לָךְ)" (Ezek 16:60). God told Moses, "I will remember My covenant with Jacob, and I will remember also My covenant with Isaac, and My covenant with Abraham as well, and I will remember the land.... I will not reject them, nor will I so abhor them as to destroy them, breaking My covenant with them" (Lev 26:42, 44). Therefore, like the Abrahamic covenant on which it is based, the Land covenant is eternal (see figure 2).

Type of Covenant	Stipulations of Covenant	Beneficiaries	Established	End

Grant	• Title to the Land
	• Three Dispersions:
	  • Assyria
	  • Babylon
	  • Rome
	• Restoration to the land
	• National Repentance
	• Victory over enemies
		Israel	In the land of Moab immediately before entering the promised land (Deut 29:1)	"Eternal covenant" Ezek 16:60

Table 7. Land Covenant

NOTES

1. Deut 30:15, 16, 18, 20. The phrase "in the land" is a common theme in Deuteron-
    omy occurring twenty-three times in reference to the land of Israel (Deut 4:5, 14,
    25; 5:31, 33; 6:1; 7:13; 11:30; 12:1, 10; 15:4, 11; 19:14; 21:1; 23:20; 25:15, 19;
    28:8, 11; 30:16, 18, 20; 32:47). Six of those twenty-three references to being "in the
    land" are in Deut 28–30, as well as 28:21 ("consumed you from the land"), 63 ("torn
    from the land"); 29:22 ("plagues of the land"); 30:5 ("into the land").

2. Arnold G. Fruchtenbaum, "Palestinian Covenant," *Dictionary of Premillennial The-
    ology* (hereafter referred to as *DPT*), gen. ed. Mal Couch (Grand Rapids, MI: Kre-
    gel, 1996) 291–92. See also Fruchtenbaum, *Israelology* 581.

3. Williamson, "Covenant," *NDBT* 424.

4. Fruchtenbaum, *Israelology* 582.

5. William E. Biederwolf, *The Second Coming Bible: The Complete Text of Every
    Scripture Passage Concerned with the Second Coming of Christ Plus Commentary
    on Each Verse* (Grand Rapids, MI: Baker, 1972) 20.

6. F. C. Cook, "Deuteronomy," in *Exodus to Esther*, Barnes' Notes, vol. 2 of 14 vols.
    (Boston: Estes and Lauriate, 1873; reprint, Grand Rapids, MI: Baker, 1998) 2:327.

7. *b. Soṭah* 37b.

8. Robertson, *Christ of the Covenants* 217–18.

9. For a notable exception see Jack S. Deere, "Deuteronomy," *BKCOT* 313–14.

10. Ryrie, *RSB* 314. See also Renald E. Showers, *There Really is a Difference: A Com-
    parison of Covenant and Dispensational Theology* (Bellmawr, NJ: The Friends of
    Israel Gospel Ministry, Inc., 1990) 77.

11. See Fruchtenbaum, "Palestinian Covenant," *DPT* 291–92; Fruchtenbaum, *Israelol-
    ogy* 582–83; Pentecost, *Things to Come* 96; J. Dwight Pentecost, *Thy Kingdom
    Come: Tracing God's Kingdom Program and Covenant Promises Throughout His-
    tory* (Grand Rapids, MI: Kregel, 1995) 104–5.

12. Brown, Driver, Briggs, *BDB* 94–95.

13. Louis Goldberg, "בַּד (*bad*)," *TWOT* 1:90–91.

14. Mendenhall, "Covenant," *IDB* 1:719.

15. We have already seen the attempt at reconciliation in *b. Soṭah* 37b.

16. *b. Berakot* 5a.

17. Jack S. Deere, "Deuteronomy," *BKCOT* 313–14.

18. Merdith G. Kline, "Deuteronomy," *Zondervan's Pictorial Bible Dictionary* (hereaf-
    ter referred to as *ZPBD*), gen. ed. Merrill C. Tenney (Grand Rapids, MI: Zondervan,
    1963) 213–15.

19. Merdith G. Kline, "Deuteronomy," *WBC* 195. See also Kline, *Structure* 139–40.

20. Keil and Delitzsch, "Deuteronomy," *Pentateuch*, COT 1:971.

21. R. K. Harrison, "Deuteronomy," *ZPEB* 2:110.

22. McCarthy, *Treaty* 202.

23. Beckman, *Hittite Diplomatic Texts* 2–3.

24. Ryken, "Deuteronomy, Book of," *DBI* 205–7.

25. Williamson, "Covenant," *NDBT* 425.

26. R. Allan Killen, John Rea, "Covenant," *WBE* 1:386–91.

27. John F. Walvoord, "Eschatological Problems VI: The Fulfillment of the Abrahamic Covenant," *BSac* 102 no. 405 (January–March 1945): 27–36.

28. Moshe Weinfeld, "Deuteronomy, Book of," *ABD* 2:168–83. See also Walton, Matthews, and Chavalas, *BBCOT* 204.

29. Walton, Matthews, and Chavalas, *BBCOT* 204.

30. Beckman, *Hittite Diplomatic Texts* 30–32, 4.1–7.

31. Ibid. 160, 31A.4.

32. Ibid. 59–64, 9.

33. Ibid. 60, 9.1.

34. Ibid. 64, no. 9, §20.

35. Walton, Matthews, and Chavalas, *BBCOT* 204.

36. Beckman, *Hittite Diplomatic Texts* 36, 5.16; 43, 6A.13; 48, 6B.8.

37. J. Dwight Pentecost, "The Godly Remnant of the Tribulation Period," *BSac* 117, no. 466 (April–June 1960): 123–43.

38. Chafer, *Major Bible Themes* 144.

39. John F. Walvoord, "Millennial Series: Part 15: The Abrahamic Covenant and Premillennialism," *BSac* 109, no. 435 (July–September 1952): 217–25.

40. See *Midr. Esth. Rab.* prologue 3 for the same interpretation.

41. Josephus, *A. J.* 10.7.4.

42. Josephus, *J. W.* 6.8.2.

43. Ibid. 6.9.2.

44. *y. Taʿanit* 68d.

45. Samuel Langhorne Clemens, *Innocents Abroad*, in *The Unabridged Mark Twain* (Philadelphia: Running, 1976) 279–82.

46. The restoration is a common theme in the prophets based upon the Land covenant (e.g., Isa 11:1–12; 14:1; 27:12–13; 43:5–6; 49:8–12; Jer 16:14–15; 23:3–8; 30:3–11; Ezek 34:11–16; Zech 8:7–8).

47. Pentecost, *Things to Come* 98.

48. Merrill F. Unger, "Ezekiel's Vision of Israel's Restoration: Part 1," *BSac* 106, no. 423 (July–September 1949): 312–24; and Merrill F. Unger, "Ezekiel's Vision of Israel's Restoration: Part 2," *BSac* 106, no. 424 (October–December 1949): 432–45.

49. Peters, *Theocratic Kingdom* 2:66.

50. Robert Jamieson, A. R. Fausset, David Brown, *Commentary Practical and Explanatory on the Whole Bible*, rev. ed. (Grand Rapids, MI: Zondervan, 1961) 163.

CHAPTER TEN

The Davidic Covenant

Covenant Type

Conclusions from the Biblical Evidence

The background for the Davidic covenant was King David's desire to build a house for the Lord; a temple (2 Sam 7:1–3; 1 Chr 17:1–3). It seemed incongruous to David that he should be living in a palace while the God of Israel had only a temporary shrine. When David voiced these concerns to the prophet Nathan, Nathan's initial reaction was enthusiasm for the project. However, later that night God spoke to Nathan (2 Sam 7:4–16; 1 Chr 17:4–14). God reminded Nathan that He did not require a house (2 Sam 7:5–7; 1 Chr 17:4–6). Then He reminded David of his humble origins (2 Sam 7:8; 1 Chr 17:7). Finally, instead of David building a house for God (temple), God revealed that He would build a house (dynasty) for David (2 Sam 7:9–16; 1 Chr 17:8–14)!

Oddly, the central passages concerning the Davidic covenant (2 Sam 7:1–17; 1 Chr 17:1–15) do not explicitly refer to God's promise to David as a covenant (בְּרִית).[1] However, we are right to think of it as a covenant for two reasons: (1) It is referred to by other Scriptures as a covenant (בְּרִית) (2 Sam 23:5; 1 Kgs 8:23–26; 2 Chr 13:5; 21:7; Ps 89:3, 28, 34, 39; 132:12; Isa 55:3; Jer 33:20–22). (2) Nathan's oracle is cast in covenant form. The passage begins with a preamble that identifies the covenant maker, "Thus says the LORD" (2 Sam 7:5a; 1 Chr 17:4a, 7). This is followed immediately by an historical prologue (2 Sam 7:5b–9a; 1 Chr 17:4b–8a), then the stipulations (2 Sam 7:9b–16; 1 Chr 17:8b–14). The divine witness is, of course, Yahweh Himself (2 Sam 7:11).

Weinfeld notes that the father-son terminology in 2 Sam 7:14 is covenantal:

> The father-son imagery, as reflected in the promise to David in II Sam. 7:14 and in its counterpart in Ps. 89:26–27 [H 27–28], also belongs to the legal conventions of grants and investiture. Thus we read in the treaty between the Hittite sovereign Šuppiluliuma and his vassal Šattiwazza (for the reading of this name, *see* Zaccagnini, *OrAnt*, XIII [1974], 25 ff.): "[The great King] grasped me with his hand and said: 'When I conquer the land of Mitanni I shall not reject you, *I shall make you my son*. I will stand by [to help you in war] and will make you sit on the throne of your father ... the word which comes out of his mouth will not turn back'" (E. Weidner, pp. 40 ff., 29–30)....
>
> The phrase "I will be his father and he shall be my son" is an adoption formula (cf. Greengus on *verba solemnia* in connection with marriage and adoption), and actually serves as the judicial basis for the gift of the eternal dynasty.[2]

Of course, from the perspective of the NT, we realize a deeper meaning (cf. Heb 1:1–14). Therefore, because of the form of Nathan's oracle and the manner in which it is viewed elsewhere in Scripture, it is clearly a covenant.

Several features may be observed in the accounts of Nathan's prophecy. First, this covenant is unilateral with the obligation being on God and not David. The phrase "I will" is prominent being used twelve times in both 2 Sam 7 and 1 Chr 17. These passages clearly conceive of the continuance of David's dynasty as a sovereign act of God. These passages are also unconditional. Although the discipline of individual kings is promised (2 Sam 7:14), it is explicitly stated that the covenant will not be abrogated by their failure (2 Sam 7:15, 16). Therefore, I note that the Davidic covenant is a unilateral covenant established sovereignly by God without any conditions that could abrogate the covenant.

The Davidic covenant adheres to the familiar form of the grant covenant. Nathan's oracle is cast in covenantal form. However, it is lacking curses. This is common in grant covenants since they are unconditional in nature, therefore, they require no curses, and the grant itself is the blessing. Therefore, in both form and function, the Davidic covenant appears to be a grant covenant.[3]

Weinfeld is also convinced that the Davidic covenant is a grant. He sees the Davidic covenant as a gracious promise of God without conditions. He notes that the Davidic covenant is described as "covenant and lovingkindness (הַבְּרִית וְהַחֶסֶד)" (1 Kgs 8:23 ASV) or "gracious covenant." This same terminology, "covenant and the lovingkindness (אֶת־הַבְּרִית וְאֶת־הַחֶסֶד)" (Deut 7:12 ASV), is used of the Abrahamic covenant by Moses. As I have shown, the Abrahamic covenant is a grant covenant. Weinfeld compares the Davidic covenant with the Abrahamic and contrasts it with the Mosaic. He notes that the Davidic and Abrahamic covenants are a pledge by God, but the Mosaic covenant is a pledge by the people to be loyal to God. Weinfeld comments that the Mosaic covenant, because of its conditional and obligatory character, "is defined as ברית and never as חסד...."[4] Mendenhall also notes the unconditional and unilateral nature of the Davidic covenant. He comments on the character of the Davidic covenant and observes that an impressive connection with the Abrahamic covenant exists. Mendenhall states that "in David, the promise to the patriarchs is fulfilled, and renewed."[5] For Mendenhall, the Davidic covenant is as unconditional as the other grant covenant, the Abrahamic covenant, to which it is related.

Ronald F. Youngblood, although agreeing with Weinfeld, points out the existence of conditional elements in the Davidic covenant. He notes Weinfeld's position concerning the grant and suzerainty covenants. However, Youngblood thinks that this is a little too simplistic. He notes that the fact that "the grant type of covenant, by its very nature, tends toward unconditionality by no means eliminates the possibility of its having conditions or obligations, which in any case are of the essence of the covenant concept itself...."[6] Kaiser strikes a correct balance between the conditional and unconditional aspects of the Davidic covenant. He notes that a particular Davidic generation's participation in the benefits of the Davidic covenant is conditional. However, this does not contradict the eternality of the promise.[7] Thus, the Davidic covenant functions in much the same manner as the Land covenant. The promise is unconditional, but the enjoyment of the promise is conditional upon obedience.

Ancient Near Eastern Parallels

Weinfeld compares both the Abrahamic and Davidic covenants with ancient Assyrian and Hittite grant covenants:

> Like the royal grants in the ancient Near East, the covenants with Abraham and David are gifts bestowed upon individuals who distinguished themselves by serving their masters loyally. Abraham is promised the land because he obeyed God and followed his mandate (Gen. 26:5, cf. 15:6–7; 22:16–18), and similarly David was

given the grace expressed in a dynasty, because he served God with truth, righteousness, and loyalty (I Kings 3:6; 9:4–5; 11:4, 6; 14:8; 15:3). The terminology employed in this context is very close to that used in the Assyrian grants. In the grant
of Ashurbanipal to his servant we read: "Baltaya ... who was devoted (lit., whose
heart was whole) to his lord, served me with faithfulness, walked in perfection in
my palace ... and kept the charge (*iṣṣur maṣṣarti*) of my kingship ... I considered
his good relations with me and decreed a gift for him" (Postgate, No. 9:11 ff.). Identical formulations are to be found in connection with the promises to Abraham and
David. With regard to Abraham it is said that he "kept my charge," וישמר משמרתי
(Gen. 26:5); walked before God (24:40; 48:15); and was expected to "be blameless"
(17:1). David's loyalty to God is couched in phrases which are even closer to the
Assyrian grant terminology: "he walked before God in truth, loyalty, and upright-
ness of heart" I Kings 3:6); walked after God "with all his heart" I Kings 14:8), etc.

"Land" and "house" (=dynasty), the subjects of the Abrahamic and Davidic
covenants, are the most prominent gifts of the suzerain in the Hittite and Syro-
Palestine realms; the Hittite grants, like the grant of land to Abraham and the grant
of "house" to David, are unconditional.[8]

There is an interesting parallel to the Davidic covenant in the Hittite treaties.
Hattusili III of Hatti made an unconditional promise of succession to Ulmi-
Teshshup of Tarhuntassa (ca. 1300 BC). However, there are conditions im-
posed on individuals in his line even up to and including the death penalty.
Nevertheless, Hattusili III promises to install someone from Ulmi-
Teshshup's line on the throne of Tarhuntassa.[9] This illustrates that ancient
Near Eastern grant covenants could be unconditional and conditional at the
same time.

Beneficiaries

In context the Davidic covenant is clearly a promise to David, David's line,
and Israel (2 Sam 7:1–3; 1 Chr 17:1–3; Ps. 89:3–4, 20–37). Jesus fulfills the
Davidic covenant (Luke 1:31–33; Rev 22:16) as the ultimate Son of David.
Fruchtenbaum summarizes that

> the Davidic Covenant promised four eternal things: an eternal house or dynasty, an
> eternal throne, an eternal kingdom, and an eternal descendent. The eternality of the
> house, throne, and kingdom are guaranteed because the Seed of David culminated in
> a person Who is Himself eternal: the Messiah, the God-Man.
>
> The unique importance of the Davidic Covenant is that it amplifies the seed as-
> pect of the Abrahamic Covenant. According to the Abrahamic Covenant, the Mes-
> siah was to be of the Seed of Abraham. This only meant that He was to be a Jew and
> could be of any of the twelve tribes. Later, in the time of Jacob, the messianic seed

aspect was limited to a member of the Tribe of Judah only (Gen. 49:10). Now the seed aspect is further narrowed to one family within the Tribe of Judah, the family of David. It will be narrowed further in Jeremiah 22:24–30 where it is decreed that while the Messiah was to be of the Seed of David, it was to be apart from Jechoniah.[10]

In spite of this, there have been attempts to transfer this covenant's promises to the Church.

Covenant Theology

One approach, often employed by covenant theologians, is to spiritualize the Scriptures to apply them in a non-literal sense to the Church. I have already examined the basis for this thinking and need not say much more here. It is an issue of presuppositions and hermeneutics. We should ask why the covenant theologian thinks that he or she must not take these Scriptures literally and where they find support for their approach. There is a special case where a two-pronged approach is taken. Some have argued that the stipulations of the Davidic covenant have all been fulfilled historically, and then go on to argue for a spiritualized interpretation. Pentecost responds to this thinking:

> Periodically the argument is raised that all the provisions of the Davidic Covenant were fulfilled during Solomon's reign. Those who hold this view contend that the land ruled over by Solomon according to 1 Kings 4:21 fulfilled the covenant, and no future fulfillment should be expected.
>
> In answer to this, it should be observed first and foremost that those who present this argument are admitting upfront that the terms of the Davidic Covenant require a literal fulfillment. Isn't it interesting, then, that most frequently these same people also argue for a "spiritual" fulfillment of the Davidic Covenant in the church? The two are mutually exclusive and make for an illogical and inconsistent theology all the way around.
>
> Regardless, in reference to the argument itself we can readily observe several details of the Davidic Covenant that were not fulfilled by Solomon. For example, there was no permanent possession of the land as promised to Abraham. Moreover, all the land was not possessed. "From the river of Egypt" (Gen. 15:18) and "from the border of Egypt" (1 Kings 4:21) are not equivalent terms geographically. Solomon did not occupy all this land; he merely collected tribute. Obviously, temporary overlordship is not everlasting possession. Finally, hundreds of years after Solomon's time the Scriptures still abound in promises concerning future possession of the land. This proves that God and His prophets realized—whether or not some modern theologians do—that Solomon did not fulfill the Abrahamic Covenant.[11]

Neither the Church nor Solomon exhausts the Davidic promises.

Progressive Dispensationalism

Hermeneutics. By employing a complementary hermeneutic, progressive dispensationalists attempt to bring the Church into Israel's promises and inaugurate the messianic kingdom now. Darrell L. Bock acknowledges that "some may object to taking passages addressed originally to Israel and applying them to the church. However, the type of complementary expansion seen in the New Covenant provides biblical precedent for this hermeneutical approach.... One should not define the meaning of these texts by using only the Old Testament sense or only the New Testament sense. A canonical reading allows both contexts to speak in a way complementary to one another."[12] Bock finds justification for complementary hermeneutics from Peter's use of Psalm 132:11 (cf. Acts 2:30) and Psalm 110:1 (cf. Acts 2:34). Several normative dispensationalists have written to answer Bock et al.[13] Space does not permit a full response here. However, a few points are worth noting.

Bock indicates that the Davidic covenant is linked to the new covenant by Ezek 34–36. He states that "this great era of the washing by the Spirit of God is associated with the presence of the great 'David.'"[14] He sees additional confirmation for this view in the prediction of John the Baptist concerning the Messiah's work of Spirit baptism (Luke 3:15). Based on this Bock sees a linkage in Acts 2 between the baptism of the Spirit and Jesus' messianic rule. Bock states, "What progressives argue is that the forgiveness of sins and the distribution of the Spirit are part of Jesus' current messianic activity that show his ruling-blessing authority as the Promised One of God."[15] Since the Church participates in the baptism of the Holy Spirit (1 Cor 12:13), they argue that the Church is brought alongside Israel in a complementary way.[16]

However, need we take these passages this way? Ezekiel 34:23–24 does predict the rule of the great "David." Assuredly, this does reflect back to the Davidic covenant. However, not until Ezek 36:25–27 do we see the promise of the Spirit that is embodied in the new covenant and also Deut 30:6. Therefore, it is hardly accurate to say that Davidic rule and the gift of the Spirit are associated by this passage. Ezekiel 36:1–24 and the Land covenant are much more connected as we saw in the last chapter. Interestingly, although the Davidic covenant contains a stipulation that touches upon the Land covenant (2

Sam 7:10), it has none that directly relate to the new covenant. It is a fair statement that all three covenants are often seen close together in the prophets, since they all are based upon the Abrahamic covenant. Nevertheless, the Davidic covenant does not contain new covenant stipulations, nor does the new covenant contain Davidic stipulations.

John the Baptist would agree that forgiveness of sins and the baptism of the Spirit are part of Jesus' present messianic activity. Jesus is the Messiah and forgiveness of sins and baptism of the Spirit are at the present part of His activity. However, these are not based on His role as the Davidic King as Bock claims. Elliott E. Johnson notes that Peter's purpose in quoting Ps. 110:1; 132:11 is to establish that Jesus is the Messiah not when He will sit upon David's throne. He admits that there is a relationship between God's throne and the throne of David (1 Chr 28:5–6; 29:23–24). However, Ps 2:4, 6 indicates a distinction.[17] With complementary hermeneutics, there is a danger of identifying things that are related or merely similar, but not the same.[18]

We must exercise extreme caution in our inferences that we are deriving our data from the text and not imposing our opinions on the text. Lightner strongly criticizes progressive dispensationalism on this point:

> Progressives, in general, and Bock and Blaising will tell you, that 2 Samuel 7 was given to Israel. They don't deny that, but in the New Testament they say, the Spirit of God took liberty to change, to enlarge that by adding a new people. Not only that, it changes the place where that covenant will be fulfilled.... Now, they say based on Acts 2 and Peter's quotation of Psalm 110 and 132 that the Church has now been brought in alongside of Israel to share in this Davidic Covenant. Furthermore, Christ is now at the right-hand of the Father on David's throne, fulfilling, in part, the Davidic Covenant....
>
> There isn't a shred of evidence, solid, exegetical evidence, for that, not in Acts 2, not in Acts 15, nor anywhere else. Bock, in his quiet, silent, sober moments would have to admit that. He says, however, it is implied in Acts 2. He is assuming that this is what is there. He is always giving this type of cautionary statements. He never says this is the result of exegesis of what Acts 2 says because in Acts 2 it doesn't say anything about Christ being now on the throne of David. It simply is referring to Psalm 16, Psalm 110, Psalm 132 to verify that Christ is, in fact, the long-promised Messiah. It says nothing about his current, present rule on the throne of David. They bring that to the passage and say it is assumed to be there by virtue of his quotation.
>
> I totally reject this assumption, but it is the bedrock basis of progressive dispensationalism, and it rests on that complementary hermeneutic. Acts 2, Peter's sermon on Day of Pentecost *complemented* what God gave to David in 2 Samuel 7.

There it was only for Israel. Now, it's to Israel and the Church. Now, it's not on
earth only, but it is in heaven, also. The people have changed and the place has
changed.[19]

I agree with Lightner that complementary hermeneutics cannot be derived
from the Scriptures. It is at best an unnecessary hypothesis and at worst it
promotes confusion by means of erroneous semantic identification.

Already/not yet. Progressive dispensationalists speak of an already/not yet
pattern and initial or partial fulfillment of covenants.[20] However, normative
dispensationalists tend to see covenant fulfillment as an all or nothing affair.[21] It is possible that the root of this conflict is semantic. *Webster's Universal Encyclopedic Dictionary* defines "fulfill" as "a : to put into effect :
EXECUTE b : to bring to an end c : to measure up to : SATISFY."[22] It would
appear that the progressive dispensationalist would define "fulfill" as "put
into effect, execute." Therefore, for the progressive dispensationalist progress in covenant fulfillment would be a continuum from partial to complete.
However, the normative dispensationalist would seem to define "fulfill" as
"bring to an end, measure up to, satisfy." Therefore, they would see individual covenant stipulations as fulfilled only when each was satisfied and the
covenant as fulfilled only when all of the stipulations were fulfilled.

A check of the Scriptures use of "fulfill" shows them to be in keeping
with the normative dispensationalist understanding (e.g., Josh 23:14; 1 Kgs
8:15–24; Neh 9:8; Jer 34:18; Luke 4:21). Indeed, I can find no mention of
partial fulfillment of an obligation.[23] Progressive dispensationalism is confused concerning the matter of the fulfillment of covenant stipulations. Bock
states, "In this writer's view one can speak of initial fulfillment when any of
the aspects are realized."[24] The corrective is to realize that, although a covenant is established at a given point in time, the stipulations of the covenant
may be instituted at different times. This is not an initial versus final fulfillment. Each individual stipulation will be completely fulfilled in its own time
and the covenant will be fulfilled when all of the stipulations are fulfilled.

In Acts 1:6 the apostles are still inquiring as to the restoration of the
kingdom to Israel. Apparently, nothing in Christ's teaching had led them to
believe that there would not be a future literal kingdom for Israel. Jesus' reply is instructive in that He does not disabuse them of the notion that He
would restore the kingdom. He merely points out that they are not given the

knowledge of when that will be (Acts 1:7). Gade comments:

> One of the questions that was going through the minds of the disciples was, "Wilt thou at this time restore again the kingdom to Israel?" (Acts 1:6). The Lord did not say, "There will be no kingdom—Israel has been put aside." He said, "It is not for you to know the times or the seasons, which the Father hath put in his own power. But ye shall receive power, after that the Holy Ghost is come upon you: and ye shall be witnesses unto me both in Jerusalem, and in all Judaea, and in Samaria, and unto the uttermost part of the earth" (Acts 1:7–8). What the Lord is actually telling them is that the kingdom is yet future.[25]

I would add that our Lord contrasts the future time of the kingdom with the present time of witnessing in the power of the Spirit, "It is not for you to know... but...." Acts 1:6 clearly teaches that this present age is in contrast with the coming messianic kingdom.

Acts 15 is another telling passage in this debate. Pentecost noted that the first church council did not consider the Davidic covenant to have been fulfilled yet:

> Another important observation we can make from the New Testament is that *the Davidic Covenant held an important place in the discussion at the first church council* (Acts 15:14–17). A close examination of this passage reveals that there is a progression of thought leading to James' conclusion. *First,* God visits the Gentiles, taking from them a people for His name. In other words, God has promised to bless the Gentiles as well as Israel, but each in his own order. The Gentile blessing is first. *Second,* Christ will return—*after* the outcalling of the people for His name. *Third,* as a result of the coming of the Lord, the tabernacle of David will be built again; that is, the kingdom will be established exactly as promised in the Davidic Covenant.[26]

Walvoord agrees and points out the distinction between this age of Gentile conversion and the messianic kingdom:

> The passage instead of identifying God's purpose for the church and for the nation, Israel, established a specific time order. Israel's blessing will not come until "I return," apparently reference to the second coming of Christ.... God will first conclude His work for the Gentiles in the period of Israel's dispersion; then He will return to bring in the promised blessings for Israel. It is needless to say that this confirms the interpretation that Christ is not now on the throne of David bringing blessing to Israel as the prophets predicted, but He is rather on His Father's throne waiting for the coming earthly kingdom and interceding for His own who form the church.[27]

The order is first God will bless the Gentiles (Rom 11:25), then Christ will return, and then the kingdom will be established (Rom 11:26–27), not before.

Jesus has gone away to receive a kingdom (Luke 19:11–15; Matt 28:18) and will one day return (Ps 110:1). Believers are now subjects of that kingdom (Col 1:13). But, since Christ has not returned to rule the Earth, our position is that of aliens (Heb 11:13–14) and ambassadors (2 Cor 5:20). If He had returned to set up His kingdom on Earth, we would be ruling with Him (1 Cor 4:8). As the author of Hebrews observes, "But now we do not yet see all things subjected to him" (Heb 2:8). In the thinking of the apostles and the author of Hebrews, it is not "already/not yet," it is "not yet!"[28]

Stipulations

The Davidic covenant promises a throne, a house, and a kingdom. The Davidic covenant's stipulations are: (1) Israel will be permanently regathered in peace (2 Sam 7:10), (2) David's dynasty will be eternal (2 Sam. 7:11b, 16; 1 Chr 17:10b), (3) Solomon will be established on the throne after David (2 Sam 7:12), (4) Solomon will build the temple (2 Sam 7:13a), (5) the throne or right to rule of David and Solomon will be established forever (2 Sam 7:13b, 16), (6) God will discipline David's descendants without destroying his line (2 Sam 7:14–15), (7) Messiah will come from David and be established upon the throne forever (1 Chr 17:11), and (8) the Messiah's throne, house, and kingdom will be established forever (1 Chr 17:12–14).[29]

Pentecost notes several implications of the Davidic covenant:

> Because the Bible anticipates a future literal fulfillment of the Davidic Covenant, certain facts present themselves concerning Israel's future. These include:
>
> (1) Israel must be preserved as a nation.
>
> (2) Israel must have a national existence, and be brought back into the land of her inheritance. Since David's kingdom had definite geographical boundaries and those boundaries were included in the promise to David concerning his descendant's reign, the nation must possess that land as their national homeland.
>
> (3) David's Son, the Lord Jesus Christ, must return to the earth, bodily and literally, in order to reign over David's covenanted kingdom. The claim that Christ is seated on the Father's throne reigning over a spiritual kingdom, the church, simply does not fulfill the promises of the covenant.
>
> (4) A literal earthly kingdom must exist over which the returned Messiah will reign.
>
> (5) This kingdom must become an eternal kingdom. Since the "throne," "house," and "kingdom" were all promised to David in perpetuity, there must be no end to Messiah's reign over David's kingdom from David's throne.[30]

Peters observes that

> the covenanted Davidic throne and Kingdom ... necessarily requires, in order to a
> future restoration, a *preservation* of the nation. This has been done; and to-day we
> see that nation wonderfully continued down to the present, although enemies, in-
> cluding the strongest nations and most powerful empires, have perished. This is not
> chance work; for, if our position is correct, this is demanded, seeing that without a
> restoration of the nation *it is impossible* to restore the Davidic Kingdom. The cove-
> nant language, the oath of God, the confirmation of promise by the blood of Jesus,
> the prophetic utterances—*all*, notwithstanding the nation's unbelief, requires *its*
> *perpetuation*, that through it finally God's promises and faithfulness may be vindi-
> cated. God so provides that *His Word* may be fulfilled. Every Jew, if we will but
> ponder the matter, that we meet on our streets is a living evidence that the Messiah
> will yet some day reign gloriously on David's throne and over his Kingdom, from
> which to extend a world-wide dominion.[31]

Messiah will rule over a regathered Israel. Therefore, Israel must be preserved and regathered. In this the Davidic covenant shows an undeniable
connection to the Land covenant.

Just as the Land covenant stipulates that Israel will be removed from the
land three times, the Davidic covenant stipulates that God will discipline disobedient Davidic kings. However, even in that discipline the throne (right to
rule), house (dynasty), and kingdom (the nation of Israel) will not be destroyed. In the same manner, the Land covenant predicts Israel's preservation
and regathering. Hosea predicts that

> the Israelites will live many days without king or prince, without sacrifice or sacred
> stones, without ephod or idol. Afterward the Israelites will return and seek the
> LORD their God and David their king. They will come trembling to the LORD and
> to his blessings in the last days (Hos 3:4–5 NIV).

Today, even if there should be no one remaining who can trace Davidic an-
cestry, Jesus the resurrected living Messiah ensures that David will always
have a descendant to sit on the throne (see table 8).

Establishment

The Davidic covenant was established and in force as soon as Nathan delivered the oracle. As I have explained, we must distinguish between the establishment of the covenant and the institution of each of its stipulations. The
tenses of Psalm 89:3–4 reflect this distinction:

I have made a covenant (כָּרַתִּי בְרִית, *qal* perfect) with My chosen;
　　I have sworn (נִשְׁבַּעְתִּי, *nipᶜal* perfect) to David My servant,
I will establish (אָכִין, *hipᶜil* imperfect) your seed forever,
　　And build up (וּבָנִיתִי, *qal* perfect with a *waw* consecutive) your throne to all generations.

Therefore, of the eight stipulations that I have identified in the Davidic covenant, only the third (Solomon will be established on the throne after David), fourth (Solomon will build the temple), fifth (the throne or right to rule of David and Solomon will be established forever), and sixth (God will discipline David's descendants without destroying his line) have been fulfilled as of this point. The Messiah has gone away to receive a kingdom (Luke 19:11–15; Matt 28:18) and will return (Ps 110:1). The remainder of the stipulations are yet future.

Type of Covenant	Stipulations of Covenant	Beneficiaries	Established	End
Grant	• Israel regatehered • David's dynasty eternal • Solomon to rule after David • Solomon to build the Temple • David's throne will be established forever • God will discipline the Davidic kings but not destroy the line • Messiah will come from David and be established forever • Messiah's throne, house, and kingdom will be forever	Israel David's line	By the oracle of the prophet Nathan (2 Sam 7:8–17 1 Chr 17:1–15)	Everlasting covenant (2 Sam 23:5; 2 Chr 13:5; Isa 55:3; Jer 33:20–22)

Table 8. Davidic Covenant

Duration

The Davidic covenant is an eternal covenant. Second Samuel 23:5 refers to it as an "everlasting covenant (בְּרִית עוֹלָם)." In 2 Chr 13:5 Abijah reminds Jeroboam, "Do you not know that the LORD God of Israel gave the rule over Israel forever (לְעוֹלָם) to David and his sons by a covenant of salt (בְּרִית מֶלַח)?"[32] Note the parallel between "forever" and "covenant of salt." Isaiah 55:3 speaks of "an everlasting covenant ... *according to* the faithful mercies shown to David (בְּרִית עוֹלָם חַסְדֵי דָוִד הַנֶּאֱמָנִים)." Jeremiah 33:20–22 states that the existence of a son of David to rule is more certain than day or night. There can be no doubt of the eternal character of this covenant (see figure 2).

NOTES

1. 1 Chronicles 17:1 does use בְּרִית, but only in the phrase "ark of the covenant of Yahweh (אֲרוֹן בְּרִית־יהוה)."

2. Weinfeld, "Covenant, Davidic," *IDB* 5:188–92.

3. McComiskey, *The Covenants of Promise* 62–63. See also Merrill, "A Theology of the Pentateuch," *A Biblical Theology of the Old Testament* 170.

4. Weinfeld, "Covenant, Davidic," *IDB* 5:189. See also Weinfeld, *The Promise of the Land* 222–64.

5. Mendenhall, "Covenant," *IDB* 1:718. See also D. J. McCarthy, *Old Testament Covenant: A Survey of Current Opinions* (Atlanta, GA: John Knox, 1972) 80–89.

6. Ronald F. Youngblood, "2 Samuel," *Deuteronomy–2 Samuel*, EBC 3:881–82.

7. Walter C. Kaiser, Jr., "The Promised Land: A Biblical-Historical View," *BSac* 138, no. 552 (October–December 1981): 302–12.

8. Weinfeld, "Covenant, Davidic," *IDB* 5:188–92.

9. Beckman, *Hittite Diplomatic Texts* 104, 18B.1.

10. Fruchtenbaum, *Israelology* 585.

11. Pentecost, *Thy Kingdom Come* 147–48. See also Pentecost, *Things to Come* 113–14.

12. Darrell L. Bock, "The Son of David and the Saint's Task: The Hermeneutics of Initial Fulfillment," *BSac* 150, no. 600 (October–December 1993): 440–57. See Darrell L. Bock, "Current Messianic Activity and OT Davidic Promise: Dispensationalism, Hermeneutics, and NT Fulfillment," *TJ* 15, no. 1 (Spring 1994): 55–87; Craig A. Blasing, Darrell L. Bock, *Progressive Dispensationalism* (Grand Rapids, MI: Baker, 1993). Also Stephen J. Nichols, "The Dispensational View of the Davidic Kingdom: A Response to Progressive Dispensationalism," *Master's Seminary Journal* (hereafter referred to as *MSJ*) 7, no. 2 (Fall 1996): 213–39 has a good comparison of normative and progressive dispensationalism.

13. Elliott E. Johnson, "Hermeneutical Principles and the Interpretation of Psalm 110," *BSac* 149, no. 596 (October–December 1992): 428–37; Charles Zimmerman, "'To This Agree the Words of the Prophets': Critical Monograph on Acts 15:14–17," *GTJ* 4, no. 3 (Fall 1963): 28–40; Mal Couch, "Progressive Dispensationalism: Is Christ Now on the Throne of David?—Part I," *CTJ* 2, no. 4 (March 1998): 32–46; Mal Couch, "Progressive Dispensationalism: Is Christ Now on the Throne of David?—Part II," *CTJ* 2, no. 5 (June 1998): 142–56; Mal Couch, "Progressive Dispensationalism: Is Christ Now on the Throne of David?—Part III," *CTJ* 2, no. 6 (September 1998): 272–85; Mal Couch, "Progressive Dispensationalism: What Really Is It?" *CTJ* 3, no. 9. (August 1999): 259–78.

14. Darrell L. Bock, J. Lanier Burns, Elliott E. Johnson, Stanley D. Toussaint, *Three Central Issues in Contemporary Dispensationalism: A Comparison of Traditional and Progressive Views*, gen. ed. Herbert W. Bateman IV (Grand Rapids, MI: Kregel, 1999) 95.

15. Ibid. 97.

16. Blaising, Bock, *Progressive Dispensationalism* 169–71.

17. Bock, Burns, Johnson, Toussaint, *Three Central Issues* 102–3.

18. Concerning NT interpretation of the OT see Fruchtenbaum, *Israelology* 843–45.

19. Robert P. Lightner, "Progressive Dispensationalism," *CTJ* 4, no. 11 (March 2000): 46–64.

20. Bock, Burns, Johnson, Toussaint, *Three Central Issues* 160.

21. Ibid. 136.

22. *Webster's Universal Encyclopedic Dictionary* (hereafter referred to as *WUED*) (New York: Barnes & Noble, 2002) 741.

23. In the LXX and the NT πληρόω ("fill, fulfill") is never used in the present of imperfect tense in a context concerning fulfilled obligations or promises. Indeed it is only used eleven times in the present in any context. In the indicative, it is used fifty-seven times in either the aorist or perfect tenses and never in the present. Twenty-three out of twenty-nine participles are either the aorists or perfects and eighteen of the twenty-two infinitives are.

24. Bock, "The Son of David and the Saint's Task," *BSac* 454.

25. Ralph M. Gade, "Is God through with the Jew?" *Grace Journal* 11, no. 2 (Spring 1970): 21–33.

26. Pentecost, *Thy Kingdom Come* 145.

27. John F. Walvoord, "Eschatological Problems VII: The Fulfillment of the Davidic Covenant," *BSac* 102, no. 406 (April–June 1945): 153–66. See also Cleon L. Rogers, Jr., "The Davidic Covenant in Acts—Revelation," *BSac* 151, no. 601 (January–March 1994): 71–84.

28. Saucy is much more hesitant than Bock or Blaising to claim that Jesus Christ is already on David's throne (Robert L. Saucy, *The Case for Progressive Dispensationalism* [Grand Rapids, MI: Zondervan, 1993] 99; 102–110).

29. See Fruchtenbaum, *Israelology* 584–85. See also John F. Walvoord, *Every Prophecy of the Bible* (Colorado Springs, CO: Chariot Victor, 1999) 52–66.

30. Pentecost, *Thy Kingdom Come* 148. See also Pentecost, *Things to Come* 114.

31. Peters, *Theocratic Kingdom* 1:351.

32. There is a possible pun here between "rule" (מֶמְלָכָה) and "salt" (מֶלַח).

CHAPTER ELEVEN

The New Covenant

Covenant Type

The main passage on the new covenant is not actually a record of that covenant but a prediction of it. This bold prophecy came in one of Israel's darkest hours, the Babylonian exile. Against this background Jer 31:31–32 announces the coming of a new covenant, "'Behold, days are coming,' declares the LORD, 'when I will make a new covenant'" (Jer 31:31). This covenant is to be qualitatively different from the Mosaic covenant, "Not like the covenant which I made with their fathers in the day I took them by the hand to bring them out of the land of Egypt" (Jer 31:32). This new covenant will be made with both "the house of Israel and with the house of Judah" (Jer 31:31), a united Israel. This striking note of hope also raises questions about the relationship of the Church to the promises of Israel.

The first task is to determine the texts that actually make up the new covenant. Scofield considers all of Jer 31:31–40 as referring to the new covenant.[1] Fruchtenbaum and Pentecost only quote Jer 31:31–34, but they reference several other verses when they enumerate the provisions of the new covenant.[2] Jeremiah 31 falls within a unit of positive oracles (Jer 30–33) referred to by David A. Dorsey as "Messages of Hope." Dorsey explains the structure of this unit:

> The fourth and central unit in the Book of Jeremiah is his collection of messages of hope. It has long been recognized that chapters 30–33 form a unit of positive messages. The beginning of the unit is well marked: it commences with Yahweh's instructions to "write in a book all of the words I have spoken to you; for the days are coming" (30:2). Shifts in topic and mood also mark the new beginning. The positive tone continues only through chapter 33; chapter 34 introduces the next unit, another collection of condemnatory messages.[3]

Dorsey suggests a threefold chiastic arrangement of this unit:

a restoration of exiled Israel and the new covenant (30:1–31:40)
- date: not given
    b symbolic-action message: purchased field (32:1–44)
    - date: tenth year of Zedekiah
a' restoration of exiled Israel and the eternal covenant (33:1–26)
- date: while Jeremiah was still confined in the courtyard of the guard.[4]

It is within the first section (30:1–31:40) of this unit that the prophecy of the new covenant is found.

Additional structure can be observed within Jer 30:1–31:40. Jeremiah 31:26 forms a boundary of sorts in that it recounts Jeremiah's awaking from the prophetic dream of Jer 30:1–31:26 that predicts Israel's glorious restoration under a Davidic King. Jeremiah 32:1 forms another boundary in that it introduces a new prophecy. The passage Jer 31:27–40 is divided into three sections that each begin with, "Behold, days are coming (הִנֵּה יָמִים בָּאִים)" (Jer 31:27, 31, 38). Almost every verse in this passage is solemnized with, "Declares the LORD (נְאֻם־יְהוָה)."[5] Actually, נְאֻם is a noun, and should be translated as Young translates, "An affirmation of Jehovah" (Jer 31:31 YLT), or as in La Bible de Jerusalem, "oracle de Yahvé" (Jer 31:31 BJ). Leonard J. Coppes notes that "this root is used exclusively of divine speaking. Hence, its appearance calls special attention to the origin and authority of what is said."[6] The first section, Jer 31:27–30, concerns restoration to the land and is not generally included with Jer 31:31–40 in discussions of the new covenant. The last section, Jer 31:38–40, also concerns restoration to the land in that it promises a secure and rebuilt Jerusalem. Only the second section, Jer 31:31–37 deals with the new covenant. In Heb 8:8–12 only verses 31–34 are quoted as making up the new covenant. However, Jer 31:35–37, with its clear message of Israel's preservation and God's forgiveness, thematically connects to the new covenant. Also, there is no structural clue that we should divide the second section. Therefore, I think it best to limit the passage under consideration to Jer 31:31–37.

As is always the case, the prophet's message is based on the covenants and so we find confirmation of the new covenant elsewhere. Jeremiah 32:38–40 bears a close resemblance to Jer 31:31–37. Especially, Jer 32:38 declares, "They shall be My people, and I will be their God (לִי לְעָם וַאֲנִי אֶהְיֶה לָהֶם לֵאלֹהִים וְהָיוּ)," which is nearly a verbatim quote from Jer 31:33b, "I will be their God, and they shall be My people (וְהָיִיתִי לָהֶם לֵאלֹהִים וְהֵמָּה יִהְיוּ־לִי לְעָם)." Certainly, Jer 32:40 could be a restatement of Jer 31:33. Walvoord sees Jer 32:37–40 as adding to the details of the new covenant concerning the regathering of Israel.[7] However, Jer 32:40–41 displays a closer affinity to the Land covenant and Deut 30:1–9. Jeremiah 32:37 also shows a strong resemblance to Deut 30:3–5. It should be noted that Jer 33:14–26 is clearly based on the Davidic covenant. Therefore, it would not be surprising for this section to be based on both the Davidic and Land covenants as well as introducing the new covenant. Thus, Israel's hope is firmly grounded on the three covenants that are based on the Abrahamic grant covenant.

Isaiah 61:8, 9 has also been linked to the new covenant by Walvoord.[8] However, since Isa 61–62 deals with the restoration of the land and Jerusalem in particular, I would think that it relates more to the Land covenant. The mention in Isa 61:8 of an "everlasting covenant (בְּרִית עוֹלָם)" need not point to the new covenant since the Davidic covenant is also called a בְּרִית עוֹלָם (2 Sam 23:5) , as is the Land covenant (Ezek 16:60) and the Abrahamic covenant (1 Chr 16:17; Ps 105:10). The *qal* imperfect in Isa 61:8 "I will make (אֶכְרוֹת)" should not lead us to think that this refers to the new covenant, since it was the only covenant not yet established in Isaiah's day. Isaiah uses a *qal* imperfect cohortative to refer to an confirmation of the Davidic covenant, "And I will make an everlasting covenant with you, *According to* the faithful mercies shown to David (וְאֶכְרְתָה לָכֶם בְּרִית עוֹלָם חַסְדֵי דָוִד הַנֶּאֱמָנִים)" (Isa 55:3). The Davidic covenant was clearly established by Isaiah's time.

Ezekiel 36:16–38 is often considered a new covenant text. It is the case that Ezek 36:25–27 speaks of the Spirit in terms that are similar to Jer 31:31–37. However, Deut 30:6 in the Land covenant also anticipates the new covenant. Moreover, Ezek 36:16–24, 28–38 speak of the land in terms similar to the Land covenant, "I will take you from the nations, gather you from all the lands and bring you into your own land " (Ezek 36:24). Ezekiel 37:21–28 has also been taken as a reference to the new covenant.[9] This identification is problematic for several reasons. First, Ezek 37:21–23 is a much closer parallel to Deut 30:1–9 and the Land covenant. Second, Ezek 37:24–25 is a clear reference to the Davidic covenant, "My servant David will be king over them.... and David My servant shall be their prince forever." Third, the phrase "covenant of peace (בְּרִית שָׁלוֹם)" is also used in Ezek 34:25 in a thoroughly Davidic context:

> Then I will set over them one shepherd, My servant David, and he will feed them; he will feed them himself and be their shepherd. "And I, the LORD, will be their God, and My servant David will be prince among them; I the LORD have spoken. "I will

make a covenant of peace with them (Ezek 34:23–25).

Finally, as I have previously shown, the phrase "everlasting covenant (עוֹלָם
בְּרִית)" does not necessarily refer to the new covenant.

Therefore, although the prophets do allude to the new covenant (e.g., Isa
59:20, 21 cf. Rom 11:27), we do not have any passage in the OT outside of
Jer 31:31–37 that contains definite additions to the new covenant. By
strengthening the new covenant with additional provisions, the case against
those who argue for a present fulfillment becomes stronger.[10] Although I disagree with Walvoord on the additions to the new covenant that he finds in
these passages, I do agree with his conclusion that the new covenant is not
fulfilled today by the Church. I will explore this issue in the section on beneficiaries of the new covenant.

The covenantal characteristics of Jer 31:31–37 indicate a covenant of the
grant type. The passage identifies itself as a "new covenant" and differenti-
ates itself from the Mosaic covenant (Jer 31:31–32). The function of a preamble identifying the Great King is served by the repeated phrase "declares
the LORD (נְאֻם־יְהוָה)" and the extended introduction in Jer 31:31–34, 36–38.
This is similar to the "thus says His Majesty, X, Great King, King of Hatti,
Hero, etc.," that we are familiar with in the Hittite covenants. The historical
prologue is brief (Jer 31:32) and is unusual for a grant covenant in that it refers to Israel's failure. However, the basis for the grant is thereby shown to
be, not the good deeds of the vassal, but rather the graciousness of the Lord.
The provisions indicate that the grant is a grant of privilege. The sovereign
unilateral commitment by the Lord is shown in the repeated use (seven instances in four verses) of "I will" (Jer 31:31, 33, 34). Of course, as we would
expect in a grant covenant, there is no separate blessing section because the
grant itself is the blessing. There is also no curse section. God himself is the
divine witness and swears His commitment to Israel (Jer 31:35–37).

The relevant NT passages (Matt 26:28; Mark 14:24; Luke 22:20; 1 Cor
11:25; 2 Cor 3:6; Heb 8:6–10, 13; 9:1, 4, 15–18, 20; 12:24) add that the new
covenant is based on Christ's sacrifice, but do not alter its character as a
grant covenant. Walvoord comments that

> the general teaching of the New Testament passages bearing upon the New Cove-
> nant is that the new covenant has been made possible by the sacrifice of Christ.…
> Whether the church of the present age or Israel is in view, the new covenant pro-
> vides a basis in grace for forgiveness and blessing secured by the blood of Jesus
> Christ. On this all conservative theologians agree whether premillennial, amillennial,

or postmillennial.[11]

Pentecost notes that "this covenant amplifies the third great area of the original Abrahamic covenant, the area of 'blessing.' Inasmuch as this is only an amplification of the original Abrahamic covenant, which has been shown to be unconditional and literal, this covenant must be also."[12] The new covenant is therefore a grant covenant and, as such, unconditional.

Beneficiaries

The identity of the beneficiaries of the new covenant is perhaps its most controversial aspect. The difficulty arises because the new covenant is made "with the house of Israel and with the house of Judah" (Jer 31:31). However, in the NT, the Church seems to be a beneficiary of the new covenant (Luke 22:20; 1 Cor 11:25; 2 Cor 3:6). Jeremiah 31:31–34 also figures prominently in the argument of the book of Hebrews, which is addressed to Jewish Christians. However, since the Church is a mystery unknown in the OT (Eph 3:9–11; Rom 16:25–26), it is difficult to imagine what relationship the Church could have to the new covenant.

Several views have developed to explain the relationship between the Church, Israel, and the new covenant: (1) the new covenant pertains only to Israel but the blood of the covenant is somehow applied to the Church (Dispensational), (2) the new covenant has two applications—Israel during the millennium and the Church during the present (Dispensational), (3) there are two new covenants—one for Israel and one for the Church (Dispensational), (4) the Church is brought alongside Israel's' promises (Progressive Dispensational), and (5) the Church has taken over Israel's promises (Covenant Theology).[13] While postmillennialism as illustrated by Hodge holds that the new covenant will be fulfilled to Israel in the golden age leading up to the second coming, amillennialists such as Allis view the Church as having replaced Israel and taken over her promises.[14] The issue is which view, if any, best fits the biblical evidence (see table 9).

The postmillennial and amillennial views fail along with their systems. Postmillennialism is to be dismissed for ignoring the biblical teaching concerning the tribulation, the second coming of Christ, and the nature of the millennium. Matthew 24:21 teaches that the tribulation is an unprecedented time of trial not just the ordinary trials of this age. Contrary to postmillennialism, there is not a one thousand year golden age followed by the return of Christ, rather Christ returns (Rev 19:11–21) and inaugurates the millennium (Rev 20:1–4). One could say that postmillennialists have a kingdom without a King, where amillennialists have a King without a kingdom. Contrary to amillennialism, there is a millennium clearly revealed in Scripture (Rev 20:1–4). Amillennialism is to be rejected for not taking the Scripture at face value concerning the millennium and other prophecies. Amillennialism spiritualizes the Scriptures rather than accept their plain meaning concerning the kingdom. Pentecost and Walvoord have well critiqued these views.[15]

View	Proponents	Number of Covenants	Church	Israel
Amillennialism	Allis	1	Replaces Israel	Replaced by Church
Postmillennialism	Hodge	1	For believing Jews	For believing Jews
Dispensationalism (1)	Darby	1	No relationship	Only for Israel
Dispensationalism (2)	Chafer, early Walvoord and Ryrie	2	One new covenant for the Church—Present	Another new covenant for Israel—Future
Dispensationalism (3)	Scofield, Walvoord, and Ryrie	1	Church participates in the spiritual blessings—Present	Israel fulfills—Future
Progressive Dispensationalism	Blasing and Bock	1	Church brought alongside in partial fulfillment	Israel fulfills—Future

Table 9. The New Covenant and the Church

There has been progress in the premillennial views. The common thread in the major premillennial views of the new covenant seems to be that the new covenant concerns Israel and requires a literal fulfillment in the millennium.[16] The earliest view, that of Darby, that there is only one new covenant and it pertains only to Israel would have few adherents today. It is difficult to reconcile with passages such as Luke 22:20; 1 Cor 11:25; and 2 Cor 3:6, which speak of the new covenant in the context of the Church. The other two views have been the center of most of the dispensational discussion. There was a difference of opinion even among the early dispensationalists. As previously mentioned, Scofield proposes one new covenant with a twofold application. Chafer, on the other hand, teaches that

> there remains to be recognized a heavenly covenant for the heavenly people, which is also styled like the preceding one for Israel a "new covenant." It is made in the blood of Christ (cf. Mark 14:24) and continues in effect throughout this age, whereas the new covenant made with Israel happens to be future in its application. To suppose that these two covenants—one for Israel and one for the Church—are the same is to assume that there is a latitude of common interest between God's purposes for Israel and His purpose for the Church.[17]

These two significant figures continued to differ on this point.

Gradually a consensus seemed to be arising. Walvoord in the decades of the 1940s and 1950s held the church's new covenant as distinct from Israel's. At that time he concludes that "of the remaining views, the position that there are two new covenants, one for Israel to be fulfilled in the millennium and another for the church in this age, was found preferable."[18] However, in 1980 Walvoord writes that Christ's death on the cross is

> the basis of grace to the church in the present age and is the legal background for salvation, justification, and all the blessings that belong to the church. The grace accomplished by Christ is also the basis for millennial blessing and the fulfillment of the many promises of an age in which there will be righteousness and peace and universal knowledge of the Lord. *A solution to the problem then is that there is one covenant with application to Israel and to the church and to anyone saved by the death of Christ. In Scripture the application of the New covenant is explicitly to the church in the present age and to Israel as a nation in the future as far as millennial blessings are concerned.* The New covenant is also the basis for a new rule of life according to the dispensational setting of those involved (emphasis mine).[19]

In this, Walvoord has taken a position similar to Scofield. Scofield says that "although certain features of this covenant have been fulfilled for believers in the present Church Age ... the covenant remains to be realized for Israel according to the explicit statement of v. 31."[20] Ryrie also takes this position:

> Concerning the Church's relation to the covenant, it seems best understood in the light of the progress of revelation. OT revelation of the covenant concerned Israel alone. The believer today is saved by the blood of the new covenant shed on the cross. All spiritual blessings are his because of this, and many of his blessings are the same as those promised to Israel under the OT revelation of the new covenant. However, the Christian believer is not promised blessings connected with the restoration to the Promised Land, and he is not made a member of the commonwealth of

Israel. He is a minister of the new covenant, for there is no other basis than the blood of that covenant for the salvation of any today. Nevertheless, in addition to revealing these facts about the Church and the new covenant, the NT also reveals that the blessings promised to Israel will be experienced by her at the second coming of Christ (Rom 11:26–27).[21]

Progressive dispensationalists would see the participation of the Church as an instance of complementary hermeneutics.[22] This approach is hardly necessary in view of the participation of the Church in the spiritual blessings of the new covenant and is ably critiqued by Ryrie.[23]

The weakness of the two new covenant view is the lack of evidence for the second new covenant. If both covenants are to be called "the new covenant" (ἡ καινὴ διαθήκη), how were the early Christians to distinguish between them? It is unlikely in the extreme that the early Christians would have thought of any other covenant than Jer 31:31–34. Fruchtenbaum observes that the Scriptures give no indication of two covenants and that any Jewish person would naturally think of Jeremiah.[24] Homer A. Kent, Jr. comments that the use of the article in "the new covenant (ἡ καινὴ διαθήκη)" (Luke 22:20) would lead the disciples to expect a specific covenant. He asserts that, given their biblical heritage, the disciples could only have concluded that Jesus was referring to Jeremiah's new covenant.[25] Jesus could only have meant, and the disciples could only have understood Him to be referring to, the new covenant of Jer 31:31–34.

Paul viewed the new covenant in the same manner. However, Paul went even farther. He saw his ministry as a ministry of the new covenant (2 Cor 3:6). Please note that He was writing to a largely Gentile church when he made that statement. There is no reason to believe that Paul meant anything different than he had in 1 Cor 11:25.[26] Therefore, Paul also knew of only one new covenant.

This leads to the conclusion that, in view of the fact that only one new covenant is known to Jesus, the disciples, and Paul, there must be only one new covenant. Kent summarizes the reasons for this position:

> The commonest explanation among premillennialists is that there is one new covenant. It will be fulfilled eschatologically with Israel but is participated in soteriologically by the church today. By this explanation the biblical distinction between national Israel and the church is recognized, the unconditional character of Jeremiah's prophecy which made no provision for any forfeiture by Israel is maintained, and the clear relationship of certain NT references to the church and the New Covenant are upheld....

The reasons supporting this understanding offer the best explanation of the biblical references. First, the normal way of interpreting the various references to "the New Covenant" is to see these as one New Covenant rather than two covenants with the same name and with virtually the same contents. Second, the crucial passages on the New Covenant in Hebrews are addressed to Christians. They may well have been Jewish Christians, but the essential fact is that they were Christians. Third, it is difficult if not impossible to maintain a consistent distinction between a New Covenant for Israel and a New Covenant exclusively for the church in the reference at Heb 12:23–24. In that passage both the church ("church of the firstborn") and OT saints ("spirits of just men made perfect") are related to the New Covenant, not two covenants. Fourth, Christ's mention of the New Covenant in the upper room discourse (Luke 22:20) would certainly have caused the apostles to relate it to Jeremiah 31. Yet Christ connected it with the symbolic bread and cup which he was instituting for the church. Fifth, the apostle Paul clearly connected the upper room instruction regarding the New Covenant to the practice of the Christian church (1 Cor 11:25). He further called himself and his associates "ministers of the new covenant" (2 Cor 3:6). Sixth, the discussion in Hebrews 8 argues that the title "New Covenant" implies a corresponding "old covenant" which is now being superseded. The Mosaic Covenant is the old one for Israel. If the church has a totally separate New Covenant, what is the old one which it replaces?[27]

Therefore, I conclude that only one new covenant is in view in the NT and it is based on Jer 31:31–37.

The answer to the dilemma of the relationship of the Church to the new covenant is rooted in the Abrahamic covenant. God promised Abraham that "in you all the families of the earth will be blessed" (Gen 12:3). Paul indicates that this is accomplished through faith in Christ, "The Scripture, foreseeing that God would justify the Gentiles by faith, preached the gospel beforehand to Abraham, *saying*, 'ALL THE NATIONS WILL BE BLESSED IN YOU.' So then those who are of faith are blessed with Abraham, the believer" (Gal 3:8–9). Paul explains that Christ took the law's curse on Himself "in order that in Christ Jesus the blessing of Abraham might come to the Gentiles, so that we would receive the promise of the Spirit through faith" (Gal 3:14). Paul explains that we participate in Abraham's blessings through our union with Christ:

> For you are all sons of God through faith in Christ Jesus. For all of you who were baptized into Christ have clothed yourselves with Christ. There is neither Jew nor Greek, there is neither slave nor free man, there is neither male nor female; for you are all one in Christ Jesus. And if you belong to Christ, then you are Abraham's descendants, heirs according to promise (Gal 3:26–29).

This is not the Church replacing Israel or being brought in alongside Israel. This is precisely the blessing predicted in the Abrahamic covenant.

Paul expounds on this concept of Gentiles sharing in the Abrahamic covenant's blessings using the horticultural image of grafting:

> But if some of the branches were broken off, and you, being a wild olive, were grafted in among them and became partaker with them of the rich root of the olive tree, do not be arrogant toward the branches; but if you are arrogant, *remember that* it is not you who supports the root, but the root *supports* you (Rom 11:17–18).

The root of the Abrahamic blessing supports the believing Gentiles. Paul responds to some early advocates of replacement theology:

> You will say then, "Branches were broken off so that I might be grafted in." Quite right, they were broken off for their unbelief, but you stand by your faith. Do not be conceited, but fear; for if God did not spare the natural branches, He will not spare you, either. Behold then the kindness and severity of God; to those who fell, severity, but to you, God's kindness, if you continue in His kindness; otherwise you also will be cut off. And they also, if they do not continue in their unbelief, will be grafted in, for God is able to graft them in again. For if you were cut off from what is by nature a wild olive tree, and were grafted contrary to nature into a cultivated olive tree, how much more will these who are the natural *branches* be grafted into their own olive tree (Rom 11:18–24)?

Indeed, Israel will be totally restored:

> For I do not want you, brethren, to be uninformed of this mystery— so that you will not be wise in your own estimation— that a partial hardening has happened to Israel until the fullness of the Gentiles has come in; and so all Israel will be saved; just as it is written, "THE DELIVERER WILL COME FROM ZION, HE WILL REMOVE UNGODLINESS FROM JACOB." "THIS IS MY COVENANT WITH THEM, WHEN I TAKE AWAY THEIR SINS" (Rom 11:25–27).

Romans 11:26–27 is the complete fulfillment of the new covenant.

In Ephesians Paul expands on the relationship of the Church to the Abrahamic blessings. First, Paul states, "Blessed *be* the God and Father of our Lord Jesus Christ, who has blessed us with every spiritual blessing in the heavenly *places* in Christ" (Eph 1:3). This is the same teaching that we see in Gal 3:26–29 that we participate in the blessings by virtue of our union with Christ. Please note that Paul says we have been blessed with "every *spiritual* blessing (ἐν πάσῃ εὐλογίᾳ πνευματικῇ)" (emphasis mine). The Greek word πνευματικός is defined as "spiritual, pertaining to the spirit, opposite σαρκικός (*fleshly, carnal*) and σάρκινος (*worldly, earthly*)...."[28] Therefore, we have not inherited every *physical* blessing. Only the *spiritual* blessings are in view. Fruchtenbaum explains:

> A better solution, and quite consistent with Dispensationalism, is to remember that these covenants contained two types of promises: physical and spiritual. The physical promises were, and still are, limited to Israel and will be fulfilled only to, in, or by Israel. However, as early as Genesis 12:3, the first passage of the first covenant, the Abrahamic Covenant, it was already promised that the spiritual blessings would extend to the Gentiles.[29]

Fruchtenbaum explains that Eph 2:11–16 and 3:5–6 teach that the law of Moses was the middle wall of partition that kept Gentiles from participating as Gentiles in the spiritual blessings of the four unconditional covenants that God made with Israel. They would have first had to become Jews in order to participate in those covenants. When Christ died on the cross, He broke down the wall of partition thus enabling Gentiles to participate in the spiritual blessings by faith. The physical promises belong only to Israel. However, in Christ, both Jew and Gentile share in the spiritual blessings.[30] The Church is now participating in the spiritual blessings of the new covenant. However, the fulfillment of the new covenant will be when all Israel will be saved at the Messiah's return to rule in His kingdom.

Stipulations

The provisions of the new covenant are expressed in the sovereign "I will" declarations of Jer 31:31–34 and the solemn declaration of Jer 31:35–37. Yahweh declares, in the covenant He "will make with the house of Israel," that He will accomplish four things.

Covenant Stipulations Written Upon Their Heart

First, "I will put my law in their inward parts, and in their heart will I write it" (Jer 31:33). Jeremiah 17:1 says that sin is engraved on the tablets of the human heart. Here God predicts a fundamental change. The phrase "I will put" (נָתַתִּי) is a *qal* perfect of נָתַן ("to give"). This is an instance of the prophetic perfect, where a future event is so certain that it is expressed as past.[31] As I have previously demonstrated, תּוֹרָה refers to the stipulations of the new covenant and need not be identified with the Mosaic covenant.[32]

1 Corinthians 9:21; Gal 6:2; and Jas 2:12 mention the "law of Christ."

Romans 8:2 mentions the "law of the Spirit," Jas 1:25 refers to the "law of liberty," and 2 Pet 3:2 speaks of the "commandment of the Lord and Savior."[33] All of these verses refer to Jesus' "new commandment" of love (John 13:34; Jas 2:8). As Jesus taught, love is the fulfillment of the law (Matt 7:12; 22:39, 40). Paul confirmed this teaching (Rom 13:10; Gal 5:14) as did James (Jas 2:8). Thomas R. Schreiner thinks that it is "unlikely that Paul understood the sayings and example of Jesus as a new law, the Torah of Christ."[34] Later he contends that "nothing in the Old Testament intimates that the new covenant (Jer. 31:31–34) would contain a different law from the old one."[35] The author of Hebrews has a different opinion when he notes that "when the priesthood is changed, of necessity there takes place a change of the law also" (Heb 7:12). As I have previously demonstrated, תּוֹרָה ("law") is the term for the stipulations of a covenant.[36] It is natural to expect that the new covenant would have its own new stipulations.

Similarities do exist between the stipulations of the Mosaic covenant and those of the new covenant. Apparently, it is not contradictory to delineate what loving behavior is.[37] Unger notes that most of the Decalogue is also to be found in the NT:

> This Mosaic system, including the Ten Commandments as a way of life, came to an end with the death of Christ (John 1:17; Rom. 10:4). The Mosaic age was preceded (Exod. 19:4) and followed by grace. In the gracious dispensation inaugurated as the result of the atonement of Christ, all the Ten Commandments appear in the epistles except that regarding the seventh day and are operative not as stern "thou shalt nots" but as gracious duties and privileges of a redeemed people, possessing the dynamic of the Holy Spirit, willingly and effectively to carry out their injunctions.[38]

However, those similarities do not constitute an identification of the two laws. After noting that "many commandments are the same as those of the Law of Moses," Fruchtenbaum notes several differences, "For example, there is no Sabbath law now (Rom. 14:5; Col. 2:16) and no dietary code (Mark 7:19; Rom. 14:20)."[39] Matthew 5:17–48, by means of the repeated "You have heard that it was said ... but I say to you," actually intensifies the demands of the Mosaic law. Fruchtenbaum explains that "while certain of the commandments of the Adamic Code were also found in the Edenic Code, it did not mean that the Edenic Code was still partially in force; it ceased to function with the fall of man."[40] Therefore, the law of the new covenant is the new law of Christ not the old law of Moses.

There is a new motivation in the new covenant. As we shall see in the following chapter, the Mosaic covenant was a suzerainty covenant and, as such, was conditional in nature. Therefore the motivation was to gain the blessings and avoid the curses. In other words, "Do, in order to be blessed." The new covenant is a grant covenant and, as such, is inherently unconditional in character. The motivation is gratitude for the great blessings that we have already received. In other words, "You have been blessed, therefore, do."[41] Kent sees the implanting of the new covenant's stipulations directly on the heart and mind as "the very essence of regeneration."[42] Feinberg comments that

> the law now becomes a principle of life (cf. Rom 8:1–4). It will become part of the nature of God's people; it will be instinctive. The core of the new covenant is God's gift of a new heart (cf. Ezek 36:25–27). Herein lies the sufficient motivation for obeying God's law. Basic to obedience is inner knowledge of God's will coupled with an enablement to perform it, all founded on the assurance that sins are forgiven.[43]

The external law was not able to secure obedience so, instead of writing the law on tablets of stone, God will write His law on hearts.

Personal Knowledge of God

The second provision of the new covenant is that "I will be their God, and they shall be My people. They will not teach again, each man his neighbor and each man his brother, saying, 'Know the LORD,' for they will all know Me, from the least of them to the greatest of them" (Jer31:33–34). Paul quotes this verse in 2 Cor 6:16 as a basis for holy behavior. The word "know" translates the Hebrew יָדַע ("know a person, be acquainted with, know"[44]). This is knowledge from a personal relationship not intellectual knowledge.[45] Feinberg explains that this knowledge does not remove the need for the teaching ministry. However, it does mean that every believer has personal firsthand experience of God without requiring the aid of others.[46] Kent notes that Jesus (John 6:45) and the apostle John (1 John 2:20) taught the same thing.[47] The new covenant predicts a change from access to God mediated by priests to direct access to God and a personal relationship for everyone.

Forgiveness of Sins

The third provision is the basis for the second, "For I will forgive their iniq-
uity, and their sin I will remember no more" (Jer 31:34). The second provision promises a personal relationship with God. This provision explains how
a holy God can have such a relationship with sinful men. Feinberg comments:

> Finally, the climax of this wonderful section comes in the revelation that the
> basis of the new covenant is forgiveness of sin. Thus gratitude for forgiveness will
> issue in spontaneous obedience. The new covenant does not envision sinlessness but
> forgiveness of sin resulting in restoration of fellowship with God. The foundation of
> the new covenant (after which the NT itself is named) is the absolute and complete
> forgiveness of all sins.... The last clause of v. 34 states that what grace forgives, di-
> vine omniscience forgets.[48]

The word "remember" translates the *qal* imperfect of the Hebrew זָכַר (*"think
(about), meditate (upon), pay attention (to); remember, recollect; mention,
declare, recite, proclaim, invoke, commemorate, accuse, confess"*[49]). Young
translates this promise, "Of their sin I make mention no more" (Jer 31:34b
YLT). Kent observes that

> the third promise of the New Covenant provides complete forgiveness to all who are
> under its provisions (Heb 8:12; Jer 31:34b). Sins would be put away permanently in
> a sense different from the old covenant. Later in the epistle the point is made that re-
> peated sacrifices reminded Israelites that no final sacrifice for sin had been offered
> (Heb 10:3, 4). The New Covenant would deal with sins in such a way that no con-
> tinued remembrance by repeated sacrifices would occur. Christ's death provided
> complete expiation for sins once-for-all. It is obviously the intention of the author to
> show that the promises of the New Covenant are all experienced by Christians.[50]

God's total forgiveness, based on the sacrificial death of the Messiah, under-
girds the entire new covenant.

Unconditional Preservation of Israel

The fourth and final provision is that Yahweh unconditionally promises the
preservation of the nation of Israel:

> Thus says the LORD,
> Who gives the sun for light by day
>   And the fixed order of the moon and the stars for light by night,
> Who stirs up the sea so that its waves roar;

The LORD of hosts is His name:
"If this fixed order departs From before Me," declares the LORD,
    "Then the offspring of Israel also will cease
From being a nation before Me forever."
Thus says the LORD,
"If the heavens above can be measured
    And the foundations of the earth searched out below,
Then I will also cast off all the offspring of Israel
    For all that they have done," declares the LORD (Jer 31:35–37).

Yahweh states this provision in the most solemn of terms. Note the extended preamble in verse 36 rivaling the most grandiose Hittite preamble. Each verse reminds us "thus says the LORD," and "declares the LORD." God's promise is as sure as the order of nature. His promise stands in spite of "all that they [Israel] have done." Feinberg comments, "Of what value is an eternal covenant if certain parties to it are limited in life span'? But such is not the case with the new covenant, for it is made with an eternal people.... The survival of Israel through the centuries can be explained only on supernatural grounds...."[51] God has promised Israel that His law will be written on their hearts, they will all have a direct personal relationship with Him, their sins will be forgiven, and their nation will be preserved. As Fruchtenbaum notes, "Not all provisions go immediately into effect."[52] The Church is presently enjoying the spiritual blessings of the new covenant, but the fulfillment awaits the return of Messiah when all Israel shall be saved (Rom 11:26–27).

Establishment

Jesus understood that He was establishing the new covenant by means of His sacrifice. The Last Supper and the institution of communion indicate this (Luke 22:20; 1 Cor 11:25). Perhaps the awareness that the new covenant was established but not fulfilled is the reason for Paul's statement, "For as often as you eat this bread and drink the cup, you proclaim the Lord's *death until He comes*" (1 Cor 11:26 emphasis mine). Hebrews 10:15–18 argues that the new covenant has been inaugurated, therefore, there is no more forgiveness by means of sacrifices. Hebrews 8:6 portrays Christ as the Mediator of the new covenant. Those who hold to two new covenants claim that the phrase "better covenant" does not refer to the new covenant. If that were the case, it is strange indeed that the context would concern the new covenant so extensively. Surely, the second covenant of Heb 8:7 is the same as the better cove-

nant in 8:6 and the new covenant in 8:8. Also, the better covenant of Heb 8:6
is founded on "better promises" than the Mosaic covenant. It is uncertain
which promises can be meant if that covenant is divorced from Jer 31:31–37.
Therefore, Heb 8:6 indicates not only that Jesus is the Mediator of the new
covenant, but also that the new covenant "has been enacted." The Greek
word translated "has been enacted" (νενομοθέτηται) is a perfect passive indicative of νομοθετέω ("ordering a matter by law *enact*; passive *be enacted,
be established*"[53]). It would be difficult to obtain a clearer statement that the
death of Christ establishes the new covenant (see table 10).

Duration

The new covenant refers to itself in terms that require eternality. Jeremiah
31:36 promises Israel's continuation "forever" (כָּל־הַיָּמִים), literally "all the
days." This is an even stronger term than עוֹלָם, which, under some circumstances, could mean a long time. The basis of the new covenant is the Abrahamic covenant, which is an eternal covenant. Therefore, there can be no
doubt that the new covenant will endure into eternity (see figure 2).

Type of Covenant	Stipulations of Covenant	Beneficiaries	Established	End
Grant	• God will write His law in Israel's heart • All Israel will know God personally • God will forgive all of Israel's sins • God will preserve Israel forever.	Israel (Church enjoys spiritual bless-ings)	By the death of Christ (Luke 22:20)	Everlasting covenant (Jer 31:35–37)

Table 10. New Covenant

NOTES

1. Scofield, *NSRB* 804.
2. Fruchtenbaum, *Israelology* 586–87 and Pentecost, *Things to Come* 116–18.
3. David A. Dorsey, *The Literary Structure of the Old Testament: A Commentary on Genesis–Malachi* (Grand Rapids, MI: Baker, 1999) 239.
4. Dorsey, *Literary Structure of the Old Testament* 240–41.
5. Jer 30:3; 31:27–28, 31–34, 36–38; 33:14.
6. Leonard J. Coppes, "נאם (*nᵉ'ūm*)," *TWOT* 2:541–42.
7. John F. Walvoord, "Eschatological Problems X: The New Covenant with Israel," *BSac* 103, no. 409 (January–March 1946): 16–27.
8. Ibid.
9. Ibid. 22
10. Ibid.
11. John F. Walvoord, *The Millennial Kingdom* (Grand Rapids, MI: Zondervan, 1959) 214.
12. Pentecost, *Things to Come* 118–19.
13. John F. Walvoord, "Part 3: Does the Church Fulfill Israel's Program," *BSac* 137, no. 547 (July–September 1980): 212–21.
14. Walvoord, *The Millennial Kingdom* 208–10.
15. Pentecost, *Things to Come* 384–90 and Walvoord, *The Millennial Kingdom* 18–108.
16. Walvoord, *The Millennial Kingdom* 209–10.
17. Chafter, *Systematic Theology* 7:98–99.
18. Walvoord, "Eschatological Problems X: The New Covenant with Israel" 24–27. See also Walvoord, *The Millennial Kingdom* 218–20.
19. Walvoord, "Part 3: Does the Church Fulfill Israel's Program" 220. See also John F. Walvoord, "Interpreting Prophecy Today—Part 2: The Kingdom of God in the Old Testament," *BSac* 139, no. 554 (April–June 1982): 111–28.
20. Scofield, *NSRB* 804.
21. Charles Caldwell Ryrie, "Covenant, New," *WBE* 1:391–92.
22. See Rodney J. Decker, "The Church's Relationship to the New Covenant (Part 1)," *BSac* 152, no. 607 (July–September 1995): 290–305; Rodney J. Decker, "The Church's Relationship to the New Covenant (Part 2)," *BSac* 152, no. 608 (October–December 1995): 431–56.
23. Ryrie, *Dispensationalism* 170–74.
24. Fruchtenbaum, *Israelology* 634.
25. Homer A. Kent, Jr., "The New Covenant and the Church," *GTJ* 6, no. 2 (Fall 1985): 289–98.
26. Ibid. 293.
27. Ibid. 297–98.
28. *ALGNT* 318.

29. Fruchtenbaum, *Israelology* 634.

30. Ibid. 635–36.

31. See Driver, *Treatise* 18–21.

32. See chapter 3. Cf. Job 22:22; Prov 1:8; 3:1; 4:2; 6:20.

33. Fruchtenbaum, *Israelology* 649–50.

34. Thomas R. Schreiner, *The Law and Its Fulfillment: A Pauline Theology of* Law (Grand Rapids, MI: Baker, 1993) 157.

35. Ibid.

36. See chapter 3.

37. Schreiner, *The Law* 147–49.

38. Merrill F. Unger, "Law," *Unger's Bible Dictionary* (hereafter referred to as *UBD*), 3rd ed. (Chicago: Moody, 1966) 646–47. See also Chafer, *Systematic Theology* 4:208–13 and Ryrie, *Dispensationalism* 57–58.

39. Fruchtenbaum, *Israelology* 650.

40. Ibid.

41. Ibid.

42. Kent, "The New Covenant and the Church" 294.

43. Charles L. Feinberg, "Jeremiah," *Isaiah–Ezekiel*, EBC 6:576. See also Keil and De-litzsch, "Jeremiah," *Jeremiah–Lamentations*, COT 8:282.

44. *BDB* 393–95.

45. Keil and Delitzsch, "Jeremiah," COT 8:283.

46. Feinberg, "Jeremiah," EBC 6:577.

47. Kent, "The New Covenant and the Church" 294–95.

48. Feinberg, "Jeremiah," EBC 6:577.

49. Andrew Bowling, "זָכַר (*zākar*),"*TWOT* 1:241–42.

50. Kent, "The New Covenant and the Church" 295.

51. Feinberg, "Jeremiah," EBC 6:578–79.

52. Fruchtenbaum, *Israelology* 636.

53. *ALGNT* 273.

♦ CHAPTER TWELVE
The Mosaic Covenant

Covenant Type

The Antiquity of the Mosaic Covenant

The antiquity and authorship of the Pentateuch has been under attack because of Wellhausen and the Documentary Hypothesis. This hypothesis is often characterized as the JEDP or JEDPR theory. Wellhausen and his students postulate four different groups of authors (<u>J</u>ahwist, <u>E</u>lohist, <u>D</u>euteronomist, and <u>P</u>riestly) that gradually added to the Pentateuch until the documents were put into their final form by R (<u>R</u>edactor). Many have supplied refutations of this view and I need not supply yet another.[1] However, it is of great interest that, although accepting the premises of the Documentary Hypothesis, even Mendenhall does see an early Mosaic source for this covenant:

> The OT criticism stemming from Wellhausen maintained that the relation between Yahweh and Israel was a "natural" one; it was a "tribal" religion in which Yahweh was little more than a symbol of the tribe, whose interests were identical to those of the deity, and consequently there could be no conditions attached to this relationship. According to this view, the prophets from Amos on were the first to maintain that the relationship had conditions of an ethical nature attached, and eventually the relationship was conceived of as a covenant in late pre-exilic times. Thus the covenant, from this point of view, was simply a theological idea, a concept for conveying religious truth.
>
> It now seems much more likely that the covenant tradition stemmed rather from events in the time of Moses....[2]

The covenant form of the Mosaic covenant is the same as the Hittite treaties of the second millennium BC. Kline argues that this indicates the antiquity of the Mosaic covenant:

> While exposing the prevalent critical histories of the formation of the canon as the

anachronistic fictions they are, orthodox Old Testament scholarship should set to work on the biblical-theological task of delineating the real history of that process. When that is done and the relevant historical realities of ancient covenant procedure are brought to bear, the formulation of the Old Testament canon will be traced to its origins in the covenantal mission of Moses in the third quarter of the second millennium B.C., providentially the classic age of treaty diplomacy in the ancient.Near East.

Our conclusion in a word, then, is that canon is inherent in covenant, covenant of the kind attested in ancient international relations and the Mosaic covenants of the Bible.[3]

The form of the Mosaic covenant locates it firmly in the second millennium BC. This covenant form is most noticeable in the books of Exodus and Deuteronomy.

Exodus

The book of Exodus displays the suzerainty covenant form. Hillers notes that "the Ten Commandments constitute an obvious parallel to the stipulations of the suzerainty treaty."[4] Mendenhall details the adherence of the Mosaic covenant to late Bronze Age Hittite treaty forms. He sees the phrase "I am the LORD your God" (Exod 20:2) as the covenant preamble. The declaration that Yahweh is the One "who brought you out of the land of Egypt, out of the house of slavery." (Exod 20:2) serves as a brief historical prologue. Mendenhall notes that the stipulation, "You shall have no other gods before Me" (Exod 20:3), is similar to the frequent obligation in the Hittite treaties excluding relationships with other sovereigns. The Hittite treaties require unwavering trust in the Suzerain and consider murmuring to be seditious. Mendenhall notes that prior to Exod 20 Israel was not punished for her murmuring (cf. Exod 17:2–7). However, after the ratification of the Mosaic covenant their murmuring was punished (cf. Num 11:1). Mendenhall discovers additional elements of the Hittite suzerainty covenant form outside of the Decalogue. The deposit of the written covenant in the Ark of the Covenant (Deut 10:5) and requirements for periodic reading (Deut 31:11) are similar to the deposition section of Hittite covenants. The requirement for all male Israelis to appear before Yahweh three times a year (Exod 34:23; Deut 16:16) is similar to Hittite requirements that vassals appear before the Great King at regular intervals. Calling heaven and earth to witness (Deut 32:1) is also found in Hittite covenants. Mendenhall considers the blessings and cursings

(Deut 27:1–28:68) to be obvious parallels to the Hittite covenants and the basis for the prophetic tradition. Finally, Mendenhall indicates that the ritual of Exod 24:5–8 may be a covenant oath.[5] Consequently, since it possesses the major elements of the form, the Exodus account is a suzerainty covenant.

Deuteronomy

Deuteronomy presents us with an unambiguous instance of the suzerainty covenant form. Michael D. Guinan remarks that

> particularly influential has been the theory (connected especially with G. Mendenhall 1954b) that the Mosaic covenant, from its beginning, was understood on the model of the suzerainty treaty (Nicholson 1986: 56–82).... the treaty pattern is clearest in the later deuteronomic literature (McCarthy 1978; M. Weinfeld 1972).[6]

Deere details the manner in which Deuteronomy conforms to the suzerainty covenant form:

> Deuteronomy follows the pattern of the vassal treaties typical of the second millennium B.C. When a king (a suzerain) made a treaty with a vassal country the treaty usually contained six elements: (a) a preamble, (b) a historical prologue (a history of the king's dealings with the vassal), (c) a general stipulation (a call for wholehearted allegiance to the king), (d) specific stipulations (detailed laws by which the vassal state could give concrete expression to its allegiance to the king), (e) divine witnesses (deities called to witness the treaty), and (f) blessings and curses (for obedience or disobedience to the treaty)....
> Deuteronomy approximates this structure, for 1:1–4 constitutes a preamble; 1:5–4:43 a historical prologue; 4:44–11:32 a general stipulation; chapters 12–26 specific stipulations; and chapters 27–28 blessings and curses. (Of course, Yahweh, being the only true God, did not call on other deities to witness the treaty.)[7]

Accordingly, both the Exodus and Deuteronomy accounts of the Mosaic covenant display the suzerainty form.

Conclusion

As I have previously demonstrated, the suzerainty form is essentially conditional and, as such, non-gracious.[8] Chafer observed that "the Mosaic Covenant is a covenant of works. Its blessings were made to depend on human faithfulness. It also provided the remedial sacrifices by which sin and failure of those under the covenant could be cared for and they restored to right relations with God."[9] Just as there are conditions within grant covenants, I am not denying that there is an element of grace even in suzerainty covenants.[10] The One covenanting with Israel was, after all, Yahweh, "Who brought you out of the land of Egypt, out of the house of slavery" (Exod 20:2). Yahweh had established a gracious relationship with Israel by delivering them before He made the Mosaic covenant with them. That deliverance has as its source the Abrahamic grant covenant's promise (Gen 15:13–16). However, the Mosaic covenant's blessings require right behavior on the part of the vassal, Israel (Deut 11:26–28).

Beneficiaries

Yahweh made the Mosaic covenant with the same people that He "brought… out of the land of Egypt, out of the house of slavery" (Exod 20:2), i.e., Israel. Moses set the law before the Israelis alone (Deut 4:44–45; 5:1–2). The Mosaic covenant set Israel apart from the nations. Moses writes, "For what great nation is there that has a god so near to it as is the LORD our God whenever we call on Him? Or what great nation is there that has statutes and judgments as righteous as this whole law which I am setting before you today?" (Deut 4:7–8). Paul taught that "the covenants and the giving of the Law" (Rom 9:4) belonged to his kindred the Jews. Ryrie comments that

> both Old and New Testaments are unanimous in this. "These are the statutes and judgments and laws, which the Lord made between him and the children of Israel in mount Sinai by the hand of Moses" (Lev. 26:46). In Romans 9:4 the recipients of the law are Paul's kinsmen according to the flesh—Jews—"who are Israelites; to whom pertaineth the adoption, and the glory, and the covenants, and *the giving of the law*, and the service of God, and the promises." This is reiterated in Romans 2:14 by contrasting the Jews who received the law with Gentiles who did not. "For when the Gentiles, which have not the law, do by nature the things contained in the law, these, having not the law, are a law unto themselves." The Mosaic Law was given to Israel and Israel only.[11]

According to Paul, the past condition of those of us who are Gentiles is "excluded from the commonwealth of Israel" (Eph 2:12). Therefore, God gave the Mosaic covenant only to Israel and it was her possession alone.

Stipulations

The law of Moses contains six hundred and thirteen commandments often divided into two hundred forty-eight positive and three hundred sixty-five negative commands. Rabbi Simlai (ca. 3rd century AD) taught that "six hundred and thirteen precepts were communicated to Moses, three hundred and sixty-five negative precepts, corresponding to the number of solar days [in the year], and two hundred and forty-eight positive precepts, corresponding to the number of the members of man's body."[12] Maimonides (AD 1135–1204) later compiled these commandments in *Sefer Hamitsvot*.[13] Philo considers the Decalogue to be general laws and the other six hundred and three commandments to be specific, "The genera and heads of all special laws, which are called 'the ten commandments,' have been discussed with accuracy in the former treatise. We must now proceed to consider the particular commands as we read them in the subsequent passages of the holy scriptures...."[14] These rabbinical scholars were not the last to divide up the law of Moses.

Many subsequent divisions of the law have been suggested such as ritual, moral, and even legal (although a legal law seems somewhat redundant). Fruchtenbaum observes that, although the division of the law into ceremonial, legal, and moral parts may be convenient for purposes of study, this division is never found in the Scriptures. He also notes that there is no warrant for separating the Decalogue from the other six hundred and thirteen commandments.[15] E. P. Sanders elaborates on the unity of the law of Moses and the folly of attempts to divide it:

> Modern scholars often try to divide the law into "ritual" and "ethical" categories, but this is an anachronistic and usually misleading division. (This was pointed out many years ago by Lake [1932: 207], but not often heeded.) In such analyses the "moral law" is often considered to be embodied in the Ten Commandments, but this puts the commandments governing use of the Lord's name, the Sabbath, and graven images into the "ethical" division, where they clearly do not belong.... People often think of the early Church as accepting the "ethical" commandments; again this is seen to be the wrong categorization. According to Acts, the commandments which the Jerusalem church wished to impose on gentile converts included the prohibitions against idolatry and eating meat with the blood in it—neither one "moral" (Acts 15:20). The major laws which govern relations between humans and God—such as the prohibition of idolatry—were maintained in all branches of Judaism, and many were inherited by Christianity. The commandments "between human and human" have of course been deeply influential.
>
> The anachronism of the moral/ritual distinction is seen in another way: "ritual" commandments not infrequently have an "ethical" aspect. Thus tithing (a "ritual" requirement) included charity (a "moral" duty), and the laws of the Sabbath provided rest for laborers and even for animals (Deut 5:14).... First-century Jews did

not see a difference between the commandment not to eat holy food when ritually impure and the requirement to pay part of the tithes to the poor—except for the difference in penalty. The same God gave both commandments, and loyalty to him required obedience of them equally.[16]

Paul writes the Galatians, "To every man who receives circumcision, that he is under obligation to keep the whole Law" (Gal 5:3). Paul sees the law of Moses as a unified whole. James writes with the same understanding, "For whoever keeps the whole law and yet stumbles in one point, he has become guilty of all" (Jas 2:10). After arguing that the Mosaic law is a unit, Aldrich observes that

> orthodox Jewish tradition, able commentators, and the Scriptures themselves recognize that the law of Moses is an indivisible unit. This presents an insurmountable problem for any degree of Mosaic legalism. No modern legalist wants to climb to the top of Mount Sinai with its fire and thunder but many think it is a good thing to take a short hike up its foothills. But to touch the mountain at the bottom was as fatal as climbing to the top (Heb 12:18–21). The unity of the Mosaic law leaves only two alternatives—either complete deliverance from or complete subjection to the entire system.[17]

The law of Moses is a unit and must be considered as a whole.

The law of Moses provided a way of life for Israel. However, it never supplied a way of salvation. Paul writes the Galatians, "If a law had been given which was able to impart life, then righteousness would indeed have been based on law (εἰ γὰρ ἐδόθη νόμος ὁ δυνάμενος ζῳοποιῆσαι, ὄντως ἐκ νόμου ἂν ἦν ἡ δικαιοσύνη)" (Gal 3:21). The εἰ in the protasis with the aorist passive indicative ἐδόθη and the ἂν in the apodosis with the imperfect indicative active ἦν indicate a second class condition in present time.[18] The nature of second class conditions is that they are assumed false for the sake of argument. Therefore, Paul could be translated, "If (and it is not the case) a law had been given which was able to impart life ..." (Gal 3:21 translation mine). In other words, no law could be given that would impart life. Consequently, the legalist is fundamentally wrong in that the law of Moses is and always was incapable of imparting life.

Establishment

The original establishment of the Mosaic covenant takes place in the wilderness at Mount Sinai three months after the Israelis left Egypt (Exod 19:1–2).

Exodus 19:3–25 details the consecration of the people of Israel in preparation for the divine visitation. Niehaus notes that the terminology of Exodus 19–20 is characteristic of a judgment theophany. Niehaus suggests that

> God is about to give the law and enter into covenant with Israel. Although he graciously brings the law, however, the law also inevitably implies judgment....
> ... it may be that Yahweh does not want Israel to be entirely unafraid. The people must understand that they are in the presence of a holy God and thus have been called upon to "consecrate" themselves (19:10–11) and to limit their approach to the mountain (vv. 12–13).[19]

With the thunder, lightning, dark clouds, fire, smoke, earthquake, and ever-louder trumpet blasts (Exod 19:16–19) announcing the impending judgment of a holy God, it is no wonder that "the people who were in the camp trembled" (Exod 19:16). The author of Hebrews equates the Mount Sinai experience with judgment and the old (i.e., Mosaic) covenant (Heb 12:18–21). He then contrasts the experience of the Hebrews at Mount Sinai with Mount Zion and the new covenant in the blood of Jesus (Heb 12:22–24). Paul makes a similar point in Gal 4:21–31. These passages underscore the fact that the Scriptures view the Mosaic covenant as essentially non-gracious. Thus, with its threatening aspect, the law is our schoolmaster to lead us to Christ and justification by grace alone through faith alone in Christ alone (Gal 3:24).

Exodus 24 recounts exactly the sort of covenant ceremony that we would expect from the ancient Near Eastern parallels. The people swear an oath *en mass* to uphold the stipulations of the Mosaic covenant (Exod 24:3). Chafer sees this oath as a fall from grace:

> While it is certain that Jehovah knew the choice the people would make, it is equally certain that their choice was in no way required by Him. His description of the relation they had sustained to Him until that moment is most tender and pleading — "Ye have seen what I did unto the Egyptians, and how I bare you on eagles' wings, and brought you unto myself." Such is the character of pure grace.... It is all of God.... He had dealt with them according to the unconditional covenant of grace made with Abraham.... Had they said at the hearing of the impossible law, "None of these things can we do. We crave only to remain in that boundless mercy of God, who has loved us, and sought us, and saved us from all our enemies, and who will bring us to Himself," it is evident that such an appeal would have reached the very heart of God. And the surpassing glory of His grace would have been extended to them without bounds; for grace above all else is the delight of the heart of God.... they confidently chose a covenant of works when they said: "All that the LORD hath spoken we will do." They were called upon to face a concrete choice between

the mercy of God which had followed them, and a new and hopeless covenant of works. They fell from grace.[20]

However, Hillers understands this oath as exactly what would be expected:

> Returning to the Sinai narrative in Exodus, where is the oath? The oath is half the treaty. It is the feature that makes the terms binding on the vassal, and if it were not present in the Israelite covenant with God, then they would have departed very far from the form of treaty which was presented in the previous chapter. We would have only the voice of God and no "Amen" from the people....
> He tells them what Yahweh has said and thus offers them the covenant. They agree, informally. Thus the stage is set for the formal oath. Moses writes out a copy of the text. Animals are slaughtered, and half the blood preserved. He reads the final and binding assent. Then he sprinkles the blood on them and identifies it as "the blood of the covenant." The idea is similar to that involved in passing between the parts of an animal; the sprinkling with blood in a similar way establishes contact and identification with the victim. The thought is "May the Lord do so to me, and more also, if I go back on my word...."[21]

Moses was obeying God's command to institute covenant proceedings (Exod 19:7). The people would hardly have been justified in refusing a divine command (Exod 19:8; Deut 27:26). Moses recounted this incident later in Deut 5:27–29. God's response was that "they have done well in all that they have spoken" (Deut 5:28). However, God knew that they will not be able to accomplish their good intentions, "Oh that they had such a heart in them (לָהֶם מִי־יִתֵּן וְהָיָה לְבָבָם זֶה, literally, 'Who will give and their heart will be this to them?'), that they would fear Me and keep all My commandments always, that it may be well with them and with their sons forever!" (Deut 5:29). Therefore, the Israelis do well, in accepting God's covenant, although God knows that they will not be able to keep it. This is the reason for the inclusion of the sacrificial system in the Mosaic covenant.

The covenant meal with God (Exod 24:9–11) would have been greatly reassuring to Israel in the context of ancient Near Eastern culture. Niehaus observes, "Exodus 24 records a communion meal that may well have been a regular way of consummating a covenant."[22] Hillers agrees, "Both among the modem bedouin and in the ancient Near East, one manner of making a league is for the prospective partners to eat together ceremonially, and perhaps that is what the author of these artless lines meant to say. This, then, would be his version of how the covenant at Sinai was ratified."[23] As I have previously observed, this act of eating with another person in the ancient Near East may well have resulted in coming under his protection.[24] It is significant that the text notes, "Yet He did not stretch out His hand against the nobles of the sons of Israel" (Exod 24:11). This covenant meal would have communicated to Israel that they were to experience Yahweh's safekeeping.

There are two covenant renewals in the Pentateuch as well as several others in the Hebrew Scriptures. The first follows the affair of the golden calf in Exod 32–33. God renews the covenant with Moses as Israel's representative. Contrary to the earlier ceremony that involved the priests and the elders (Exod 24:9–11), this time Yahweh commands, "No man is to come up with you" (Exod 34:3). The first tablets of the Mosaic covenant were "written by the finger of God" (Exod 31:18). However, when God reaffirmed the Mosaic covenant, He commands Moses to "write down these words, for in accordance with these words I have made a covenant with you and with Israel" (Exod 34:27). Several passages speak of the law coming through angels (Deut 33:2 LXX; Acts 7:38, 53, Gal 3:19; Heb 2:2). Since the Greek ἄγγελος and the Hebrew מַלְאָךְ both have the same basic meaning of "messenger" and God is clearly speaking with Moses, perhaps the messenger referred to is human, i.e., Moses.[25] This would be stating the same thing as Gal 3:19–20 that God gave the law through a mediator. In all of the covenants before the Abrahamic covenant, God speaks directly to the individuals with whom He is covenanting. After the inauguration of the Mosaic covenant, God begins to use mediators. It is as if, with the giving of the law, God began to distance Himself. The problem is, of course, with humankind, as Isaiah said, "But your iniquities have made a separation between you and your God and your sins have hidden *His* face from you, so that He does not hear" (Isa 59:2).

The second covenant renewal takes place on the plains of Moab and is contained in Deut 1–28. Deuteronomy consists of seven Mosaic discourses arranged to correspond to the form of an ancient Near Eastern suzerainty covenant with an epilogue concerning the succession of covenant leadership upon the death of Moses. This covenant renewal was necessary because, with a few exceptions, the original Exodus generation had died in the wilderness (Deut 1:34–36). God intends that the people know the covenant was not with the fathers alone, but also with their children. Moses writes, "The LORD our God made a covenant with us at Horeb. The LORD did not make this covenant with our fathers, but with us, *with* all those of us alive here today" (Deut 5:2–3). After the Israelis had entered the land, Joshua renewed the Mosaic covenant again (Josh 24:24–25). Other renewals of the Mosaic covenant take place under Asa (2 Chr 15:9–15); Jehoiada (2 Kgs 11:17; 2 Chr 23:16);

Hezekiah (2 Chr 29:10); and Josiah (2 Kgs 23:1–3; 2 Chr 34:31–32). The repeated renewal of the Mosaic covenant betrays awareness that Israel did not keep the Mosaic law (see table 11).

Duration[26]

A Statement of the Problem

The early Church fathers evidently believed that the law of Moses had been superseded. Tertullian (AD 160–225) argues, based on the new covenant, that the Mosaic covenant was temporary:

> And in another passage: "Behold, the days come, saith the Lord, that I will make a new covenant with the house of Jacob, and with the house of Judah; not according to the covenant that I made with their fathers in the day when I arrested their dispensation, in order to bring them out of the land of Egypt." He thus shows that the ancient covenant is temporary only, when He indicates its change; also when He promises that it shall be followed by an eternal one.[27]

This was a cause of much disagreement in early Jewish-Christian dialogue. In the Talmud we find this story concerning Rabbi Gamaliel II (ca. AD 80) [Not the teacher of Paul, Gamaliel I (ca. AD 50)]:

> Imma Shalom, R. Eliezer's wife, was R. Gamaliel's sister. Now, a certain philosopher lived in his vicinity, and he bore a reputation that he did not accept bribes. They wished to expose him, so she brought him a golden lamp, went before him, [and] said to him, 'I desire that a share be given me in my [deceased] father's estate.' 'Divide,' ordered he. Said he [R. Gamaliel] to him, 'It is decreed for us, Where there is a son, a daughter does not inherit.' [He replied], 'Since the day that you were exiled from your land the Law of Moses has been superseded and another book given, wherein it is written, 'A son and a daughter inherit equally.' The next day, he [R. Gamaliel].... Said he to them, 'Look at the end of the book, wherein it is written, I came not to destroy the Law of Moses nor to add to the Law of Moses, and it is written therein, A daughter does not inherit where there is a son.[28]

As I will explain, this is a misinterpretation of Matt 5:17. Nevertheless, it does demonstrate an awareness of the conflict.

This conflict is not limited to the early centuries of this era. Many Christians today would assert the continuance of the Mosaic covenant. Berkhof writes that

> it is equally contrary to Scripture to say ... that the law does not apply in the New

Testament dispensation. Jesus taught the permanent validity of the law, Matt. 5:17–19. Paul ... holds his readers responsible for keeping the law, Rom. 13:9....

> There is another sense, however, in which the Christian is not free from the law.... *It is pure Antinomianism to maintain that Christ kept the law as a rule of life for His people,* so that they need not worry about this any more. The law lays claim, and justly so, on the entire life of man in all its aspects, including his relation to the gospel of Jesus Christ.... The law not only demands that we accept the gospel and believe in Jesus Christ, but also that we lead a life of gratitude in harmony with its requirements....
>
> The Reformed do full justice to the second use of the law [as a schoolmaster to lead us to Christ] ... but they devote even more attention to the law in connection with the doctrine of sanctification. *They stand strong in the conviction that believers are still under the law as a rule of life* and gratitude (emphasis mine).[29]

I will examine Matt 5:17–19 fully later. However, I would note in passing that Berkhof's reference to Rom 13:9 is strange in that, in context, Paul is arguing that love, which is Jesus' new commandment (John 13:34), replaces the need for the Mosaic law.

Some see the ethic of love as insufficient for Christian living. Donald G. Bloesch writes that

> in Reformed theology, the law is a means to salvation—but only when united with the gospel. Psalm 19:7–8 is often cited: "The law of the Lord is perfect, reviving the soul.... The commands of the Lord are radiant, giving light to the eyes" (NIV). The law saves by directing us to the gospel, by relaying the message of the gospel to us. The law by itself does not save but only condemns. It is when Christ speaks to us through the law, it is when we perceive the law through the lens of the gospel, that we are convicted of sin and assured by the promise of the gospel.
>
> *Reformed theology takes strong exception to grounding ethics simply in the spirit of love.* With the Reformed fathers "ethics was grounded not upon love but upon obeying the commandments as *God's* commandments. The Law keeps its place beside the Gospel as another, a second reality, equally true and commanding and necessary because the one God stands behind both, because the one Holy Spirit imparts both to men" (emphasis mine).[30]

Chafer complains that the

> notion that people will not live righteous lives unless placed upon a works basis of relationship to God has permeated the church to a large degree. This ignorance is manifest in the church by the fact that the greatest incentive to holy living that the human heart can know is ignored, which is, to "walk worthy of the vocation wherewith we are called" (Eph 4:1). The individual who comprehends that he has attained by faith through grace to the perfect righteousness of God, will be incited by so great an honor and trust to walk more faithfully in the path of God's own choosing than

will the individual who hopes—against hope, for it is recognized as an impossible task—to satisfy a holy God by his ever-failing works.[31]

As Paul writes, "For in Christ Jesus neither circumcision nor uncircumcision means anything, but faith working through love" (Gal 5:6).

Other Christians assert, with varying degrees of assurance, that the Mosaic law has, in some sense, come to an end. Unger comments with conviction that "this Mosaic system, including the Ten Commandments as a way of life, came to an end with the death of Christ (John 1:17; Rom. 10:4).... The Mosaic law was thus a temporary divine administration in effect only until Christ should come."[32] Schreiner, after making an excellent case for the termination of the law,[33] seems to want to leave some role for the law after all:

> The Mosaic covenant has passed away because Messiah has come. Nevertheless, this cessation of the Mosaic covenant does not constitute an abrogation of the law but a fulfillment and establishment of the law (Rom. 3:31). In other words, one cannot give an unqualified "yes" or "no" answer concerning the cessation of the law in Paul. In one sense it has passed away, and in another sense it has been fulfilled.[34]

At the conclusion of his analysis, Schreiner is still somewhat indefinite:

> Paul's understanding of the continuing validity of the law is complex. One cannot respond with a simple "yes" or "no" as to whether the law remains in force. Paul argues that the Mosaic covenant has ended in one sense.... The Mosaic covenant, however, has ceased because it is fulfilled in Christ....
> The moral absolutes of the Mosaic law, however, are also fulfilled in Christ. The fulfillment of these commands, however, does not necessitate a change in the content of the commands. What is new is that the gift of the Holy Spirit now provides the power to obey what the law enjoins.[35]

Thus, some Christians see the Mosaic law as still in effect while others are quite sure that it has ended. Still others seek to find some role for the law of Moses in the Christian life.[36]

Some Clarification of the Issues

Many of those who seek to find a valid role for the Mosaic covenant today are concerned about God's eternal ethical absolutes. Aldrich clarifies this issue by differentiating between God's eternal moral standard and the law of Moses. He points out that God's absolute moral standard is the character of God Himself. Therefore, it existed before the Mosaic covenant and would still exist after the Mosaic covenant.[37] Dispensationalists are not asserting that God has surrendered His moral absolutes. Nor are they ignoring the fact that the law of Moses is an expression of those moral absolutes. What dispensationalists are asserting is that the Mosaic covenant has been abolished and that, under the new covenant, we have a different rule of life that also expresses God's moral absolutes.

Theologians have distinguished three uses for the law. In the first use, the *usus politicus* ("political use") or *usus civilis* ("civil use"), the law restrains sin and promotes righteousness. In the second use, the *usus elenchticus* ("convicting use") or *usus pedagogicus* ("pedagogical use"), the law brings us to faith in Christ. However, in the third use, the *usus didacticus* ("didactic use") or *usus normativus* ("normative use"), also called the *tertius usus legis* ("third use of the law"), the law is used as a rule of life for believers.[38] One can question the effectiveness of the first use, since Paul asserts that the law has the effect of increasing sin (Rom 5:20). To be sure, the problem lies with sinful human beings and not with the law (Rom 7:12, 13; 8:3). The second use is scriptural, since it derives directly from Gal 3:21–25. However, the third use of the law is the point of controversy.

Salvation by Grace through Faith Alone

The foundational principle that must guide our thinking on this matter is that God justifies human beings by grace alone through faith alone in Jesus Christ alone and not by works. This is the consistent teaching of Jesus (John 3:14–18, 36; 5:24; 6:28–29, 40; 11:25–27), Paul (Rom 3:21–22; 4:5; Eph 2:8–10), and the apostles (Acts 10:43; 15:7–11; 1 John 5:11). To depart from this principle is to depart from the orthodox Christian faith.

John makes it plain that there is an inherent contrast between grace and law (John 1:17). Paul teaches in Rom 3:21, 22 that righteousness is apart from the law. Paul even asserts that God justifies "the one who does not work, but believes in Him who justifies the ungodly" (Rom 4:5). According to Paul, there exists a danger in placing oneself under the law as a rule of life (Gal 3:1–5; Col 2:16–23; 1 Tim 1:3–7). Walvoord comments on the danger of confusing law and grace:

> One of the serious errors of the covenant theologians is their disregard of the essentially legal and non-gracious rule provided by the Mosaic Covenant. The New Testament in no uncertain terms describes it as a ministry of death and condemnation, and it is never described as a way of salvation.... It is hard to reconcile such a

theory to the direct statement of Scripture that "the law was given by Moses, but grace and truth came by Jesus Christ" (John 1:17). According to Galatians 2:16, justification is impossible by the law. Paul denounced this concept as a perversion of the gospel (Gal 1:7–9) which deserved the severest condemnation. If the Mosaic law could provide salvation, then it was a salvation by religious works and not of faith. Such a viewpoint does violence to the pure grace of God provided in Christ.[39]

As I have previously shown, the new covenant is a grant covenant and, as such, is unconditional and gracious.[40] However, the Mosaic covenant is a suzerainty covenant, and, therefore, is conditional and obedience-oriented. These two covenants are very different in form and purpose and must not be confused. Now, let us consider the scriptural evidence that the Mosaic covenant is temporary and has come to and end.

Scriptural Evidence

Romans 7:1–6. In Rom 7:1–6 Paul formulates an analogy based on the law concerning marriage. Paul explains in Rom 7:1–3 that a married woman who joined herself to another would be an adulteress, but, if her husband were to die, she would be free to remarry. This illustrates the principle of Rom 7:1 that "the law has jurisdiction over a person as long as he lives." Paul's purpose in mentioning this legal principle is to show that we, through our union with Christ in His death, "were made to die to the Law through the body of Christ" (Rom 7:4). Consequently, Paul concludes that "we have been released (καταργέω) from the Law, having died to that by which we were bound" (Rom 7:6). The Greek καταργέω is defined as

> from the basic sense *cause to be idle* or *useless*, the term always denotes a nonphysical destruction by means of a superior force coming in to replace the force previously in effect, as, e.g. light destroys darkness ... as release by removal from a former sphere of control *free from*; passive *be discharged from, be freed from* ... as destruction by replacement *abolish, destroy, cause to cease, put an end to*....[41]

Joseph H. Thayer agrees and defines καταργέω as

> *to render idle, unemployed, inactive, inoperative* ... to deprive of its strength, make barren ... to cause a person or a thing to have no further efficiency; to deprive of force, influence, power.... *to cause to cease, put an end to, do away with, annul, abolish*....[42]

Bauer, Arndt, and Gingrich also define καταργέω as

to cause someth[ing] to lose its power or effectiveness, *invalidate, make power-less*.... to cause someth[ing] to come to an end or to be no longer in existence, *abolish, wipe out, set aside*.... to cause the release of someone from an obligation ... *be discharged, be released*.[43]

Therefore, Rom 7:6 teaches that the law of Moses is abolished in that it is inoperative or useless, being deprived of force, influence, and power.

Romans 10:4. Paul writes to the Romans, "For Christ is the end of the law for righteousness to everyone who believes (τέλος γὰρ νόμου Χριστὸς εἰς δικαιοσύνην παντὶ τῷ πιστεύοντι)" (Rom 10:4). The Greek word γὰρ ("for") indicates that Rom 10:4 is the reason for Paul's statement in Rom 10:3 that those who sought to establish their own righteousness were not subjecting themselves to the righteousness of God. The Greek word τέλος comes first in this verse for emphasis and is central to the understanding of this verse.

Τέλος has been explained as either "end" or "goal." The meaning of "goal" would possibly avoid the implication of the cessation of the Mosaic covenant. Henry Alford explains τέλος as "the object at which the law aimed."[44] He then referred to 1 Tim 1:5, which is the only verse in the NT in which τέλος has the meaning of "goal." However, Friberg defines τέλος as "an action *achievement, carrying out, fulfillment* ... a closing act *end, termination, cessation* ... as a goal toward which movement is being directed *outcome, end (result), purpose*...."[45] Bauer, Arndt, and Gingrich agree and define τέλος as "a point of time marking the end of a duration, *end, termination, cessation*.... the last part of a process, *close, conclusion*.... the goal toward which a movement is being directed, *end, goal, outcome*...."[46] Thayer also defines τέλος as "*end*, i.e. **a.** *termination, the limit* at which a thing ceases to be.... *the end* i.e. *the last in any succession or series*.... *that by which a thing is finished*, its *close, issue*.... *the end to which all things relate, the aim, purpose*...."[47] In each case, the least likely meaning has been that of "goal" or "aim." The basic range of meaning seems to involve "end," "termination," "cessation," "close," and "conclusion." Even in the subsidiary meanings of "achievement," "fulfillment," and "goal," the meaning is "*that by which a thing is finished*." Thayer cites Rom 10:4 as an example of the meaning "*termination, the limit* at which a thing ceases to be." As Lenski comments, "Τέλος is not aim, object, or fulfillment; it is 'end,' finish, windup."[48] Even the Vulgate translates τέλος as *finis*. Therefore, the normal way to define τέλος is as an end, termination, conclusion, or cessation.

The papyrus evidence supports this conclusion. Moulton and Milligan cite several examples of τέλος from the papyri:

> P Eleph I[12] (B.C. 311–0) (=*Selections*, p. 3) ἐγ δίκης κατὰ νόμον τέλος ἐξούσης, "as if a formal decree of the court had been obtained,"....
>   P. Tebt I 14[8] (B.C. 114) μέχρι δὲ τοῦ τὸ προκείμενον ἐπὶ τέλος ἀχθῆναι, "until the matter was concluded" (Edd.), P Oxy IV. 724[9] (A.D. 155) ἐπὶ τέλει τοῦ χρονου, *ib.* VIII. 1128[20] (A.D. 173) ἐπὶ τέλει ἑκαστοῦ ἐνιαυτοῦ, "at the end of each year," *ib.* XIV. 1694[23] (a lease—A.D. 280) ἐπὶ τέλει τοῦ χρονοῦ....[49]

Please note the similarities between Rom 10:4 and these papyri. In the first instance we have τέλος and νόμος together in the phrase "ἐγ δίκης κατὰ νόμον τέλος ἐξούσης," referring to the conclusion of a legal matter. I would translate this instance literally, "As if concerning the legal case an end (or conclusion) had been obtained." Τέλος is used with the genitive in the sense of "end" or "conclusion": "μέχρι δὲ τοῦ ... ἐπὶ τέλος," "ἐπὶ τέλει τοῦ χρονου," and "ἐπὶ τέλει ἑκαστοῦ ἐνιαυτοῦ." Therefore, I conclude that it is highly probable that we should understand τέλος as meaning "end," "termination," "cessation," or "conclusion."[50]

There has been some considerable discussion over the phrase "of the law" (νόμου). Lenski comments that

> the emphasis is on the predicate which is placed forward, "an end of law," both nouns are anarthous: everything in the nature of law, including, of course, the Mo-saic law, but also all use made of law by moralists of any kind for attaining right-eousness before God, has been brought to an "end" by Christ....[51]

Denney states that "νόμου without the article is 'law' in the widest sense; the Mosaic law is only one of the most important instances which come under this description; and it, with all statutory conceptions of religion, ends when Christ appears."[52] However, Colwell's rule as normally understood would in-dicate that νόμου should be taken as definite even though anarthous.[53] There-fore, the NASB and all of the other English, German, French, and Spanish translations that I surveyed, with the sole exception of Young, translate νόμου as "of the law," thus indicating the law of Moses. As Alford comments, "νόμου is here plainly *the law of Moses*."[54] Even through he modifies Colwell's rule, Daniel B. Wallace still ranks Rom 10:4 as an instance of a definite anarthous predicate nominative.[55] These details, in conjunction with the immediate context which concerns the law of Moses, lead me to agree with the common translation of νόμου as "of the law," i.e., of the law of

Moses.

The phrase "for righteousness" (εἰς δικαιοσύνην) may be taken as either an εἰς of reference or of result.[56] If it is an εἰς of reference, the meaning would be that "Christ is the termination of the law with reference to righteousness" (Rom 10:4 my translation). However, this leads to two questions: First, does this indicate that the law was once a means of righteousness? Paul has been clear in such verses as Rom 3:19–21; 4:1–16; Gal 3:10–12 that no one ever was or will be justified by the law. In Gal 3:12 Paul quotes the same verse (Lev 18:5) that he does in Rom 10:5. The point that he is making in both contexts is that, because all sin and fall short of God's law, there is no one who is righteousness by law (Gal 3:10, cf. Jas 2:10). Second, if Christ is the "termination of the law with reference to righteousness to all that believe" (Rom 10:4 my translation), is there perhaps some group, other than believers, for whom the law would be for righteousness? Schreiner writes that

> the words "to everyone who believes" support the idea that in verse 4 Paul does not make a global statement on the relationship between gospel and law. Christ is not the end of using the law for righteousness for all people. Verse 3 demonstrates that some Jews wrongly try to use the law for their own righteousness. Thus, verse 4 claims that only those who believe, who trust in Christ for their righteousness, cease trying to use the law to establish their own righteousness.[57]

Everett F. Harrison also comments that "Paul adds a certain qualification to the statement about Christ as the end of the law for righteousness. He is that 'for everyone who believes.' This seems to suggest that the law is still applicable to those who do not believe."[58] Please note that neither Schreiner nor Harrison is saying that the law of Moses justifies anyone. Schreiner is referring to the misuse of the law and Harrison is referring to the condemning work of the law. However, in neither of these senses can one truly say that the law is "with reference to righteousness." Paul is in fact making a global statement that applies to the particular instance of those that sought to establish their own righteousness.

The other possibility, that it is an εἰς of result, solves many of these problems. The translation would then be, "Christ is the end of the law so that there may be righteousness for everyone who believes" (Rom 10:4 NIV).[59] This would fit well with Pauline theology. The termination of the Mosaic covenant and the establishment of the new covenant do have the result that there is "righteousness for everyone who believes." This also answers the misguided attempt to establish one's own righteousness. Therefore, I think that, in this case, the NIV translation is to be preferred. Thus, Rom 10:4 should be translated, "For Christ is the termination of the law [of Moses] so that [there might be] righteousness for all who trust" (my translation). Thus, Rom 10:4 teaches the cessation or termination of the Mosaic covenant.[60]

2 Corinthians 3:7–11. In 2 Cor 3:7–11 Paul contrasts the glory of the law of Moses with the new covenant. When Paul refers to "the ministry of death, in letters engraved on stones" (2 Cor 3:7), there can be no doubt that he means the tablets of the testimony of the Mosaic covenant. He acknowledges that the Mosaic law has a glory, but it is fading just like the divine light on Moses' face (2 Cor 3:7 cf. Exod 34:29–35). Paul concludes, "For if that which fades away *was* with glory, much more that which remains *is* in glory (εἰ γὰρ τὸ καταργούμενον διὰ δόξης, πολλῷ μᾶλλον τὸ μένον ἐν δόξῃ)" (2 Cor 3:11). This is a first class condition in the Greek. Therefore, Paul's "if" does not express any doubt, rather he is assuming the truth of the statement. Young brings out the meaning of καταργέω, translating, "For if that which is being made useless *is* through glory, much more that which is remaining *is* in glory" (2 Cor 3:11 YLT). Schreiner comments that

> Paul contrasts the two covenants here, asserting that one is "passing away" while the other is permanent. The word for "passing away" (καταργούμενου, *katargoumenou*) [*sic*] must refer to the temporary nature of the Mosaic covenant, in comparison with the new covenant "which remains" (μένον, *menon*). Paul evidently has constructed an antithesis in which one covenant is said to remain forever, while the other (the Mosaic) is coming to an end.[61]

The law of Moses in general and especially the Ten Commandments are "being made useless." They are of a temporary nature. The new covenant is "that which is remaining."

This passage has strong implications for those who hold the doctrine of the third use of the law. Frequently they narrow their definition of the law down to the Ten Commandments. However, Ryrie explains that

> in some ways this passage is stronger, because it is more particular. Here the comparison is made between what was ministered through Moses and what is ministered through Christ. That which Moses ministered is called a ministration of death and it is specifically said to have been written and engraven in stones. What was so written? The Ten Commandments, of course. Thus, this passage declares that the Ten Commandments are a ministration of death. Furthermore, Paul says that they are done away (v. 11), and this specifically applies to the Ten Commandments. Lan-

guage could not be clearer, and yet there are fewer truths of which it is harder to convince people. Any argument that it is not right or safe to take the Ten Commandments away from people must be directed to Paul and ultimately to the Holy Spirit, who superintended the writing of this passage.[62]

Fruchtenbaum comments:

> In verses three and seven the spotlight is on the Ten Commandments since it is these which were *engraven on stones*. The main point then is that the Law of Moses, especially as represented by the Ten Commandments, is a "ministration of death" and a "ministration of condemnation." If the Ten Commandments were still in force today, this would still be true. However, they are no longer in force, for it states in verses seven and eleven that the law has "passed away." The Greek word used is *katargeo*, which means "to render inoperative." Since the emphasis in this passage is on the Ten Commandments, this means that the Ten Commandments have passed away. The thrust is very clear. The Law of Moses, and especially the Ten Commandments, is no longer in effect.[63]

It is precisely the Ten Commandments that have been discontinued. Therefore, any attempt to reintroduce them as a rule of life is a serious mistake.

Galatians 3:19–4:7. In Gal 3:6–18 Paul makes three main points. Paul explains to the Galatians that Abraham was justified by faith (Gal 3:6–9). Then he demonstrates that the law brings only a curse since no one keeps it (Gal 3:10–14). Finally, he explains that the law of Moses did not set aside the Abrahamic covenant (Gal 3:15–18). This gives rise to the natural question, "Why the Law then?" (Gal 3:19). Paul answers, "It was added because of transgressions." Then the passage proceeds to explain the second use of the law (Gal 3:19–4:7). However, in so doing, Paul mentions a temporal aspect to the existence of the law in Gal 3:19.

Paul writes that the law had been added "*until* (ἄχρι) the seed would come to whom the promise had been made" (Gal 3:19 emphasis mine). Galatians 3:16 clarifies that the seed referred to is Christ. The conjunction ἄχρι seems to normally be temporal with rare exceptions such as Acts 28:15 where it is spatial. It is generally to be translated "until," and occasionally "as long as" (e.g., Heb 3:13). Friberg defines it "as a conjunction expressing time up to a point *until*...."[64] Thayer calls ἄχρι "a particle indicating the terminus ad quem."[65] Thus, Paul establishes the coming of Christ as the *terminus ad quem* of the law of Moses.

Next, Paul uses an illustration from Roman life to explain the change in salvation history from life under the law to faith in Christ (Gal 3:24–4:7). Paul speaks of the law as a "tutor (παιδαγωγὸς)" (Gal 3:24). The παιδαγωγὸς ("literally *boy leader*, a trusted attendant who supervised the conduct and morals of a boy before he came of age *guardian, trainer, instructor....*"[66]) was the slave who led the child to his lessons. This custom is familiar not only in Greco-Roman society, but also in Jewish culture. The *Midrash Exodus Rabbah* 21.8 (R. Absalom?); 42.9 (R. Nahman? ca. 4th century AD), by means of haggadah, refers to Moses as Israel's pedagogue (פדגוג, a loan word from the Greek, παιδαγωγὸς). Although the midrash does not refer to the law as a pedagogue explicitly, Moses may well be metonymy for the law of Moses as in 2 Cor 3:15. Schreiner observes that

> the word *pedagogue* is used for temporal reasons in Galatians 3:23–25. One who was still "under a pedagogue" had not yet grown up. Paul's intention here is to make a salvation-historical point. Now that Christ has come the pedagogue is no longer needed....
>
> Pedagogues, guardians, and managers, therefore, are appropriate illustrations since they contrast childhood with adulthood.... He uses these words to stress that the law was not intended to be in force forever. It has a temporal limit in salvation history.[67]

Since he is under a slave's authority, the heir is no better than a slave (Gal 4:1–3). However, with the coming of Christ at the "fullness of time" (Gal 4:4), we are no longer "children (νήπιος)" (Gal 4:3), but have received the "adoption as sons (υἱοθεσία)" (Gal 4:5). The Greek νήπιος is "a very young child *infant....*"[68] The Greek υἱοθεσία ("adoption") is from υἱός ("mature son") and θέσις ("placing"). All of this serves to confirm that "now that faith is come, we are no longer under a tutor" (Gal 3:25).

Some have sought to identify the problem that Paul is addressing in Galatians 3 as legalism, not the law of Moses. Schreiner criticizes this position arguing that it does not explain the abolition of circumcision. Schreiner also notes that Paul uses the term "law" and not "legalism." He argues that, since the word law in Gal 3:17, 19, 21 must refer to the law of Moses, the law of Moses is in view in Gal 3:15–25 not legalism.[69] Paul is not merely arguing that legalism is wrong. He is teaching that the Mosaic covenant has passed away.

Ephesians 2:14–16. Paul asks the Ephesian Gentiles to remember their condition before Christ (Eph 2:11–12). They were the uncircumcision, separate from Christ, excluded from Israel, strangers to the covenants of promise, without hope and without God. Now God brings these Gentiles into a new relationship by virtue of union with Christ (Eph 2:13). The Church, the body of Christ, makes both Jew and Gentile into one body (Eph 2:14). Christ accomplishes this by breaking down the barrier between the groups. Ryrie notes that the dividing wall is "an allusion to the wall which separated the Court of the Gentiles from the Court of the Jews in the Temple. An inscription warned Gentiles of the death penalty for going beyond it."[70] Christ "broke down the barrier of the dividing wall by abolishing (καταργέω) in His flesh the enmity" (Eph 2:14–15). The enmity of which Paul speaks is clarified as "the Law of commandments contained in ordinances" (Eph 2:15).[71] As I have demonstrated above, the use of the Greek verb καταργέω means that the law of Moses is abolished in that it is inoperative or useless being deprived of force, influence, and power. In Eph 2:16 Paul restates that, by means of the cross, Christ has put to death the enmity. Since Eph 2:15 equates the enmity and "the Law of commandments contained in ordinances," this is equivalent to saying that Christ by the cross put the law of Moses to death.

Colossians 2:13–14. In a passage reminiscent of Eph 2:14–16, Paul reminds the Colossians that, although they were dead in their "transgressions and … uncircumcision" (Col 2:13), God forgave them and made them alive in union with Christ. This forgiveness is accomplished by having "canceled out (ἐξαλείφω) the certificate of debt consisting of decrees against us and which was hostile to us (καθ' ἡμῶν χειρόγραφον τοῖς δόγμασιν ὃ ἦν ὑπεναντίον ἡμῖν)" (Col 2:14). The Greek ἐξαλείφω is defined as "of a written record *do away with, erase* … of a record of misdeeds *remove, elimi-nate….*"[72] Thayer defines χειρόγραφον as

> *a handwriting; what one has written with his own hand* … specifically, a note of hand, or writing in which one acknowledges that money has either been deposited with him or lent to him by another, to he returned at an appointed time … *meta-phorically, applied in Col. 2:14 … to the Mosaic law, which shews men to be chargeable with offenses for which they must pay the penalty* (emphasis mine).[73]

F. F. Bruce observes the similarity to Eph 2:15 and its implications:

> One must also take account of the dative τοῖς δόγμασιν attached to χειρόγραφον. This writer has translated this as a dative of accompaniment: "the bond, *ordinances and all*".... This takes τοῖς δόγμασιν in the same sense as the par-

allel ἐν δόγμασιν in Ephesians 2:15. But if the words are rendered "ordinances and all" or "consisting of ordinances," is this not equating the bond with the Law itself? Yes. There is no doubt a natural reluctance to think of the Law itself as being blotted out by God; but one must remember the different ways in which Paul speaks of the Law of God.... Those who undertook to observe the Law either as a means of getting right with God or as the way to higher attainment in spiritual experience soon found that the Law, instead of helping them, bore witness against them....

The canceled bond of Colossians 2:14, then, seems to be the Law, bearing witness against those who tried to use it as the way to justification or sanctification. Its cancellation is expressed in two figures: it has been blotted out, and it has been nailed to the cross.[74]

Here, as in Eph 2:15, the cross is shown to be the *terminus ad quem* of the law of Moses.

Hebrews 7:11–18. In Hebrews 7–8 the author makes a case for the priesthood of the Messiah. The argument centers on the similarities between Jesus and the OT character Melchizedek (Heb 7:1–10) and the promise of a Melchizedekan priesthood made to David (Ps 110:4). Psalms 110 is a Psalm of David, and our Lord Jesus quoted it as messianic in Matt 22:41–46. This Psalm teaches that Messiah will be both a king (Ps 110:1–3, 5–6) and a priest (Ps 110:4). Ryrie observes, "Verse 1 refers to the present position of Christ sharing the Father's kingly authority; verse 2, to His rule on earth during the millennial kingdom."[75] The talmudic sages sought to avoid the troubling implications of Ps 110:4 of a priesthood that rivaled the Aaronic priesthood:

R. Zechariah said on R. Ishmael's [ca. 2nd century AD] authority: The Holy One, blessed be He, intended to bring forth the priesthood from Shem, as it is written, And he [sc. Melchizedek] was the priest of the most high God. But because he gave precedence in his blessing to Abraham over God, He brought it forth from Abraham; as it is written, And he blessed him and said. Blessed be Abram of the most high God, possessor of heaven and earth, and blessed be the most high God. Said Abraham to him, 'Is the blessing of a servant to be given precedence over that of his master?' Straightway it [the priesthood] was given to Abraham, as it is written, The Lord said unto my Lord, Sit thou at my right hand, until I make thine enemies thy footstool; which is followed by, The Lord hath sworn, and will not repent, Thou art a priest for ever, after the order of Melchizedek,' meaning, 'because of the words of Melchizedek.' Hence it is written, And he was a priest of the most High God, [implying that] he was a priest, but not his seed.[76]

However, the clear implication of Ps 110:4 is that the Messiah will be a priest, but not of the order of Aaron.

The author of Hebrews demonstrates that, if the Mosaic covenant were still in effect, Jesus would be disqualified from being a priest. Jesus, as a descendant of David, was from the tribe of Judah, not from the tribe of Levi (Heb 7:13–14). Since the Levitical priesthood was part of the Mosaic covenant, a change in the priesthood meant "a change (μετάθεσις) of law" (Heb 7:12). The Greek μετάθεσις is defined as "figuratively *changeover* from one state or institution to another, *transformation, change.*"[77] Hebrews 7:18 speaks of "setting aside (ἀθέτησις)" the commandments. The terms "law" and "commandment" refer to the stipulations of the Mosaic covenant. Therefore, they are a synecdoche for the Mosaic covenant in this passage. Friberg notes that ἀθέτησις is "a legal technical term *annulment, setting aside* as being no longer in force...."[78] Nowhere in this passage does it say that only the ceremonial law has been abolished. The law is a unit and, therefore, the entire law must change.[79] Ryrie agrees and observes that

> the writer concludes that if the Levitical priesthood could have brought perfection to the people, there would not have been a need for the Melchizedek priesthood (v. 11). "For the priesthood being changed, there is made of necessity a change also of the law" (v. 12). If the priests of Levi could satisfy, we would not need Christ. And if we need Christ, we must have a Melchizedekan order of priests, for Christ being of the tribe of Judah could never qualify as a Levitical priest. And when the priesthood is changed there is of necessity a change made of the law. Thus if the law has not been done away today, then neither has the Levitical priesthood; and, if this be true, Christ is not our high priest. But if Christ is our high priest, we cannot be under law. Every time we pray in the name of Christ we are affirming that the Mosaic Law is done away.[80]

The case of King Uzziah is instructive. Uzziah was of the Davidic line but was struck with leprosy when he attempted to usurp the priestly office (2 Chr 26:16–21). However, if the Mosaic covenant has its *terminus ad quem* at the death of Christ, then there is no hindrance to Christ exercising His priesthood. Thus, the present high priestly ministry of Christ is another evidence for the abolition of the Mosaic covenant.

Hebrews 8:7–13. After presenting his argument that the change in the priesthood has necessitated setting aside the Mosaic covenant, the author of Hebrews argues that this change of covenant was predicted by Jeremiah's prophecy of the new covenant (Jer 31:31–34). The author of Hebrews quotes all of Jer 31:31–34 in Heb 8:8–12. He apparently considers it self-explanatory, since he adds only one verse to the beginning and one to the end of the quote. The first point that he makes is that the Mosaic covenant was deficient. This is not in contradiction to Paul, who teaches that "the Law is holy, and the commandment is holy and righteous and good" (Rom 7:12). The deficiency of the law was the inability of sinful human beings to keep it (Rom 8:3). The establishment of the new covenant remedied this deficiency. This strongly indicates that the new covenant is not just a restatement of the Mosaic covenant. It is not a renewal of the old covenant, it is a new covenant.

The second point that the author of Hebrews makes is that speaking of a new covenant makes the Mosaic covenant obsolete (Heb 8:13). Therefore, the Mosaic covenant is disappearing, "When He said, 'A new covenant,' He has made the first obsolete (πεπαλαίωκεν). But whatever is becoming obsolete (παλαιούμενον) and growing old is ready to disappear" (Heb 8:13). The phrase "made ... obsolete" (πεπαλαίωκεν) in Heb 8:13a is the perfect active indicative of παλαιόω ("*make old, declare* or *treat as obsolete*"[81]). The use of the perfect tense indicates that the first covenant (i.e., the Mosaic covenant) has from the author's point of view been made obsolete in the past with the result that it now stands obsolete in the present. However, the phrase "becoming obsolete" (παλαιούμενον) in Heb 8:13b is a present passive participle. Is the author saying that the Mosaic covenant has been made obsolete or is he saying that it is becoming obsolete? The answer is that Heb 8:13b states a general principle that whatever is becoming obsolete and growing old is ready to disappear. The author has already told us in Heb 8:13a that the law has been "made ... obsolete." In syllogistic form, the author is arguing:

- All that is obsolete disappears.
- The Mosaic covenant has become obsolete
- Therefore, the Mosaic covenant has disappeared.

The logical conclusion that the author of Hebrews expects us to draw is that the Mosaic covenant has disappeared.

Matthew 5:17–19. Matthew 5:17–19 is often cited in an attempt to prove that the law of Moses is still in force. Jesus says, "Do not think that I came to abolish the Law or the Prophets; I did not come to abolish but to fulfill (Μὴ νομίσητε ὅτι ἦλθον καταλῦσαι τὸν νόμον ἢ τοὺς προφήτας· οὐκ ἦλθον καταλῦσαι ἀλλὰ πληρῶσαι)" (Matt 5:17). The phrase "do not think" (Μὴ νομίσητε) is a prohibitive subjunctive. Wallace explains that "this is the use of the subjunctive in a prohibition.... It is used to forbid the occurrence of an action."[82] Colloquially, we might say, "Don't even think it!" The word "that" (ὅτι) is a declarative ὅτι. The word "abolish" (καταλύω) is defined as having

> the basic sense *put down, loosen*, various meanings are derived ... literally, of buildings with their stones *destroy, demolish, dismantle* ... opposite οἰκοδομέω (*build*) ... figuratively, as invalidating an institution, such as law or sacrifice *do away with, annul, abolish*....[83]

Wallace observes that "this summarizes the views of Jesus' opponents. The supposed direct discourse would have been, 'He has come to destroy the law.'"[84] Keener explains that "Jewish teachers said that one 'abolished' the law by disobeying it (cf. Deut 27:26), because one thereby rejected its authority. Such highhanded rebellion against the law—as opposed to particular sins—warranted social and spiritual expulsion from the Jewish community."[85] The word "but" (ἀλλὰ) is a contrastive conjunction.[86] In contrast to abolishing the law and the prophets, Jesus asserts that He has come to "fulfill" (πληρόω) them. In Matthew πληρόω is used fairly consistently of prophetic fulfillment. The key is that Christ fulfills both *the law and the prophets*. This points toward prophetic fulfillment. A close parallel is Matt 26:56 that reads, "*Fulfill* the Scriptures *of the prophets*" (emphasis mine). In Matt 11:13 Jesus says, "For all *the prophets and the Law* prophesied until John" (emphasis mine). In Luke 24:44 Jesus states, "All things which are written about Me in *the Law of Moses and the Prophets* and the Psalms must be *fulfilled*" (emphasis mine). In this verse we have all three divisions of the Hebrew Scriptures mentioned: the law (*Torah*), the prophets (*Neviʾim*), and Psalms as a synecdoche for all of the writings (*Ketuvim*)—the entire *Tanak*. Phillip tells Nathanael that Jesus of Nazareth is He "of whom Moses in *the Law and also the Prophets* wrote" (John 1:45 emphasis mine). Jesus did not abolish the Hebrew Scriptures, rather He fulfilled all that they contained about Him.

Of course, in His sinless life, Jesus also "fulfilled all righteousness" (Matt 3:15). However, Jesus' life did not end the law of Moses. His death did. Matt 5:17–19 was uttered during His life when He was obligated to fulfill all of the Mosaic law. Fruchtenbaum notes that even Jesus in Mark 7:19, implies the abolition of the dietary laws.[87] With the destruction of the temple the Jews abandoned sacrificial law, as it states in *Midrash Deuteronomy*

Rabbah (R. Simeon ben Halafta (?), ca. 2nd century AD):

> This bears out what the Scripture says, To do righteousness and justice is more acceptable to the Lord than sacrifice (Prov. XXI, 3). Scripture does not say, As much as sacrifice, but 'More than sacrifice'. How? *Sacrifices were operative only so long as the Temple stood*, but righteousness and justice held good during the time when the Temple stood and also hold good now when the Temple is no longer (emphasis mine).[88]

Covenant theologians would abolish the dietary laws, ceremonial laws, and circumcision. Many would restrict the meaning of the law to the Ten Commandments, but even there, they would change the Sabbath. Thus, out of six hundred and thirteen commandments, they would retain nine or 1.47%. Fruchtenbaum criticizes such thinking, "Such lofty statements break down when one comes to specifics and, in practice, none of the claimants really believe it.... This is wishful thinking at best and sloppy exegesis at worst. This is trying to prove a theology by ignoring the details."[89] Taken as a statement that the law of Moses remains in force, Matt 5:17 proves too much. In fact, those that are most zealous for the law have abandoned a lot of jots and tittles along the way.

Jesus says, "For truly I say to you, until heaven and earth pass away, not the smallest letter or stroke shall pass from the Law until all is accomplished" (Matt 5:18). The phrase "not... shall pass (οὐ μὴ παρέλθῃ)" is an emphatic negation. Wallace notes that "emphatic negation is indicated by οὐ μὴ plus the aorist subjunctive.... This is the strongest way to negate something in Greek.... οὐ μὴ rules out even the idea as being a possibility...."[90] Law may well be a synecdoche for the entire Scriptures. In this case, it is highly significant that Christ mentions the new heaven and new earth. The new heaven and new earth are among the last things fulfilled in the prophetic Scriptures (Isa 65:17; 66:22; Rev 21:1). If Jesus means this saying to endorse the view of the eternal validity of the law of Moses, then why would He say "until all is accomplished," and not "forever." However, if He is referring to prophetic fulfillment of all the Scriptures, it makes perfect sense.

Matthew 5:18 speaks to the inspiration and preservation of the Scriptures. Rabbinical sources also attest to the view that each letter is important. In *Midrash Leviticus Rabbah* we find:

> R. Ze'era [ca. 3rd century AD] said:... Even those things in the Torah which appear [useless], for instance the thin strokes [of letters] (kozin), are taltale taltalim, [i.e. mounds upon mounds], meaning they have it in their power to bring about the

destruction of the world and make it into a mound (tel), as it is said, And it shall be a heap (tel) forever; it shall not be built again (Deut. XIII, 17).

It is written, Hear, O Israel, the Lord our God, the Lord is One—ehad (Deut. VI, 4); if you make [the letter] daleth into [the letter] resh [אחר ("strange") instead of אחד ("one")] you cause the destruction of the whole of the Universe.

It is written, For thou shalt bow down to no other god (Ex. XXXIV, 14). If you change the resh into a daleth [אחד ("after") instead of אחר ("other")], you bring as a result destruction upon the world.

It is written, And ye shall not profane (tahallelu) My holy name; if you make the letter heth into the letter he [לא תהללו ("you shall not praise") instead of לא תחללו ("you shall not profane")] you bring as a result destruction upon the world.

It is written, Let everything that hath breath praise (tehallel) the Lord, Hallelu-jah (Ps. CL, 6). If you make the letter he into the letter heth [תחלל ("shall profane God") instead of תהלל "shall praise God"] you bring as a result destruction upon the world.

It is written, They have acted deceptively against the Lord (Jer. V, 12). If you make the letter beth into a kap [כה ("like the Lord") instead of בה ("against the Lord")] you bring as a result destruction upon the world.

It is written, They have dealt treacherously against the Lord (Hosea V, 7). If you make the letter beth into a kaf [כיהוה "as the Lord" instead of ביהוה ("against the Lord")], you bring, as a result, destruction upon the world.

It is written, There is none holy as the Lord (X Sam. II, 2). If you make the let-ter kaf into a beth [בה ("there is nothing holy in the Lord") instead of כה ("as the Lord")], you bring as a result destruction upon the world.[91]

Keener notes that

later rabbis told the story that when God changed Sarai's name to Sarah, the *yod* that was removed complained to God for generations till he reinserted it, this time in Joshua's name. Jewish teachers used illustrations like this to make the point that the law was sacred and one could not regard any part as too small to be worth keeping.[92]

Jesus is expressing the highest regard for the Scriptures.

Finally, Jesus teaches that "whoever then annuls one of the least of these commandments, and teaches others *to do* the same, shall be called least in the kingdom of heaven; but whoever keeps and teaches *them*, he shall be called great in the kingdom of heaven" (Matt 5:19). Please note that one's relation-ship to the commandments is not determinative of one's salvation, but of one's standing in the kingdom. Therefore, I take Matt 5:19 as referring to eternal rewards.[93] At the time that Jesus said this, the Mosaic covenant was still in force and one's rewards would be determined by one's relationship to the law of Moses. However, with the abolition of the Mosaic covenant, now

one's fulfillment of the law of Christ determines one's rewards. Paul writes
to the Corinthians that, in order to gain an audience with Jewish people, he
became "as under the Law, though not being myself under the Law" (1 Cor
9:20–21). Paul proceeds to explain that he is "not ... without the law of God
(ἄνομος θεοῦ) but under the law of Christ (ἔννομος Χριστοῦ)" (1 Cor 9:21).
Fruchtenbaum notes that Covenant Theologians who quote this text are not
consistent with it. Although they use differing terminology, they all clearly
believe that some of the 613 commandments have been done away with.
However, Matt 5:19 adds the phrase "the least of these commandments"
which surely includes all 613 commandments.[94] Therefore, Christ is saying
that He holds the entire Scriptures in the highest regard and would never destroy any of them in the slightest. He is teaching the verbal plenary inspiration of the Scriptures, their preservation, and fulfillment in total. He teaches
that our position in the kingdom will depend on the reaction to God's revealed will.[95] At the time of the Sermon on the Mount, that standard was the
law of Moses. It no longer is (see figure 2).

Type of Covenant	Stipulations of Covenant	Beneficiaries	Established	End
Suzerainty	613 commandments Talmud and Maimonides: • 365 negative commands • 248 positive commands Philo: • 10 general commands • 603 specific commands consisting of: • Apodictic law: "You shall / You shall not…" • Case law: "If / When…"	Israel	At Mount Sinai (Mount Horeb) mediated by Moses (Exod 20–24) Renewed by: • Moses (Exod 34) • Moses (Deut 1–28) • Joshua (Josh 24:24–25) • King Asa (2 Chr 15:9–15) • King Jehoiada (2 Kgs 11:17; 2 Chr 23:16) • King Hezekiah (2 Chr 29:10) • King Josiah (2 Kgs 23:1–3; 2 Chr 34:31–32)	The Mosaic covenant ended with the death of Christ (Rom 7:1–6; 10:4; 2 Cor 3:7–11; Gal 3:19–4:7; Eph 2:14–16; Col 2:13–14; Heb 7:11–18; 8:7–13)

Table 11. Mosaic Covenant

NOTES

1. See Dyson Hague, "The History of the Higher Criticism," *The Fundamentals*, 4 vols. (Los Angeles: Bible Institute of Los Angeles, 1917; reprint, Grand Rapids, MI: Baker, 1998) 1:9–42; Geo. Fredrick Wright, "The Mosaic Authorship of the Pentateuch," *The Fundamentals* 1:43–54; Franklin Johnson, "Fallacies of the Higher Criticism," *The Fundamentals* 1:55–75; Josh D. McDowell, *The New Evidence that Demands a Verdict* (Nashville, TN: Nelson, 1999) 389–533; Norman L. Geisler, "Pentateuch, Mosaic Authorship of," *Baker Encyclopedia of Christian Apologetics* (Grand Rapids, MI: Baker, 1999) 586–88; Norman L. Geisler, "Redaction Criticism, Old Testament," *Baker Encyclopedia of Christian Apologetics* 635–38; Norman L. Geisler, "Wellhausen, Julius," *Baker Encyclopedia of Christian Apologetics* 769–71; and Gleason L. Archer, *A Survey of Old Testament Introduction*, rev. ed. (Chicago: Moody, 1994) 89–189.

2. Mendenhall, "Covenant," *IDB* 1:718–19.

3. Kline, *Structure* 43–4.

4. Hillers, *Covenant* 50.

5. Mendenhall, "Covenant," *IDB* 1:719–20. For a contrary opinion see McCarthy, *Treaty and Covenant* 243–76. He agrees that Exod 19–24 is covenantal, but disagrees that it is in the Hittite form.

6. Michael D. Guinan, "Mosaic Covenant," *ABD* 4:905–9.

7. Deere, *BKCOT* 260.

8. See chapter 2.

9. Lewis Sperry Chafer, *Systematic Theology* 1:43.

10. See chapters 8 and 10.

11. Charles Caldwell Ryrie, *The Grace of God: A Handbook of Bible Doctrine* (Chicago: Moody, 1963) 59.

12. *b. Makkot* 23b, *The Soncino Talmud*.

13. Moses Maimonides, *The 613 Commandments*, trans. Charles B. Chavel (Brooklyn, NY: Soncino, 1967). Maimonides' list of *Mitsvot* is available from Paul Halsall, ed., *Maimonides: The 613 Mitzvot* [list on-line], in *Internet Medieval Sourcebook* (New York: Fordham University, accessed 29 March 2002); available from http://www.fordham.edu/halsall/source/ rambam613.html; Internet.

14. Philo, *De specialibus legibus I* 1.1, in *The Works of Philo*, trans. C. D. Yonge, in The Master Christian Library ver. 8.0 [CD-ROM] (Albany, OR: AGES Software, 1997) 1219.

15. Fruchtenbaum, *Israelology* 641.

16. E. P. Sanders, "Law," *ABD* 4:242–65.

17. Roy L. Aldrich, "Has the Mosaic Law Been Abolished?" *BSac* 116, no. 464 (October–December 1959): 322–35.

18. Daniel B. Wallace, *Greek Grammar Beyond the Basics: An Exegetical Syntax of the*

New Testament with Scripture, Subject, and Greek Word Indexes (Grand Rapids, MI: Zondervan, 1996) 689–96.

19. Niehaus, *God at Sinai* 195–97.
20. Lewis Sperry Chafer, *Grace: The Glorious Theme* (Grand Rapids, MI: Zondervan, 1922) 115–16. Curiously, *Midr. Deut. Rab.* 7:10 is similar to Chafer's position. However, see Ryrie, *Dispensationalism* 110–11 for a different view.
21. Hillers, *Covenant* 55–57.
22. Niehaus, *God at Sinai* 197.
23. Hillers, *Covenant* 57.
24. See chapter 2.
25. An alternative view would be that the angel spoken of was the "angel of Yahweh" or the pre-incarnate Christ. See Irenaeus, *Adv. haer.* 4:12:4.
26. Much of the material in this section appeared as an article in *Bibliotheca Sacra* (Hal Harless, "The Cessation of the Mosaic Covenant," *Bibliotheca Sacra* 160, no. 639 [July–September 2003]: 349–66). I am grateful to *Bibliotheca Sacra* for permission to include it here.
27. Tertullian, *Against Marcion* 4.1, in *The Ante-Nicene Fathers*, 10 vols., trans. Peter Holmes, eds. Alexander Roberts, James Donaldson, in The Master Christian Library ver. 8.0 [CD-ROM] (Albany, OR: AGES Software, 1997) 3:624–25.
28. *b. Shabbat* 116a–b, *The Soncino Talmud*.
29. Berkhof, *Systematic Theology* 613–15.
30. Donald G. Bloesch, "Law and Gospel in Reformed Perspective," *GTJ* 12, no. 2 (Fall 1991): 179–88.
31. Lewis Sperry Chafer, "Soteriology," *BSac* 103, no. 411 (July–September 1946): 261–83.
32. Unger, "Law," *UBD* 646–47. See also Chafer, *Systematic Theology* 4:234–51.
33. Schreiner, *The Law* 123–43.
34. Ibid. 160–61.
35. Ibid. 177–78.
36. David A. Dorsey, "The Law of Moses and the Christian: A Compromise," *JETS* 34, no. 3 (September 1991): 321–34.
37. Aldrich, "A New Look at Dispensationalism" 48.
38. Berkhof, *Systematic Theology* 614–15.
39. Walvoord, *The Millennial Kingdom* 91.
40. See chapter 11.
41. *ALGNT* 221.
42. Joseph Henry Thayer, *Greek-English Lexicon of the New Testament being Grimm's Wilke's Clavis Novi Testamenti* (hereafter referred to as *GELNT*) (Grand Rapids, MI: Zondervan, 1962) 336.
43. *BDAG* 525–26.
44. Henry Alford, *Acts—I II Corinthians*, Alford's Greek Testament: An Exegetical and

Critical Commentary, 6 vols. (London: Rivingtons, 1874–5; reprint, Grand Rapids, MI: Guardian, 1976) 2:417.

45. *ALGNT* 377–78.

46. *BDAG* 998–99.

47. *GELNT* 619–20.

48. R. C. H. Lenski, *The Interpretation of St. Paul's Epistle to the Romans*, Commentary on the New Testament, 11 vols. (n.p.: Lutheran Book Concern, 1936; reprint, n.p.: Hendrickson, 1998) 6:645.

49. *MM* 630–31.

50. So also Schreiner, *The Law* 133–36. Although he agrees concerning the meaning of τέλος, Schreiner does differ as to the general applicability of this verse to the argument. I disagree and would assert that Paul is citing a general principle that explains Rom 10:3.

51. Lenski, *Romans* 6:645.

52. James Denney, "St. Paul's Epistle to the Romans," *Apostles, Romans, First Corinthians*, The Expositor's Greek Testament, ed. W. Robertson Nicoll, 5 vols. (Grand Rapids, MI: Eerdmans, 1990) 2:669.

53. Wallace, *Greek Grammar Beyond the Basics* 256–57.

54. Alford, *Acts—I II Corinthians* 2:417.

55. Wallace, *Greek Grammar Beyond the Basics* 257–70.

56. Wallace, *Greek Grammar Beyond the Basics* 369–71. See also H. E. Dana, Julius R. Mantey, *A Manual Grammar of the Greek New Testament* (n.p.: Macmillan, 1957) 103.

57. Schreiner, *The Law* 135–36.

58. Everett F. Harrison, "Romans," *Romans—Galatians*, EBC 10:111.

59. So also the RSV, "For Christ is the end of the law, that every one who has faith may be justified," NRSV, "For Christ is the end of the law so that there may be righteousness for everyone who believes," NLT, "All who believe in him are made right with God," JB, "so that all who have faith will be justified," Luther, "Denn Christus ist des Gesetzes Ende; wer an den glaubt, der ist gerecht," and Die Einheitsübersetzung, "Denn Christus ist das Ende des Gesetzes, und jeder, der an ihn glaubt, wird gerecht."

60. See Charles Caldwell Ryrie, "The End of the Law," *BSac* 124, no. 495 (July–September 1967): 239–47.

61. Schreiner, *The Law* 132.

62. Ryrie, *The Grace of God* 60–61.

63. Fruchtenbaum, *Israelology* 646.

64. *ALGNT* 85.

65. *GELNT* 91.

66. ALGNT 291.

67. Schreiner, *The Law* 79–80. See also Richard N. Longenecker, "The Pedagogical Na-

ture of the Law in Galatians 3:19–4:7," *JETS* 25, no. 1 (March 1982): 53–61, for a wealth of historical background.

68. *ALGNT* 271.

69. Schreiner, *The Law* 139–40.

70. Ryrie, *RSB* 1782.

71. Fruchtenbaum, *Israelology* 645

72. *ALGNT* 153. See also *MM* 687; Deissmann, *Light*, 333–34; and G. Adolf Deissmann, *Bible Studies: Contributions Chiefly from Papyri and Inscriptions to the History of the Language, the Literature, and the Religion of Hellenistic Judaism and Primitive Christianity*, trans. Alexander Grieve (Edinburgh: T. & T. Clark, 1901; reprint, Peabody, MA: Hendrickson, 1988) 247.

73. *GELNT* 668.

74. F. F. Bruce, "Colossian Problems—Part 4: Christ as Conqueror and Reconciler," *BSac* 141, no. 564 (October–December 1984): 291–301.

75. Ryrie, *RSB* 905.

76. *b. Nedarim* 32b, *The Soncino Talmud.*

77. *ALGNT* 260.

78. *ALGNT* 36.

79. Fruchtenbaum, *Israelology* 644–45.

80. Ryrie, *The Grace of God* 60.

81. *ALGNT* 292.

82. Wallace, *Greek Grammar Beyond the Basics* 469.

83. *ALGNT* 220.

84. Wallace, *Greek Grammar Beyond the Basics* 456.

85. Keener, *BBCNT* 57.

86. Wallace, *Greek Grammar Beyond the Basics* 671.

87. Fruchtenbaum, *Israelology* 648. See also Chafer, *Systematic Theology* 5:105–8.

88. *Midr. Deut. Rab.* 5:3, *The Soncino Midrash Rabbah* 5:103.

89. Fruchtenbaum, *Israelology* 640–41.

90. Wallace, *Greek Grammar Beyond the Basics* 468.

91. *Midr. Lev. Rab.* 19:2, *The Soncino Midrash Rabbah* 3:236–37.

92. Keener, *BBCNT* 57–8; cf. *b. Sanhedrin* 107a. See John Lightfoot, *Matthew — Mark, A commentary on the New Testament from the Talmud and Hebraica: Matthew — I Corinthians*, 4 vols. (Oxford: Oxford University Press, 1859; reprint, Grand Rapids, MI: Baker, 1979) 2:100–1.

93. See Dillow, *The Reign of the Servant Kings* 67–68.

94. Fruchtenbaum, *Israelology* 647–48.

95. See Dillow, *The Reign of the Servant Kings* 551–83.

PART THREE

The Dispensations in the Light of the Divine Covenants

CHAPTER THIRTEEN

The Dispensation of Innocence

Duration and Characteristics

Preliminary Observations Concerning Dispensations

Dispensationalists have not always agreed on the name and number of dispensations. Ryrie notes that:

> Occasionally a dispensationalist may hold to as few as four, and some hold as many as eight. The doctrinal statement of Dallas Theological Seminary (Article V) mentions only three by name (the Mosaic Law, the present dispensation of Grace, and the future dispensation of the Millennial Kingdom). Why is there this difference? Probably the answer lies in the fact that the three—Law, Grace, and Kingdom—are the subject of so much of the material in the Bible, whereas the others, however many there may be, are not.[1]

Ryrie goes on to express confidence that the remaining four dispensations may be deduced. The case has already been made very well for the seven-dispensation approach and need not be replicated here.[2]

Ryrie defines a dispensation as "*a distinguishable economy in the outworking of God's purpose.*"[3] There are two aspects to a dispensation. Ryrie explains that "a dispensation is from God's viewpoint an economy; from man's, a responsibility...."[4] This definition is in keeping with the Greek word οἰκονομία ("literally, relating to the task of an οἰκονόμος (*steward*) in household administration, *stewardship, management...*"[5]) that is translated "dispensation." Dispensations are descriptive both of God's administration and man's responsibility. However, what God is administering and man is responsible for are the covenantal stipulations that have been instituted at any given point. Dispensations are descriptive and the divine covenants are prescriptive. Therefore, the dispensations are covenantally driven.

Other elements such as testing, failure, judgment, and transitional periods may be observed, but do not define the dispensation. Thus, Ryrie's definition is to be preferred over Scofield's, "A dispensation is a period of time during which man is tested in respect of obedience to some specific revelation of the will of God."[6] The administration takes place during a period but is not synonymous with it. Along with responsibility comes the possibility of failure and with failure comes divine judgment. Therefore, it is not surprising that we will observe failure and judgment in conjunction with dispensations. However, these do not define the dispensations, they accompany them. We must distinguish between the definition of a dispensation and its ancillary features.

The Characteristics of the Dispensation of Innocence

The first commonly held dispensation is that of Innocence. Concerning the dispensation of innocence, it is sufficient to note with Ryrie that "before the fall of man the arrangement was certainly distinguishably different from that after the Fall."[7] Ryrie prefers to describe the dispensation of innocence as unconfirmed creaturely holiness, but notes that is too long to be a good name for a dispensation. He notes that this dispensation is characterized by humankind's condition of freedom from sin before the fall. Ryrie observes that the key person in this dispensation was Adam, who failed the test of not eating the fruit. God judged humankind but also made the first promise of a Redeemer. The Scriptures concerning this dispensation are recorded in Genesis 1:28–3:6.[8] God administered the pre-fall world with only one rule, a perfect environment, and two perfect humans. This dispensation would test humankind in a perfect environment.

The Duration of the Dispensation of Innocence

Dispensations are not identical to ages. However, there is a finite period of time during which a particular administration of God is in force. We can observe the dispensation of innocence beginning with the creation of humankind in Gen 1:27 and certainly with the announcement of the one condition in Gen 2:15–17. It seems reasonable that Gen 1:1–27 be seen as a transitional period leading up to man's creation. However, that need not lead us to assume that all dispensations have transitional periods. In any case, we can discern the dispensation of innocence's duration to be from the creation of man to his fall (Gen 1:27–3:7). This failure resulted in the judgment of expulsion from Eden (see table 12).

Administration	Responsibility	*Terminus ad quo*	*Terminus ad quem*	Failure	Judgment
Innocence	Humankind is to obey God's one rule.	Adam's Creation (Gen 1:27–28)	Expulsion from Eden (Gen 3:22–24)	The Fall (Gen 3:1–7)	Curse (Adamic Covenant) (Gen 3:8–21)

Table 12. Characteristics of the Dispensation of Innocence

Covenants in Force

As previously indicated, the only covenant in force in the pre-fall world was the Edenic covenant. The Edenic covenant was a suzerainty covenant that defined Adam's vassal relationship with Yahweh. God gave Adam the earth and a position of authority over it, with but one condition. Adam was not to eat from the tree of the knowledge of good and evil (Gen 2:16–17). When he did so the covenant was broken (Gen 3:7). We should note that the establishment and the violation of the Edenic covenant form the *terminus ad quo* and *terminus ad quem* of the dispensation of innocence (see figure 2).

Stipulations in Force

The Edenic covenant, which is the only covenant in force during the dispensation of innocence, has three stipulations. First, man, as a vassal of Yahweh, was to cultivate and keep the garden (Gen 2:15). This, in effect, gave him a position. Second, man's need for sustenance was provided for (Gen 2:16). The third stipulation formed the condition under which the others would be enjoyed. Man was not to eat of the fruit of the knowledge of good and evil (Gen 2:17). All three of these stipulations were in force and formed the basis for the administration of God that we call the dispensation of innocence.

As is often observed, the dispensations seem to end in humankind's failure to fulfill their God-given responsibilities and a resulting judgment. This is what led Scofield to his definition of dispensation as "a dispensation is a period of time during which man is tested in respect to his obedience to some *specific* revelation of the will of God."[9] While I prefer Ryrie's definition, Scofield's point concerning testing is well taken. In this dispensation the revelation of the will of God, the basis for God's governing arrangement was, of course, the Edenic covenant. Man failed to obey God's one condition and so brought upon himself the curses of this divine suzerainty covenant. At that point we enter a new distinguishable administration in the outworking of God's purpose (see table 13).

Covenant In Force	Beneficiaries	Covenant Stipulation	Covenant Duration	Dispensational Characteristic	Duration
Edenic	Humankind	Man is to cultivate and keep the garden.	Creation–Fall (Gen 1:27–3:4)	Man lives in a perfect environment.	Creation–Fall (Gen 1:27–3:4)
		Man is free to eat of all trees save one.		All of man's needs are supplied.	
		Do not eat of the tree of the knowledge of good and evil.		There is the moral test of the forbidden tree.	

Table 13. Dispensation of Innocence and Covenant Stipulations

NOTES

1. Ryrie, *Dispensationalism* 46–47.
2. Ibid. 45–59. See also Charles C. Ryrie, "The Necessity of Dispensationalism," *BSac* 114, no. 455 (July–September 1957): 243–54.
3. Ibid. 28.
4. Ibid. 30.
5. *ALGNT* 279. Cf. Eph 1:10.
6. Scofield, *NSRB* 3; cf. English, *A Companion to the NSRB* 54. See also Unger, "Dispensations," *UBD* 269.
7. Ryrie, *Dispensationalism* 47.
8. Ryrie, *Dispensationalism* 51–52.
9. Scofield, *NSRB* 3.

CHAPTER FOURTEEN

The Dispensation of Conscience

Duration and Characteristics

God states that "the man has become like one of Us, knowing good and evil" (Gen 3:22). Of course, this knowledge came to Adam and Eve because they had chosen evil, whereas God knows good and evil by continually choosing the good. With this knowledge humankind became responsible to conscience. Cain is told that "sin is crouching at the door; and its desire is for you, but you must master it" (Gen 4:7). Ryrie explains that referring to this dispensation as the dispensation of conscience does not mean that man had no conscience either before of after this dispensation. Instead it indicates that the main way that God governed humankind was by the dictates of his conscience. The record of this dispensation is contained in Gen 4:1–8:14.[1]

This dispensation began with the establishment of the Adamic covenant (Gen 3:14–21) that invoked the curses of the Edenic covenant. Blood sacrifice was instituted during this dispensation (Gen 3:21; 4:4). Although a few responded, such as Abel, Enoch, and Noah (Gen 6:8), most like Cain (Gen 4:3, 7) did not. Unnatural affection (Gen 6:2), violence, and corruption filled the earth (Gen 6:5). God sent the Flood and saved only Noah's family (1 Pet 3:20). Noah is mentioned as being "a righteous man," and finding "favor in the eyes of the LORD" (Gen 6:8–9). This means that he followed the dictates of his conscience (Gen 6:8–9, 22; 7:5) and offered blood sacrifices for his sin (Gen 8:20–22). I would also note in passing that during this dispensation the death penalty is forbidden (Gen 4:14–15, 23–24) whereas it is later commanded (Gen 9:5–6).

Violence and sin, again demonstrating humankind's failure, characterize the dispensation of conscience. We have the first murder (a religious murder at that!) in Gen 4:3–15. There is the first recorded instance of polygamy in

Gen 4:19, 23. The husband of those two wives, Lamech, was a violent man who boasted of killing two people (Gen 4:23–24). There is the obscure reference in Gen 6:2–4 to the "Nephilim" (הַנְּפִלִים), literally "the fallen ones," and the "sons of God" (בְּנֵי הָאֱלֹהִים), coming "in to the daughters of men" (Gen 6:4). Ryrie takes this to be a reference to fallen angels cohabiting with human women, as alluded to in Jude 6 and 2 Pet 2:4.[2] The only other texts in which the phrase "sons of God" (בְּנֵי הָאֱלֹהִים) appears are Job 1:6 and 2:1. In those texts the reference is clearly to angels. In any case, a declaration of humankind's wickedness and God's judgment followed this development (Gen 6:5–7). Noah alone was righteous, i.e., he lived in accordance with the Adamic covenant (Gen 6:8). God ended this corrupt and violent dispensation in the judgment of the Flood (Gen 6:11–8:19).

This is not to say that conscience is not a factor in our current dispensation. Paul in Rom 2:14–16 indicates that in this dispensation conscience is still an essential factor in God's judgment of human intentions. We are to be careful of searing and defiling our consciences (1 Cor 8:7; 1 Tim 4:2). Paul writes that "the goal of our instruction is love from a pure heart and a good conscience and a sincere faith" (1 Tim 1:5). He also cautioned that, without a good conscience, some had "suffered shipwreck in regard to their faith" (1 Tim 1:19). However, Chafer says that "*the Dispensation of Conscience*, which extended from Adam's fall to the flood, in which age conscience was, apparently, the dominating feature of human life on the earth and the basis of man's relationship with God."[3] Therefore, the issue is not whether or not conscience is a factor in a given dispensation, but rather whether conscience the main factor in God's administration (see table 14).

Administration	Responsibility	*Terminus ad quo*	*Terminus ad quem*	Failure	Judgment
Conscience	Humankind is to obey their conscience.	Adamic Covenant (Gen 3:14–21)	Flood (Gen 8:19)	Humankind full of wickedness (Gen 6:5–7)	Flood (Gen 6:11–8:19)

Table 14. Characteristics of the Dispensation of Conscience

Covenants in Force

When humankind broke the Edenic covenant (Gen 3:1–7), the curses were enacted (Gen 3:8–24).[4] The suzerainty covenant that codifies the curses that are now in effect is the Adamic covenant.[5] The Edenic covenant was broken and only the Adamic covenant had been established during the dispensation of conscience. As previously indicated, the Adamic covenant continues until the new heaven and new earth, although the effects of the curse are lessened during the millennium. This indicates that the Adamic covenant endures well past the end of this dispensation. Therefore, the sole covenant in force during the dispensation of conscience is the Adamic covenant (see figure 2).

Stipulations in Force

The stipulations of the Adamic covenant address Satan, in the person of the Serpent, and Eve and Adam, who represented all of their posterity. Satan was humbled and told that "dust shall you eat" (Gen 3:14). This stipulation was instituted immediately. It was also predicted that he would one day suffer total defeat under the heel of one of Eve's descendants (Gen 3:15). Although this was a living hope during the dispensation of conscience (Gen 4:1), it was not fulfilled until the crucifixion. Eve was told that her pain in childbirth would be increased and that her relationship with her husband would be distorted (Gen 3:16). This stipulation was instituted immediately and was in force during this dispensation. Adam was informed that he would endure painful labor (Gen 3:17–19) and eventually die and return to the dust. These stipulations were instituted immediately and were in force during this dispensation. Finally, Yahweh performed the first blood sacrifice in order to clothe the nakedness of Adam and Eve. In Gen 4:1–5 we have a sacrificial system. Therefore, with the institution of the stipulations of the Adamic covenant God instituted blood sacrifice. Thus, there is a conspicuous correspondence between the characteristics of the dispensation of conscience and the Adamic covenant's stipulations in force at the time (see table 15).

Dispensations are not ways of salvation. Salvation has always been by grace, through faith, and based on Christ's atonement either past or future. However, due to progressive revelation, the content of faith is not the same in each dispensation. In the dispensation of conscience a simple sacrificial system was in place. Moreover, no sacrificial system existed before the fall. Therefore, it is fair to conclude that the sacrifices have some connection with

the awareness of sin. The NIV captures the correct sense of שָׁעָה ("gaze, regard") when it translates Gen 4:4, "The LORD looked with favor on Abel
and his offering" (Gen 4:4 NIV). It also translates Gen 4:5, "But on Cain and
his offering he did not look with favor" (Gen 4:5 NIV). Abel is called "righteous" (Matt 23:25). Hebrews 11:4 adds that the decisive factor in God's ac-
ceptance was faith. There was a promise of a future significant victory over
Satan (Gen 3:15), but little detail had been given. It is worthy of note that
Cain's was the only non-blood sacrifice offered until the Mosaic law. I conclude that the content of faith during the dispensation of conscience was that
God exists and would forgive when a blood sacrifice was offered in faith .

Covenants In Force	Beneficiaries	Covenant Stipulation	Covenant Duration	Dispensational Characteristic	Duration
Adamic	Serpent	Satan is humbled ("eat dust") but his total defeat is future at this time.	Fall–New Heavens and New Earth (Gen 3:5 – Rev 22:3)	Nephilim. Violence and sin.	Fall–Flood (Gen 3:4–8:14)
	Woman	The woman is to experience pain in childbirth.		First birth is prominent in Gen 4:1. Growth of the human population.	
		Her relation-ship with her husband is distorted.		Polygamy and possible co-habitation with fallen angels.	
	Man	Adamic		Occupations prominent in this dispensation. Note Cain's banishment.	
	Humankind	Under a sen-tence of death. But blood sacrifice is instituted.		Man is to approach God via blood sacrifice.	

Continued on the next page

Table 15 (*Continued*)

Covenants In Force	Beneficiaries	Covenant Stipulation	Covenant Duration	Dispensational Characteristic	Duration
Adamic	Humankind	The negative development of the Fall left humankind knowing good and evil.	Fall–New Heavens and New Earth (Gen 3:5–Rev 22:3)	Man is morally responsible, "to do all known good, to abstain from all known evil...."[6]	Fall–Flood (Gen 3:4–8:14)

Table 15. Dispensation of Conscience and Covenant Stipulations

NOTES

1. Ryrie, *Dispensationalism* 52–53.
2. Ryrie, *RSB* 1874, 1891.
3. Chafer, *Systematic Theology* 1:40.
4. See chapter 5 above.
5. See chapter 6 above.
6. Scofield, *NSRB* 7.

CHAPTER FIFTEEN

The Dispensation of Human Government

Duration and Characteristics

The dispensation of human government began with the Noahic covenant.[1] God began to govern humankind based upon external justice administered collectively by men instead of the internal basis of conscience. This was set against the backdrop of the divine promise that there would be no more universal floods. God set aside universal judgment by flood and delegated authority to humankind to judge on His behalf. Chafer observes that *"the Dispensation of Human Government,* which extended from the flood to the call of Abraham, is characterized by the committing of self-government to men...."*[2] Ryrie explains the features of the dispensation of human government and its failure:

> The chief personage during this economy was Noah. The new revelation of this time included animals' fear of man, animals given to man to eat, the promise of no further floods, and the institution of capital punishment. It is the latter that gives the distinctive basis to this dispensation as that of human, or civil, government. God gave man the right to take the life of man, which in the very nature of the case gave man the authority to govern others. Unless government has the right to the highest form of punishment, its basic authority is questionable and insufficient to protect properly those it governs.
>
> Failure to govern successfully appeared on the scene almost immediately, for Noah became drunk and incapable of ruling. The people, instead of obeying God's command to scatter and fill the earth, conceived the idea of staying together and building the tower of Babel to help achieve their aim. Fellowship with man replaced fellowship with God. As a result, God sent the judgment of the tower of Babel and the confusion of languages. He also graciously intervened in that He did not utterly destroy the nations but chose to deal graciously with Abraham and his descendants. The scriptural revelation of this stewardship is found in Genesis 8:15–11:9.[3]

Therefore, humankind was responsible in this dispensation to protect life and rule for God.

Unger seems to confuse the duration of the Noahic covenant with the dispensation of human government. Unger states that "the world is still Gentile-governed, and hence this dispensation overlaps other dispensations, and will not strictly come to an end until the second coming of Christ."[4] Scofield notes that "the dispensation of Human Government was followed ... by that of Promise.... However, man's responsibility for government did not cease but will continue until Christ sets up His kingdom."[5] Since the Noahic covenant is an eternal covenant, humankind's responsibility remains to rule for God. The ultimate expression of this will be Messiah's kingdom. However, as with conscience, the issue is what characterizes God's administration of humankind. God's establishment of human government characterizes this dispensation. The notable failure of human government to rule for God was the tower of Babel (Gen. 11:1–9) which ended in divine judgment and the confusion of tongues. Therefore, the dispensation of human government has its *terminus ad quo* with the establishment of the Noahic covenant and its *terminus ad quem* with the tower of Babel (Gen 11:1–26), from the standpoint of the biblical narrative, but historically with the call of Abraham (Gen 12:1–3) (see table 16). The establishment of the Abrahamic covenant began the next significant shift in God's interaction with humankind.

Administration	Responsibility	*Terminus ad quo*	*Terminus ad quem*	Failure	Judgment
Human Government	Humankind is to protect life and rule for God.	Noahic Covenant (Gen 8:20–9:17)	Tower of Babel (Gen 11:26)	Tower of Babel (Gen 11:26)	Confusion of Tongues (Gen 11:5–9)

Table 16. Characteristics of the Dispensation of Human Government

Covenants in Force

Two covenants were in force during the dispensation of human government. The Adamic covenant, a suzerainty covenant, was in force, since it continues until the new heaven and new earth. The Noahic covenant, a grant covenant, was established at the inauguration of this dispensation. A pattern may be observed in that each of the dispensations that we have considered begins with the establishment of a new covenant. The establishment of the Edenic covenant inaugurated the dispensation of innocence, the Adamic covenant inaugurated the dispensation of conscience, and now the establishment of the Noahic covenant inaugurates the dispensation of human government (see figure 2).

Stipulations in Force

Since two covenants (the Adamic and the Noahic) are in force during the dispensation of human government, the stipulations in force are a combination of the stipulations of both of these covenants. From the Adamic covenant, we have the following stipulations that are in force in this dispensation: Satan is humbled but still active. Women experience pain in childbirth and distortion in their relationships with their husbands. Men experience pain in their work. Both men and women die. In addition, humankind is to approach God by means of blood sacrifice.[6] These stipulations are the same as we have already observed during the dispensation of conscience.[7]

However, the Noahic covenant introduced new stipulations that formed the unique character of this dispensation.[8] The Noahic covenant, as a grant covenant, stipulated four things: Humankind is to rule the earth as God's vassals. Humankind may now eat meat and thus rules over the animal kingdom. God will no more destroy all life by a flood. Humankind is given authority and responsibility to take the life of murderers. The death penalty is, of course, extremely controversial today and yet one wonders why this should be the case among those who believe the Scriptures. Since the meaning of Gen 9:6 is unambiguous and that covenant stipulation is in force eternally, there should be no debate.[9] These stipulations established the institution of human government that gave this dispensation its character.

These stipulations align with the conditions that we observe in the dispensation of human government. As we would expect from the Adamic covenant, sin and rebellion (Gen 9:20–27; 11:1–26), the growth of the human population (Gen 10:1–32; 11:10–26), humankind's occupations, blood sacrifice (Gen 8:20) and moral responsibility all continue in this dispensation. In keeping with the Noahic covenant there is also an emphasis on human government and divine judgment in a manner that is not universally lethal. In this dispensation, too, the covenants form the basis for the dispensation.

As in the previous dispensation, blood sacrifice continued (Gen 8:20). No additional revelation is recorded concerning God's forgiveness, although much had been revealed of His judgment (Gen 6–8). Therefore, the content of faith remains the same in the dispensation of human government. Man was to trust that God existed and would forgive when blood sacrifices are offered in faith. There was a promise of a future significant victory over Satan (Gen 3:15). However, as yet, little detail had been given (see table 17).

Covenants In Force	Beneficiaries	Covenant Stipulation	Covenant Duration	Dispensational Characteristic	Duration
Adamic	Serpent	Satan is humbled ("eat dust") but his total defeat is future at this time.	Fall–New Heavens and New Earth (Gen 3:5– Rev 22:3)	Sin and rebellion (Gen 9:20–27; 11:1–26).	Establishment of the Noahic Covenant to the Tower of Babel (Gen 8:20–11:9)
	Woman	The woman is to experience pain in childbirth.		Growth of the human population (Gen 10:1–32; 11:10–26).	
		Her relationship with her husband is distorted.			
	Man	The man is to experience pain in his labor.		Farming (Gen 9:20), hunting (Gen 10:9), and building (Gen 10:11; 11:3, 4) are mentioned.	
	Humankind	Humankind is under a sentence of death, but blood sacrifice is instituted.		Noah approaches God via blood sacrifice (Gen 8:20).	

Continued on the next page

Table 17 (*Continued*)

Covenants In Force	Beneficiaries	Covenant Stipulation	Covenant Duration	Dispensational Characteristic	Duration
Adamic	Humankind	The negative development of the Fall left humankind knowing good & evil.	Fall–New Heavens and New Earth (Gen 3:5–Rev 22:3)	Man is morally responsible to do all known good, to abstain from all known evil.	Establishment of the Noahic Covenant to the Tower of Babel (Gen 8:20–11:9)
Noahic		Rule Earth as God's Vassals	From Establishment to Eternity (Gen 9:16)	Human governments are ordained by God. However, humankind organizes in rebellion against God (Gen 11:1–26).	
		No More Universal Floods		God's judgments did not destroy on a universal level.	
		The Authority and the Responsibility to Judge Murder.		Death Penalty was ordered by God.	
		Permission to Eat Meat		Meat was allowed for the human diet, thus affirming humankind's rule over the animal kingdom.	

Table 17. Dispensation of Human Government and Covenant Stipulations

NOTES

1. See chapter 7.
2. Chafer, *Systematic Theology* 1:40–41.
3. Ryrie, *Dispensationalism* 53.
4. Unger, "Dispensations," *UBD* 269.
5. Scofield, *NSRB* 14.
6. See chapter 6.
7. See chapter 14.
8. See chapter 7 for the details of the stipulations of the Noahic covenant.
9. Walter C. Kaiser Jr., Peter H. Davids, F. F. Bruce, Manfred T. Brauch, *Hard Sayings of the Bible* (Downers Grove, IL: InterVarsity, 1996) 114–17.

CHAPTER SIXTEEN

The Dispensation of Promise

Duration and Characteristics

With the call of Abraham (Gen 11:27–12:3), we encounter a new distinguishable economy in the outworking of God's purpose. Previously, God had been administering humankind as a whole. Now, although all humankind still had responsibilities before God, the focus of God's administration shifted to one man and his family. Through that family and the nation that is to arise from them God intended to bless all humankind (Gen 12:2, 3). Ryrie explains that "the title Promise comes from Hebrews 6:15 and 11:9, where it is said that Abraham obtained the promise and sojourned in the land of promise."[1] The distinguishing feature of the dispensation of promise is that, while previously God had dealt with all humankind, now God selected one family and one nation to deal with directly. Ryrie suggests that this dispensation could be best designated the dispensation of Patriarchal Rule. The patriarchs were responsible to simply trust God. They failed repeatedly and finally became slaves in Egypt. However, God graciously provided a deliverer in Moses. This dispensation covers the Scriptures from Gen 11:10–Exod 18:27. Ryrie defends the distinctiveness of the dispensation of promise:

> Is this a dispensation distinct from that of the Mosaic Law, or is it merely a preparatory period? The answer seems to be clear from Galatians 3:15–29. Though it is true that God was dealing with the same people during both the Patriarchal and Mosaic dispensations, that is not the determining factor. After all, up to the call of Abraham, God had been dealing in different ways with the same group—the entire population of the earth. In the first and second dispensations God was dealing with the same people—Adam and Eve. So the fact that He was dealing with Israel during both the patriarchal and legal eras is not determinative. What does determine the distinguishability of the two dispensations is simply the different bases on which He dealt with them. Promise and law are sharply distinguished by Paul in Galatians 3

even though he maintains that the law did not annul the promise. And the Mosaic Law is kept so distinct from the promise to Abraham that it is difficult not to recognize a different dispensation. This is the essence of the definition, and if anything is kept distinct in that chapter, the law is. Therefore, the separate dispensation of promise, or of the Patriarchs, is justified.[2]

Chafer notes that

during this age the divine promise alone sustains Abraham and his posterity. While Hebrews 11:13, 39 refer to Old Testament saints generally in that no major Old Testament promise was realized during its own period, these passages are specifically true of those who lived within the age of promise.[3]

God's promises to the patriarchs characterize this dispensation. The patriarchal responsibility before God was faith in God's promises (Gen 15:6).

God's promise to Abraham made a grant to him and his descendants of the land of Canaan (Gen 12:1, 7; 13:14–15, 17; 15:7; 18–21; 17:8; 26:3; 28:13). It has been noted that matters seem to go well for the patriarchs when they are in the land and badly when they go down to Egypt (e.g., Gen 12:10–20). God even commanded Isaac to stay in the land and not go down to Egypt (Gen 26:2, 3). Egypt seems to have been a sort of "security-blanket" to the patriarchs. If there is a famine, then go to Egypt (Gen 12:10; 42:1–3; 43:2). If the land is good, it is like Egypt (Gen 13:10) . The patriarchs tended to live as close to Egypt as they could and still reside in the promised land (Gen 12:9; 13:1; 20:1; 21:31–33; 22:19; 24:62; 26:23). Finally, as predicted (Gen 15:13–16), they permanently moved to Egypt (Gen 46:5–7) where they eventually become enslaved (Exod 1:1–14). Perhaps they did not understand the danger of continually going down to Egypt because Gen 15:13–16 did not name the nation that would enslave them. While Egypt was God's providential means of preserving Israel under Joseph's administration (Gen 45:5–8), moving there was a violation of the divine command of Gen 13:17; 26:2, 3. Going down to Egypt was a means of meeting their needs without requiring any trust in God Who had promised blessing in the land (Gen 26:2, 3). Because of God's covenant love he protected Israel even when, through a lack of faith, they failed in their responsibility to trust Him.

There is a failure on the part of the Egyptians that we should not overlook. God had promised Abraham, "I will bless those who bless you, and the one who curses you I will curse" (Gen 12:3). This is demonstrated in a small way in Gen 12:10–20. Abraham, although lacking trust in God and practicing falsehood (Gen 12:10–13), is rescued from Pharaoh by "great plagues" (נֶגַע,

cp. Gen 12:17 with Exod 11:1 which uses the same word). Abraham is expelled with great riches from Egypt (Gen 12:16, 19–20; 13:2). In similar
fashion, Egypt fails in its responsibility to bless God's chosen people and
thus incurs God's curse (Exod 3:16–22).

The duration of the dispensation of promise extends between two main
events. The first, the giving of the Abrahamic covenant inaugurates God's
new administration. The last, the exodus from Egypt, marks the transition to
a new means of administration, law. These two events mark the *terminus ad
quo* and the *terminus ad quem* of the dispensation of promise (see table 18).

Administration	Responsibility	*Terminus ad quo*	*Terminus ad quem*	Failure	Judgment
Promise	The patriarchs are to have faith in God's promises.	Call of Abraham/ Abrahamic Covenant (Gen 11:27– 12:3)	Mosaic Covenant at Mount Sinai (Exod 20:1)	Egyptian Bondage (Gen 15:13– 16)	Exodus Plagues (Exod 1– 19)

Table 18. Characteristics of the Dispensation of Promise

Covenants in Force

As previously noted, the dispensation of promise is inaugurated with the establishment of the Abrahamic covenant. Thus, the pattern that covenants inaugurate dispensations is still preserved. In addition to the Abrahamic
covenant, the Adamic and Noahic covenants are still in force during the dispensation of promise. The interplay between these three covenants forms the
basis for this dispensation. The new features of this dispensation are a direct
result of the Abrahamic covenant. Although God remained concerned with
the whole of humankind, with the inauguration of the Abrahamic covenant
He began a plan to ultimately bless all humankind through one chosen people. Through that chosen seed all the families of the earth would be blessed
(Gen 12:3) (see figure 2).

Stipulations in Force

The stipulations already instituted of the three covenants in force (Adamic,
Noahic, and Abrahamic) define the responsibilities and characteristics of

God's administration called the dispensation of promise. As previously noted, the Adamic covenant contains the following stipulations that are still in force in this dispensation: Satan is humbled but still active. Women experience pain in childbirth and distortion in their relationships with their husbands. Men experience pain in their work. Both men and women die. And humankind is to approach God by means of blood sacrifice.[4] In the Noahic covenant it is stipulated: Human governments are responsible to rule as God's vassals even to the point of taking human life in punishment for murder. Humans are to rule over the animal kingdom. Moreover, all destructive divine judgments will be local and not threaten life on a universal scale.[5] Although the Adamic and Noahic covenants are foundational, the Abrahamic covenant provides the stipulations that give the dispensation of promise its unique character.

In general, God promised Abraham a land, a seed, and a blessing.[6] Not all of those stipulations are instituted during the dispensation of promise. The stipulations in force can be distilled to six general promises: The Abrahamic covenant stipulated that Abraham would, with Sarah, begin a line that, through Isaac and, as was later confirmed, Jacob, would grow to be a great nation, Israel. Membership in that covenant people was contingent on the sign of circumcision. That nation is to be enslaved for four hundred thirty years. It also stipulated that Abraham would be the progenitor of other nations. Abraham is to be blessed personally and bless others. Those who bless him and his family would be blessed and those who curse them would be cursed. The remaining stipulations were not yet instituted during the dispensation of promise. They were to be apprehended by faith (Heb 11:13–16).

These covenant stipulations accurately define the conditions that prevail during the dispensation of promise. The Abrahamic line did grow from its beginning with Abraham and Sarah's son, Isaac, through Jacob and his twelve sons to become the people, Israel. In addition, Abraham is the progenitor of the Arabs through Ishmael (Gen 16:10–12) and, through Esau, the Edomites (Gen 25:30). Membership in the covenant people does require not only descent from Abraham, Isaac, and Jacob but also circumcision (Gen 17:22–27). Abraham was personally wealthy and gave to others (Gen 13:2; 14:20). Abraham's descendants, Israel, did go down to Egypt and were enslaved there (Gen 46:1–7; Exod 1:1–14). In Egypt, God heard their cry and delivered them by bringing His curses on those that had cursed His people (Exod 3:16–22).

In this dispensation, the content of faith underwent its first changes since the fall. For the vast mass of humankind, all was the same. They were to trust that God exists and will forgive those who offer blood sacrifices in faith. However, the patriarchs were to trust as well in God's promise of a seed from Whom would come a universal blessing (Gen 15:6) (see table 19).

Covenants In Force	Beneficiaries	Covenant Stipulation	Covenant Duration	Dispensational Characteristic	Duration
Adamic	Serpent	Satan is humbled ("eat dust") but his total defeat is future at this time.	Fall – New Heavens and New Earth (Gen 3:5 – Rev 22:3)	Sins of lying, lust, adultery, sexual sin, strife, violence, murder, kidnapping, slavery, wickedness, rebellion, etc.	Establishment of the Abrahamic Covenant to the Exodus from Egypt (Gen 11:27– Exod 19:25)
	Woman	The woman is to experience pain in childbirth.		Growth of the human population.	
		Her relationship with her husband is distorted.		Conflict between the patriarchal wives is prominent.	
	Man	The man is to experience pain in his labor.		Occupation of shepherd prominent.	
	Humankind	Humankind is under a sentence of death.		Patriarchs continue to approach God via blood sacrifice.	
		The negative development of the Fall left humankind knowing good and evil.		Man is morally responsible, "to do all known good, to abstain from all known evil...."[7]	

Continued on the next page

Table 19 (*Continued*)

Covenants In Force	Beneficiaries	Covenant Stipulation	Covenant Duration	Dispensational Characteristic	Duration
Noahic	Humankind	Rule Earth as God's Vassals	From Establishment to Eternity (Gen 9:16)	Human governments are ordained by God. However, Egypt oppresses Israel.	Establishment of the Abrahamic Covenant to the Exodus from Egypt (Gen 11:27– Exod 19:25)
		No More Universal Floods		God judges Sodom and Gomorrah, Egypt.	
		The Authority and The Responsibility to Judge Murder.		Death Penalty was ordered by God.	
		Permission to Eat Meat		Animal husbandry practiced.	
Abrahamic	Israel	Abraham's line, through Sarah, Isaac, and Jacob, to become a great nation, Israel.	From Establishment to Eternity (Gen 13:15; 17:7)	Israel grew from Jacob's household to a nation while in Egypt.	
		Circumcision of males is required.		Circumcision was practiced with some lapses (Exod 4:24–26; Josh 5:3–8)	
		The nation was to be enslaved 430 years.		Israel enslaved in Egypt.	
		Abraham was to be personally blessed and a source of blessing.		Abraham was wealthy (Gen 13:2) and gave 10% to Melchizedek.	

Continued on the next page

Table 19 (*Continued*)

Covenants In Force	Beneficiaries	Covenant Stipulation	Covenant Duration	Dispensational Characteristic	Duration
Abrahamic	Gentiles	Abraham was to be the progenitor of nations.	From Establishment to Eternity (Gen 13:15; 17:7)	Abraham is also the ancestor of the Arabs and the Edomites.	Establishment of the Abrahamic Covenant to the Exodus from Egypt (Gen 11:27–Exod 19:25)
		Those that blessed Israel were blessed, those that cursed Israel were cursed.		Judgments on those who came against the patriarchs (Gen 12:17; 20:3) and ultimately God's judgment of Egypt (Exod 3:16–22).	

Table 19. Dispensation of Promise and Covenant Stipulations

NOTES

1. Ryrie, *Dispensationalism* 53–54.
2. Ibid.
3. Chafer, *Systematic Theology* 1:41.
4. See chapter 6.
5. See chapter 7.
6. See chapter 8.
7. Scofield, *NSRB* 7.

CHAPTER SEVENTEEN

The Dispensation of Law

Duration and Characteristics

With the dispensation of promise, the focus of God's administration of humankind shifted to the people of Israel. This is even more evident in the dispensation of law. Ryrie describes the prominent features of the dispensation of law:

> To the children of Israel through Moses was given the great code that we call the Mosaic Law. It consisted of 613 commandments covering all phases of life and activity. It revealed in specific detail God's will in that economy. The period covered was from Moses until the death of Christ, or from Exodus 19:1 to Acts 1:26 [*sic*].
>
> The people were responsible to do all the law (James 2:10), but they failed (Rom. 10:1–3). As a result, there were many judgments throughout this long period. The ten tribes were carried into Assyrian captivity; the two tribes were carried into Babylonian captivity; and later, because of their rejection of Jesus of Nazareth, the people were dispersed into all the world (Matt. 23:37–39). All during their many periods of declension and backsliding, God dealt with them graciously from the very first apostasy with the golden calf, when the law was being delivered to Moses, to the gracious promises of final regathering and restoration in the millennial age to come. These promises of a glorious future are guaranteed secure by the Abrahamic promises, which the law in no way abrogated (Gal. 3:3–25). We are also told clearly in the New Testament (Rom. 3:20) that the law was not a means of justification but of condemnation.[1]

This does not mean that God was unconcerned with Gentiles during the dispensation of law. Nevertheless, the focus of attention was clearly on Israel.

Again, as with the other dispensations, the dispensation of law begins with the giving of a covenant. The *terminus ad quo* of the dispensation of law is the establishment of the Mosaic covenant at Mount Sinai in Exod 19:1.

The fact that the Mosaic covenant underwent several covenant renewal ceremonies under Moses, Joshua, and various kings indicates awareness that Israel did not keep the law of Moses. Israel's failure resulted in several exiles as predicted in the Land covenant.[2] The Land covenant in Deut 28–30 charts the course of Israel's fate in this dispensation. Israel progresses from natural disasters, to invasion and foreign domination, to three major exiles: Assyria, Babylon, and Rome.[3] The *terminus ad quem* is the death of Christ that ends the Mosaic covenant and introduces the new covenant.[4] Thus, the duration of the Mosaic covenant sets the bounds for the dispensation of law (see table 20).

Administration	Responsibility	*Terminus ad quo*	*Terminus ad quem*	Failure	Judgment
Law	Israel is to obey God's law.	Mosaic Covenant at Mount Sinai (Exod 20:1)	Death of Christ (Rom 7:1–6; 10:4; 2 Cor 3:7–11; Gal 3:19–4:7; Eph 2:14–16; Col 2:13–14; Heb 7:11–18; 8:7–13)	Israel fails re-peatedly to keep the law	Assyrian Exile Babylo-nian Exile Roman Exile (Deut 28–30)

Table 20. Characteristics of the Dispensation of Law

Covenants in Force

During the dispensation of law, the Adamic and Noahic covenants continued to govern humankind in general. Israel received the Abrahamic covenant be-fore the Mosaic covenant. Therefore, subsequent covenants in no way abro-gated the Abrahamic covenant (Gal 3:15–17). However, the covenant that marks the watershed change in this dispensation was the Mosaic covenant. This covenant provided Israel with a rule of life in this dispensation. Two of the three covenants that expand on the Abrahamic covenant were established against the background of the dispensation of law. The first, the Land cove-nant, specified the conditions under which Israel will enjoy possession of the land. The next, the Davidic covenant, made promises concerning David's throne, dynasty, and kingdom. Jeremiah prophesied the third covenant that expands on the Abrahamic covenant during this dispensation (Jer 31:31–37). However, the new covenant was not established until this dispensation ended at the crucifixion of Christ.

As I have demonstrated, the Mosaic covenant is temporary in nature and ends with the establishment of the new covenant.[5] Scriptural support for this fact is found in such passages as Rom 7:1–6; 10:4; 2 Cor 3:7–11; Gal 3:19–4:7; Eph 2:14–16; Col 2:13–14; Heb 7:11–18; 8:7–13. In addition, the Mosaic covenant is given to Israel alone and, therefore, has no bearing on Gentiles during the dispensation of law (see figure 2).

Stipulations in Force

The stipulations already instituted of the six covenants in force (Adamic, Noahic, Abrahamic, Mosaic, Davidic, and Land covenants) define the responsibilities and characteristics of the divine administration referred to as the dispensation of law. The Adamic and Noahic covenants delineate God's general administration of humankind. The Adamic covenant contains the following stipulations that are still in force: Satan is humbled but still active. Women experience pain in childbirth and distortion in their relationships with their husbands. Men experience pain in their work. Both men and women are mortal. Moreover, humankind is to approach God by means of blood sacrifice.[6] The Noahic covenant stipulates that human governments are responsible to rule as God's vassals even to the point of taking human life in punishment for murder. Humans are to rule over the animal kingdom. Moreover, all destructive divine judgments will be local and not threaten life on a universal scale.[7] These characteristics and responsibilities define conditions in the dispensation of law for all humankind.

The other four covenants determine the characteristics and responsibilities for Israel during the dispensation of law. On one hand, Israel is to trust in the promises of the Abrahamic covenant and the related Land and Davidic covenants. On the other hand, Israel's failure to keep the law of Moses results in God's judgment. There is a certain tension in the dispensation of law between God's gracious promise and His non-gracious law. In this dispensation, God is beginning to fulfill the land aspect of the Abrahamic covenant with the conquest under Joshua. However, as I mentioned above, the predicted curses and exiles of the Land covenant form the basis for Israel's history during this dispensation. The Davidic covenant holds the great promise of an eternal throne, dynasty, and kingdom for the Seed of David. However, it also promised divine judgment on David's descendants who are disobedient. The subsequent history of the kings of Judah was a working out of these covenant stipulations. Of course, God has not yet installed the ultimate Davidic King on the throne of David in His kingdom during this dispensation. In addition, the new covenant, although prophesied by Jeremiah, is not yet established in the dispensation of law.

In the dispensation of law, the content of faith remained the same for the mass of humankind. They are to trust that God exists and will forgive those who offer blood sacrifices in faith. Israel is still to trust in God's promise of a seed from Whom would come a universal blessing (Gen 15:6). However, two things are different. Israel has in the law a clearer revelation of her sin and the need for forgiveness and God augments the sacrificial system. Walvoord explains the faith basis of the sacrificial system:

> Under the system of sacrifices, God provided an outward means of manifesting inward faith. The sacrifices in themselves could not save. An unbeliever who offered sacrifices was still lost. A believer who really trusted in Jehovah would, on the other hand, be sure to offer his sacrifices. The sacrifices while not work which was acceptable as a ground of salvation before God were nevertheless a work which demonstrated faith. Faith in the Old Testament therefore took a definite outward form of manifestation. In offering the sacrifice, the offerer was assured that he was performing an act of recognition of God as His Savior and in particular a recognition of the promise of the coming seed of the woman, the Son of God Himself. The institution of the Mosaic covenant did not fundamentally alter the way of salvation. It specified more particularly the way of sacrifice. It provided moreover a detailed rule of life and the obligation to obey as a condition for blessing in this life. Salvation was still a work of God for man, not a work of man for God.[8]

The sacrifices increase in educational value and point in a clearer manner to the coming ultimate Sacrifice in the next dispensation (see table 21).

Covenants In Force	Beneficiaries	Covenant Stipulation	Covenant Duration	Dispensational Characteristic	Duration
Adamic	Serpent	Satan is humbled ("eat dust") but his total defeat is future at this time.	Fall–New Heavens and New Earth (Gen 3:5 – Rev 22:3)	Satan still active (e.g., 1 Chr 21:1; Zech 3:1–2)	Estab-lishment of the Mosaic Covenant to the Cross
	Woman	The woman is to experience pain in childbirth.		Growth of the human population.	
		Her relation-ship with her husband is distorted.		Family strife is prominent in David's family and his de-scendants as well as others.	(Exod 20:1–Matt 27:50; Mark 15:37; Luke 23:46; John 19:30)
	Man	The man is to experience pain in his labor.		Occupations continue to be laborious.	
	Humankind	Blood sacrifice is instituted.		Men continue to approach God via blood sacrifice.	
		Humankind knowing good and evil		Man is morally responsible.	
Noahic		Rule Earth as God's Vassals	From Estab-lishment to Eternity (Gen 9:16)	God ordains human governments.	
		No More Universal Floods		God judges locally.	
		The Author-ity and The Responsibil-ity to Judge Murder.		Death Penalty in effect.	
		Permission to Eat Meat		Animal husbandry	

Continued on the next page

Table 21 (*Continued*)

Covenants In Force	Beneficiaries	Covenant Stipulation	Covenant Duration	Dispensational Characteristic	Duration
Abrahamic	Israel	Abraham's line, through Sarah, Isaac, and Jacob, to become Israel.	To Eternity (Gen 13:15; 17:7)	Israel grew from Jacob's household to a nation while in Egypt.	Establishment of the Mosaic Covenant to the Cross (Exod 20:1–Matt 27:50; Mark 15:37; Luke 23:46; John 19:30)
		Circumcision of males is required.		Circumcision is practiced.	
		The nation was to be enslaved 430 years.		Israel freed from Egypt.	
	Gentiles	Abraham to be father of nations.		Arabs and the Edomites	
		Those that blessed Israel were blessed, those that cursed Israel were cursed.		Cycle: Israel sins, God punishes them by allowing oppressors, Israel repents, God brings deliverance, God punishes the oppressors	
Mosaic	Israel	613 Commands	Mosaic covenant ended at death of Christ Rom 7:1–6; 10:4; 2 Cor 3:7–11; Gal 3:19–4:7; Eph 2:14–16; Col 2:13–14; Heb 7:11–18; 8:7–13	Blessings for obedience Curses for disobedience	

Continued on the next page

Table 21 (*Continued*)

Covenants In Force	Beneficiaries	Covenant Stipulation	Covenant Duration	Dispensational Characteristic	Duration
Land	Israel	Title to the Land	"Eternal covenant" Ezek 16:60	Israel takes possession of the Land.	Establishment of the Mosaic Covenant to the Cross (Exod 20:1–Matt 27:50; Mark 15:37; Luke 23:46; John 19:30)
		Three Exiles Predicted (Deut 28–30)		• Assyrian exile • Babylonian exile • Roman exile	
Davidic	Israel David's line	David's throne, dynasty, and kingdom established forever.	Everlasting covenant (2 Sam 23:5; 2 Chr 13:5; Isa 55:3; Jer 33:20–22)	Israel has a line of Davidic kings.	
		Solomon to rule after David and build the Temple		Solomon rules and builds the Temple.	
		God to discipline Davidic kings but not destroy the line		Ten tribes split off under Rehoboam. No Davidic kings on the throne of Judah after the Babylonian exile.	

Table 21. Dispensation of Law and Covenant Stipulations

NOTES

1.   Ryrie, *Dispensationalism* 55.
2.   See chapter 9.
3.   The Roman exile actually occurs in the next dispensation.
4.   See chapter 12.
5.   See chapter 12.
6.   See chapter 6.
7.   See chapter 7.
8.   John F. Walvoord, "Series in Christology—Part 4: The Preincarnate Son of God," *BSac* 104, no. 416 (October–December 1947): 415–25.

CHAPTER EIGHTEEN

The Dispensation of Grace

Duration and Characteristics

Although they may have varying opinions of the continuity or discontinuity between the periods of law and grace, most Christians agree that an crucial change occurs at the cross of Christ. Paul the apostle refers to this current dispensation as "the dispensation of the grace of God (τὴν οἰκονομίαν τῆς χάριτος τοῦ θεοῦ)" (Eph 3:2 YLT) that he was entrusted with. Paul also refers to "the dispensation of the mystery (ἡ οἰκονομία τοῦ μυστηρίου)" (Eph 3:9 ASV) as something that had existed long before himself. Indeed the dispensation that Paul speaks of is a part of God's "eternal purpose (πρόθεσιν τῶν αἰώνων)" (Eph 3:11). Michel observes that οἰκονομία "also means 'plan of salvation,' 'administration of salvation,' 'order of salvation.'"[1] It is apparent in Eph 3:1–11 that Paul is a minister of the dispensation but the dispensation is not synonymous with Paul's ministry. Paul indicates in Gal 3:23–4:7 that there is a radical discontinuity between the current dispensation and the dispensation of law. Paul says that "the law is not based on faith; on the contrary, 'The man who does these things will live by them'" (Gal 3:12). As a suzerainty covenant, the Mosaic covenant was non-gracious in character. Therefore, the dispensation that resulted from its stipulations was also non-gracious in character. However, the new covenant, as a grant covenant, is inherently gracious. Therefore, its stipulations result in a dispensation characterized by grace.

Both progressive dispensationalists[2] and covenant theologians[3] have disputed the meaning of mystery. This dispensation is a "mystery (μυστήριον)" (Eph 3:9). It is a mystery that "the Gentiles are fellow heirs and fellow members of the body" (Eph 3:4–6). That Christ indwells the entire body, both Jew and Gentile, is a mystery (Col 1:26–27). The Greek μυστήριον ("mystery") was a technical term among the mystery cults of the Hellenistic world for "secret, secret rite, secret teaching, mystery"[4] or "a religious secret confided only to the initiated, secret rite"[5] The usage in the NT has a somewhat different meaning, "what can be known only through revelation mediated from God, *what was not known before*"[6] or

> the unmanifested or private counsel of God, (God's) secret, the secret thoughts, plans, and dispensations of God ... which are hidden fr[om] human reason, as well as fr[om] all other comprehension below the divine level, and await either fulfillment or revelation to those for whom they are intended.[7]

This indicates that the word μυστήριον ("mystery") itself conveys the idea that the mystery was previously unknown.[8] Moreover, if any doubt remains, this is the mystery "which for ages has been hidden in God" (Eph 3:9) and "which in other generations was not made known to the sons of men" (Eph 3:5). It is clear from the context that the nature of the Church as the body of Christ and this dispensation were not merely less well understood. They were unknown. This explains the otherwise puzzling omission of the present age from the prophecy of Daniel's seventy weeks (Dan 9:24–27). Thus, I must disagree with Robert L. Saucy that "the former hiddenness thus relates as much to their not being realized or actualized in history as to any new disclosure of information."[9] Saucy reaches this conclusion because he thinks that the mysteries "are best understood as fulfillments of Old Testament prophecies."[10] This is a case of invalid semantic identification.[11] Gentile salvation is predicted in the OT (Gen 12:3; Isa 42:6; 49:6). However, the present dispensation and the nature of the Church are not. There are points of similarity in these concepts. Nevertheless, they are not identical.

From the above I conclude that our present dispensation has two main characteristics. It is gracious in character and it is a mystery unforeseen in the OT. Ryrie explains that grace existed before the dispensation of grace. However, the coming of Christ displayed God's grace in a manner that eclipses all previous displays. Ryrie notes that humankind's current responsibility is to accept the gift of righteousness by faith (Rom. 5:15–18). He observes that, with this dispensation, God is again working with the whole of humankind although they fail for the most part to accept God's free offer of grace.[12] The Scriptures involved in this dispensation are from the death of Christ (Matt 27:50; Mark 15:37; Luke 23:46; John 19:30)–Rev 19:21. Therefore, the distinguishable economy in the present outworking of God's plan is that God is administering humankind according to grace. Humankind's responsibility is to respond in faith to God's free offer of salvation. Humankind's failure is that the majority reject God's grace (see table 22).

The question of the duration of this dispensation is largely dependent on whether one considers it the dispensation of the Church (e.g., James M. Gray) or the dispensation of grace (e.g., Scofield).[13] If one considers this dispensation to be the dispensation of the Church, then logically one would expect it to begin and end with the presence of the Church. The Church begins at Pentecost. Matthew 16:18 reads, "I will build my Church." Therefore the Church is future at that point. Acts 1:5 indicates that the Spirit baptism was future at that point. This is, of course, post-resurrection. In Acts 2, although not explicitly called "the baptism of the Spirit," the baptism of the Spirit takes place. Acts 11:15–17 confirms that Acts 2 was, in fact, the baptism of the Spirit. 1 Corinthians 12:12–13 indicates that the body of Christ is formed by the baptism of the Spirit. Ephesians 1:22, 23 and Col 1:17, 18 indicate that the Church is His body. Therefore, the Church begins at Pentecost and so would this dispensation, if this is the dispensation of the Church.

However, does God administer humankind through the Church in this dispensation? The distinguishable economy in the outworking of God's purpose during this dispensation is that His administration is by means of grace. That is exactly what Paul called this dispensation: "the dispensation of the grace of God (τὴν οἰκονομίαν τῆς χάριτος τοῦ θεοῦ)" (Eph 3:2 YLT). Therefore, it is best to consider this dispensation to be the dispensation of grace. In that case, the *terminus ad quo* would not be the day of Pentecost, when the Church was born, but rather the crucifixion of Christ, when the new covenant was established. As I have previously demonstrated, believing Jews and Gentiles alike participate in the spiritual blessings of the new covenant.[14] This is the basis for God's grace in this dispensation. Thus, the pattern persists that links the inauguration of each dispensation to the establishment of a covenant.

This understanding has implications for the *terminus ad quem* of the dispensation of grace. Since the Church is not the distinguishable means of divine administration during the dispensation of grace, the dispensation of grace need not end immediately with the rapture.[15] Thus, the tribulation falls within the dispensation of grace. Ryrie concludes that, since the Church will be raptured before the Tribulation, from the Church's viewpoint the Tribulation would seem to have no relation to this dispensation. Nevertheless, from the viewpoint of God's administration of the world it is better to see the Tribulation as the conclusion of the dispensation of grace rather than a separate dispensation.[16] This would fit the often observed pattern of dispensations ending in failure and judgment as God's judgment will fall on those who reject Him. Therefore, the *terminus ad quem* of the dispensation of grace is the second coming of Christ and the establishment of the millennial kingdom.

There appears to be confusion in this matter between dispensations and ages. These are related but not synonymous terms. A dispensation is a distinguishable economy that describes the manner in which God is managing the world. An age is a period of time that may or may not be associated with a dispensation. In this case, both the Church age and the tribulation fall within the dispensation of grace (see figure 3).

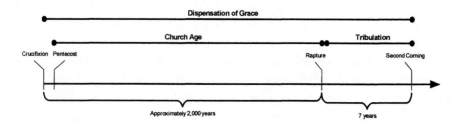

Figure 3. Dispensation of Grace vs. Church Age and Tribulation

Administration	Responsibility	*Terminus ad quo*	*Terminus ad quem*	Failure	Judgment
Grace	Believe the gospel.	Death of Christ (Gal 3:19–4:7; Eph 3:1–11)	Second coming of Christ (Rev 19:1)	Majority fails to believe Apostasy in the visible church	The Great Tribulation

Table 22. Characteristics of the Dispensation of Grace

Covenants in Force

During the dispensation of grace, the Adamic and Noahic covenants continue to direct humankind in general. Although the Mosaic covenant has ended, Israel remains under the Abrahamic covenant. Subsequent covenants by no means cancel the Abrahamic covenant (Gal 3:15–17). With the establishment of the new covenant, the three covenants that develop the Abrahamic covenant are all in force during the dispensation of grace. The first, the Land covenant, continues to specify the conditions under which Israel will enjoy possession of the land. The next, the Davidic covenant, makes promises concerning David's throne, dynasty, and kingdom. The death of Christ established the new covenant that Jeremiah prophesied during the dispensation of law. It is the new covenant spiritual blessings that give the dispensation of grace its unique character (see figure 2).

Stipulations in Force

The instituted stipulations of the six covenants in force (Adamic, Noahic, Abrahamic, Land, Davidic, and new covenants) define the responsibilities and characteristics of the dispensation of grace. The Adamic and Noahic covenants define God's general administration of humankind. The Adamic covenant's stipulations are still in force: Satan is humbled but still working. Women still experience pain in childbirth and distortion in their relationships with their husbands. Men still experience pain in their work. All human beings are still mortal. However, humankind is no longer to draw near to God by means of blood sacrifice. Rather men are to trust in the ultimate sacrifice, God's own Son.[17] The Noahic covenant stipulates that human governments are still responsible to rule as God's vassals even to the extent of taking human life as retribution for murder. Humans are still to rule over the animal kingdom. Additionally, all destructive divine judgments will be local and not threaten life on a universal scale. Even the tribulation at the end of the dispensation leaves some survivors.[18] These characteristics and responsibilities define the general conditions in the dispensation of grace.

The other four covenants determine the characteristics and responsibilities for Israel during the dispensation of grace. Israel is to trust in the promises of the Abrahamic covenant and the related Land, Davidic, and new covenants. Jesus, as the Davidic messiah, made an offer to Israel of the messianic kingdom. The leadership of Israel refused. Therefore, the kingdom is

postponed (Matt 21:43). In judgment Israel suffered the Roman exile predicted in the Land covenant (Deut 28:63–68; Dan 9:26). Although the Jewish
people have begun to return physically, their spiritual renewal awaits the
kingdom and the institution of the new covenant's provisions. Revelation 12
and Matt 24 indicate that Israel will yet suffer persecution during the tribulation.

The new covenant has superseded the old Mosaic covenant.[19] Schreiner
explains that the Mosaic sacrifices have lost their efficacy:

> Paul can threaten those who return to the law with the curse, not because he does not
> believe in the forgiveness of Yahweh, but because he believes that, now that Mes-
> siah has come, atonement can only be obtained through his death. The sacrifices of
> the old covenant once were sufficient—probably in Paul's mind only provisionally
> since they pointed to Christ's death—but to return to them now rules out the impor-
> tance of the death of the Messiah. If Old Testament sacrifices do atone, then "Christ
> died needlessly" (Gal. 2:21). The fact that Old Testament sacrifices no longer atone
> reveals the salvation-historical shift in Paul's thinking. What the Old Testament sac-
> rifices anticipated and pointed to has arrived, and now that the fulfillment has come
> that which predicted the fulfillment is set aside.
>
> In fact, Paul's sustained polemic against the law only makes sense if there is a
> shift in salvation history.[20]

Schreiner also notes that, even where moral stipulations carry over, the appropriate response is now different:

> Even if the moral principles of the Old Testament law are accepted as norma-
> tive, that does not mean the penalties attached to the law are still in force. The penal-
> ties were probably stricter for Israel because she was supposed to be a holy nation,
> unique in all the earth. The church constitutes the people of God in the midst of
> many nations. None of these nations, though, intrinsically comprises God's special
> and peculiar people. The law commanded that those who commit incest be put to
> death (Lev. 18:6–18, 29). Paul in I Corinthians 5 still finds such a practice to be evil,
> but he does not suggest that the offender be put to death. Instead, the offender is to
> be put out of the church until he repents.[21]

The law of Moses functions as a pedagogue to lead us to Christ. However,
now that Christ is come we are no longer under that pedagogue (Gal 3:19–
4:7).

The spiritual blessings of the new covenant are available to Jew and Gentile alike in this dispensation through union with Christ, although all of the
stipulations of the new covenant are not yet instituted.[22] As always, salvation
is by grace alone through faith alone and based on Christ's atonement alone.

However, in this dispensation of grace God has fully revealed the content of faith. No longer is there need to offer animal sacrifices, Jesus is revealed as the final Sacrifice. He alone is the object of our faith.

Covenants In Force	Beneficiaries	Covenant Stipulation	Covenant Duration	Dispensational Characteristic	Duration
Adamic	Serpent	Satan is humbled ("eat dust") but his total defeat is future.	Fall–New Heavens and New Earth (Gen 3:5 – Rev 22:3)	Satan still active (e.g., 1 Pet 5:8)	Establishment of the new covenant to the second coming of Christ (Matt 27:50; Mark 15:37; Luke 23:46; John 19:30– Rev 19:1)
	Woman	Woman experiences pain in childbirth.		Growth of the human population continues.	
		Her relationship with her husband is distorted.		Family strife continues.	
	Man	Man experiences pain in his labor.		Occupations continue to be laborious.	
	Humankind	Blood sacrifice is abolished.		Humans approach God via Jesus' sacrifice.	
		Knowing good and evil subject to death		Humans are morally responsible and mortal.	
Noahic		Rule Earth as God's vassals	From Establishment to Eternity (Gen 9:16)	God ordains human governments	
		No more universal floods		God judges locally.	
		Authority to judge murder.		Death Penalty in effect (Rom 13:2–4).	

Continued on the next page

Table 23 (*Continued*)

Covenants In Force	Beneficiaries	Covenant Stipulation	Covenant Duration	Dispensational Characteristic	Duration
Abrahamic	Israel	Abraham's line, through Sarah, Isaac, and Jacob, to become a great nation, Israel.	From Establishment to Eternity (Gen 13:15; 17:7)	Israel grew from Jacob's household to a nation while in Egypt.	Establishment of the new covenant to the second coming of Christ (Matt 27:50; Mark 15:37; Luke 23:46; John 19:30– Rev 19:1)
		Circumcision of males is required.		Circumcision continues to be practiced for Jews. But it is not a requirement for salvation.	
	Gentiles	Abraham was to be the progenitor of nations.		Arabs and the Edomites (Jordanians)	
		Those that blessed Israel were blessed, those that cursed Israel were cursed.		God continues to bless nations and individuals that bless Israel and punish those who curse them.	
Land	Israel	Title to the Land	Eternal covenant (Ezek 16:60)	Physical return has begun. Spiritual return is yet future.	
		Third Exile		Exiled by Rome in AD 70	
Davidic		David's throne, dynasty, and kingdom established forever.	Everlasting covenant (2 Sam 23:5; 2 Chr 13:5; Isa 55:3; Jer 33:20– 22)	Jesus offered the kingdom to Israel and was rejected. The kingdom was postponed.	

Continued on the next page

Table 23 (*Continued*)

Covenants In Force	Beneficiaries	Covenant Stipulation	Covenant Duration	Dispensational Characteristic	Duration
New	Israel (Spiritual Blessings to Church in Christ)	Stipulations not yet all instituted.	Forever (Jer 31:36)	Church, both Jew and Gentile, participate in the spiritual blessings of the new covenant by union with Christ.	Establishment of the new covenant to the second coming of Christ (Matt 27:50; Mark 15:37; Luke 23:46; John 19:30– Rev 19:1)

Table 23. Dispensation of Grace and Covenant Stipulations

NOTES

1. Otto Michel, "οἰκονομία," *Theological Dictionary of the New Testament* (hereafter referred to as *TDNT*), ed. Gerhard Friedrich, trans. Geoffrey W. Bromiley, 10 vols. (Grand Rapids, MI: Eerdmans, 1967) 5:151–53.
2. Saucy, *The Case for Progressive Dispensationalism* 143–73.
3. Pentecost, *Things to Come* 136.
4. *BDAG* 661–62. See also *MM* 420.
5. *ALGNT* 267.
6. Ibid.
7. *BDAG* 661. See also *MM* 420.
8. Pentecost, *Things to Come* 134–38.
9. Saucy, *The Case for Progressive Dispensationalism* 173.
10. Ibid.
11. See chapter 10.
12. Ryrie, *Dispensationalism* 56. See also Chafer, *Systematic Theology* 4:180–233
13. Ibid. 71.
14. See chapter 11.
15. Chafer, *Major Bible Themes* 135.
16. Ryrie, *Dispensationalism* 51.
17. See chapter 6.
18. See chapter 7.
19. See chapter 12.
20. Schreiner, *The Law* 63.
21. Ibid. 143.
22. See chapter 11.

CHAPTER NINETEEN

The Dispensation of the Kingdom

Duration and Characteristics

Rabbi Hiyya ben Abba (late 3rd–early 4th centuries AD) claims that "all the prophets prophesied only for the Messianic age...."[1] In fact, biblical prophecy does extend past the messianic age to the new heaven and new earth (Isa 65:17; Rev 21:1). However, we can forgive Rabbi Hiyya for hyperbole when we consider that all of the covenants come to full implementation in the dispensation of the kingdom.

In the dispensation of the kingdom the distinguishable economy in the outworking of God's purpose is the personal rule of the earth from Israel of God's Messiah and Son, Jesus Christ. Chafer comments:

> Likewise, the divine government cannot remain the same in the earth after the world-transforming temporal victories of the second coming, as it has been under the reign of grace. All this is reasonable; but, what is far more impelling and compelling, this is what is precisely revealed by God in His Word.[2]

The main characteristic of this dispensation is the establishment of the millennial kingdom at the second coming of Christ (Rev 19:1–21) and His righteous rule over the entire world for one thousand years (Rev 20:3, 4). Satan will be bound during this time of perfect government (Rev 20:1–3). Humankind will be responsible to obey King Messiah. However, as in the other dispensations, humankind will fail and the millennium will end with a brief ill-fated rebellion (Rev 20:7–9).[3] The Scriptures concerning this dispensation are Rev 19:1–20:10. Chafer observes that "the great key words under the Mosaic system were 'law' and 'obedience,' the great key words in the present age are 'believe' and 'grace,' while the great key words in the kingdom are 'righteousness' and 'peace.'"[4] The future messianic kingdom is the subject of several OT passages such as Isa 60:1–22; 62:1–12; 65:17–25; 66:10–

24; Jer 30:1–31:40; Ezek 40:1–48:35. Consequently, it is scarcely a new subject when John speaks of the kingdom in Rev 20:1–15.

The previously unrevealed detail that John provides is the duration of the kingdom. In Rev 20:2–7 John tells us six times that the duration of the messianic kingdom is one thousand years, thus the term millennium from the Latin, *mille annis* ("thousand years"). There is no reason to take this duration as figurative when John's other time references (e.g., Rev 11:2, 3) are quite precise. Therefore, the messianic kingdom is the personal reign of the ultimate descendant of David, Jesus Christ, on the earth for one thousand years.

The dispensation of the kingdom answers humankind's age-old desire for perfect government and good leaders. In the dispensation of the kingdom the earth will be renewed, and health, prosperity, and peace will provide a perfect environment. The Messiah will be ruling in perfect righteousness and justice. He is Himself perfect God and perfect Man—Peace and prosperity, righteousness and justice, and the perfect King! How could there be a better world? Nevertheless, the end of the millennium will find rebels in sufficient numbers to constitute a huge army willing to join with Satan in rebellion (Rev 20:7–8). God will destroy the rebels with fire from heaven (Rev 20:9) and, thus, even the dispensation of the kingdom will end with humankind's failure. Consequently, God has demonstrated, in every conceivable dispensation, humankind's failure. At the judgment none will be able to impugn God's justice for He has demonstrated it throughout all of the dispensations (see table 24).

Righteousness and justice will characterize Messiah's reign. The Messiah's rule will tolerate no rebellion (Ps 2:9–12; Isa 60:12) and the standards will be higher than the law of Moses (Matt 5:17–48). Chafer considers the kingdom to be a return to law:

> This body of Scripture is found in the Old Testament portions which anticipate the Messianic kingdom and in large portions of the Synoptic Gospels. The essential elements of a grace administration—faith as the sole basis of acceptance with God, unmerited acceptance through a perfect standing in Christ, the present possession of eternal life, an absolute security from all condemnation, and the enabling power of the indwelling Spirit— are not found in the kingdom administration. On the other hand, it is declared to be the fulfilling of "the law and the prophets" (Matt. 5:17–18; 7:12), and is seen to be an extension of the Mosaic Law into realms of merit-seeking which blast and wither as the Mosaic system could never do (Matt. 5:20–48).[5]

Ryrie's reply is that the idea of the reintroduction of law during the tribulation is "highly doubtful," since the law ended with the death of Christ (Rom 10:4; 2 Cor 3:7–11).[6] I consider it much more likely that the law the Messiah will enforce during the dispensation of the kingdom will consist of the covenant stipulations in force (see table 25).

Administration	Responsibility	Terminus ad quo	Terminus ad quem	Failure	Judgment
Kingdom	Obey the King	Second coming of Christ (Rev 19:1)	1,000 years after the second coming of Christ (Rev 20:1–9)	Large numbers join Satan in rebellion at the end of the millennium (Rev 20:7–9).	The Great White Throne Judgment (Rev 20:11–15)

Table 24. Characteristics of the Dispensation of the Kingdom

Covenants in Force

During the dispensation of the kingdom, the Adamic covenant is still in force, although its effects have diminished. The Adamic covenant with its curses ends at the completion of the dispensation of the kingdom (Rev 21:4; 22:3). The Noahic covenant is still in force. These two covenants stipulate the responsibilities of Gentiles during the dispensation of the kingdom. Although the Mosaic covenant ends with the inauguration of the dispensation of grace, Israel is still under the Abrahamic, Land, Davidic, and new covenants. The stipulations of these covenants are instituted in full during the dispensation of the kingdom (see figure 2).

Stipulations in Force

The stipulations of these six covenants (Adamic, Noahic, Abrahamic, Land, Davidic, and new covenants) constitute the governing arrangement for the dispensation of the kingdom. Several important changes occur that moderate the effect of the Adamic covenant's curses. First, Satan, will be not merely humbled as before, but will be bound for the millennium (Rev 20:1–3). Thus,

God will prevent Satan from deceiving humankind during the dispensation of the kingdom. Although humankind will be still mortal during the dispensation of the kingdom, life spans will be extended (Isa 65:20). Although animal sacrifice for atonement is abolished, Ezek 40:1–43:27 seems to indicate that sacrifices will take place during the dispensation of the kingdom. Perhaps these sacrifices are of a memorial character. Although men will still labor, Isa 60:5–17 indicates that the dispensation of the kingdom will be a time of unparalleled prosperity. Although unglorified humans still possess sin natures, yet violence will be unheard of (Isa 60:17, 18). Presumably, the general climate of peace will also affect family relationships and the general health will diminish childbearing difficulties as well. The Adamic curse is diminishing and will cease at the new heaven and new earth (Rev 21:4; 22:3).

The Noahic covenant stipulations are all in force during the dispensation of the kingdom. As the Noahic covenant stipulates, human governments are to rule for God as His vassals.[7] That relationship becomes much more direct in the dispensation of the kingdom when Jesus Christ, the King of kings, rules the world from Jerusalem (Ps 2:6–9; Isa 60:12; Rev 19:16). King Jesus will dispense swift and sure justice and will rule in absolute righteousness. The result will be a *pax Israhelis* under Messiah's rule. Humankind will continue to rule over the animal kingdom, but even wild animals will be at peace (Isa 65:25). The dispensation of the kingdom will be a time of unparalleled peace and perfect government under God's anointed King.

The stipulations of the Abrahamic covenant and all three related covenants (the Land, Davidic, and new covenants) will be completely instituted and in full force during the dispensation of the kingdom. God stipulated that Abraham and his descendants through Isaac and Jacob would inherit a land, a seed, and a blessing (Gen 12:1–3). The land promised is the land of Canaan, and Gen 15:18–21 stipulates the boundaries. In the dispensation of the kingdom, Israel will possess for the first time, fully and permanently, the land in its entirety. The Land covenant reveals that God, after three exiles (Deut 28–29) will regather Israel forever (Deut 30:1–10) . Also in the Land covenant are stipulations that anticipate the Davidic (Deut 30:5) and new covenants (Deut 30:6) as well.

The seed stipulations of the Abrahamic covenant, as expanded by the Davidic covenant, will also be fully implemented in the dispensation of the kingdom. Abraham is promised a seed in that he was to have numerous descendants. Deuteronomy 30:5 indicates that, during the dispensation of the kingdom, the population of Israel will grow beyond any past numbers. David was promised an eternal kingdom and that Israel would dwell forever in peace (2 Sam 7:10–11). Thus, the age-old prayer for peace will be finally fulfilled during the dispensation of the kingdom (Ps 122:6). Israel will endure forever (Jer 31:35–37). The Davidic covenant also stipulates that David's throne (i.e., government) and house (i.e., dynasty) would endure forever. This finds realization in Jesus the Messiah, Who will rule "on the throne of David and over his kingdom ... from then on and forever more" (Isa 9:6–7).

The blessing promises of the Abrahamic covenant will come to completion in the stipulations of the new covenant. Although all that place faith in Jesus Christ in this and the previous dispensation participate in the spiritual blessings of the new covenant, the promise to Israel will be fulfilled only with the dispensation of the kingdom. Israel will possess an enablement to obey the stipulations of the new covenant as God's moral law is written on their hearts (Jer 31:33; Deut 30:6). Each Israeli will enjoy a close personal relationship with God (Jer 31:33–34). God will forgive all of Israel's sin (Jer 31:34). Additionally, in language reminiscent of both the Davidic (2 Sam 7:10–11) and land covenants (Deut 30:5), God promises that Israel will be preserved as a nation forever (Jer 31:35–37). Thus, as God promised Abraham, "I will bless you ... and so you shall be a blessing ... and in you all of the families of the earth shall be blessed" (Gen 12:2–3) (see table 25).

Some brief consideration of the eternal state is in order. Ryrie comments that

> when temporal history ends, the household arrangement, which is the basis for a dispensational stewardship, also ends. In other words, the dispensational economies are related to the affairs of this present world, and they are no longer needed when the history of this world comes to a conclusion. Thus, in eternity there is no need for the economic arrangements of a dispensation as they are known in history.[8]

With all due respect, I must disagree. In fact, this is an example of the problem of viewing dispensations in a vacuum, rather than from a covenantal perspective. If covenant stipulations are the basis of dispensations and those covenants are eternal, so must be the "household arrangement."[9] Admittedly, although the Noahic covenant is eternal, it is hard to imagine that there will be the slightest concern in eternity about murders. In addition, the Adamic covenant will have ended (Rev 22:3). However, even the new heaven and earth has a Jerusalem (Rev 21:1–22:5). Israel will be "a nation ... forever"

(Jer 31:36). The Messiah, Jesus Christ, will rule with "no end," and "forevermore" (Isa 9:7). Taken literally, these promises cannot be fulfilled in a mere one thousand years (see table 26). As the Psalmist writes, "Forever, O LORD, Your word is settled in heaven" (Ps 119:89), and

> He has remembered His covenant forever,
> > The word which He commanded to a thousand generations,
>
> *The covenant* which He made with Abraham,
> > And His oath to Isaac.
>
> Then He confirmed it to Jacob for a statute,
> > To Israel as an everlasting covenant (Ps 105:8–10).

God's covenant promises hold true forever.

Covenants In Force	Beneficiaries	Covenant Stipulation	Covenant Duration	Dispensational Characteristic	Duration
Adamic	Serpent	Satan humbled and will suffer total defeat.	Fall–New Heavens and New Earth (Gen 3:5 – Rev 22:3)	Satan bound for the millennium (Rev 20:1–3)	The second coming of Christ to the end of the millennium (Rev 19:1–20:10)
	Woman	Experience pain in childbirth.		The earth is repopulated by survivors of the Tribulation. Health and longevity.	
	Woman	Relationship with her husband is distorted.		Family strife should be lessened by general climate of peace.	
	Man	Experience pain in his labor.		Unprecedented time of prosperity.	
	Humankind	Blood sacrifice is abolished.		Men approach God via Jesus' sacrifice. There will be memorial sacrifices.	
		Knowing good and evil, subject to death.		Morally responsible and mortal.	

Continued on the next page

Table 25 (*Continued*)

Covenants In Force	Beneficiaries	Covenant Stipulation	Covenant Duration	Dispensational Characteristic	Duration
Noahic	Humankind	Rule earth as God's vassals	From Estab-lishment to Eternity (Gen 9:16)	Jesus Christ rules all nations from Jerusalem.	The second coming of Christ to the end of the mil-lennium (Rev 19:1– 20:10)
		No more universal floods		God judges the final rebellion at the end of the millennium (Rev 20:7–9).	
		The Author-ity and The Responsibil-ity to Judge Murder.		Death Penalty in effect, Messiah's rule will be firm and just (Ps 2:9–12; Isa 60:12).	
		Permission to eat meat		Animals at peace also (Isa 65:25).	
Abrahamic	Israel	Abraham's line, through Sarah, Isaac, and Jacob, to become a great nation, Israel.	From Estab-lishment to Eternity (Gen 13:15; 17:7)	Israel will grow to its greatest popu-lation during the millennium (Deut 30:5).	
		Circumci-sion of males		Circumcision continues to be practiced.	
	Gentiles	Abraham was to be the progenitor of nations.		Saved Arabs and the Edo-mites blessed in the Kingdom (Isa 19:18–25).	
		Those that blessed Is-rael were blessed, those that cursed Israel were cursed.		God continues to bless nations and individuals that bless Israel and punish those who curse them.	

Continued on the next page

Table 25 (*Continued*)

Covenants In Force	Beneficiaries	Covenant Stipulation	Covenant Duration	Dispensational Characteristic	Duration
Land	Israel	Title to the Land	Eternal covenant (Ezek 16:60)	Israel in the land forever.	The second coming of Christ to the end of the millennium (Rev 19:1–20:10)
		Final Return from Exile			
Davidic		David's throne, dynasty, and kingdom established forever.	Everlasting covenant (2 Sam 23:5; 2 Chr 13:5)	Jesus Christ will rule the world from Jerusalem.	
New		Forgiveness	Forever (Jer 31:36)	Gentiles participate in the spiritual blessings by union with Christ. Jews are forgiven, enabled to obey, and given an intimate relationship with God. Israel a nation forever.	
		Law written on hearts			
		Each will know God.			
		Israel will be a nation forever.			

Table 25. Dispensation of the Kingdom and Covenant Stipulations

Covenants In Force	Beneficiaries	Covenant Stipulation	Covenant Duration	Characteristic
Noahic	Humankind	Blood sacrifice is abolished.	From Establishment to Eternity (Gen 9:16)	All are glorified and sinless.
		Rule Earth as God's Vassals		Jesus Christ rules all nations
		No more universal floods		No more curse (Rev 22:3).
		The Authority to judge murder		No more sin

Continued on the next page

Table 26 (*Continued*)

Covenants In Force	Beneficiaries	Covenant Stipulation	Covenant Duration	Characteristic
Abrahamic	Israel	Abraham was to be the progenitor of nations.	From Establishment to Eternity (Gen 13:15; 17:7)	Saved Gentiles will be blessed eternally (Rev 5:9; 22:3–4).
		Those that blessed Israel were blessed, those that cursed Israel were cursed.		No more curse (Rev 22:3).
		Abraham's line, through Sarah, Isaac, and Jacob, to become a great nation, Israel.		Israel will be a nation forever (Jer 31:35–37).
		Circumcision is required.		Circumcision of the heart.
Land		Title to the Land	Eternal covenant (Ezek 16:60)	Israel in the land forever.
		Final Return from Exile		Peace forever.
Davidic		David's throne, dynasty, and kingdom established forever.	Everlasting covenant (2 Sam 23:5; 2 Chr 13:5)	Jesus Christ will rule the world from Jerusalem.
New		Forgiveness	Everlasting covenant (2 Sam 23:5; 2 Chr 13:5) Forever (Jer 31:36)	Gentiles participate in the spiritual blessings by union with Christ.
		Law written on hearts		Jews are forgiven, enabled to obey, and given an intimate relationship with God.
		Each will know God.		
		Israel will be a nation forever.		Israel will be a nation forever.

Table 26. Eternal State and Covenant Stipulations

NOTES

1. *b. Berakot* 34b; *b. Shabbat* 63a.
2. Chafer, *Systematic Theology* 4:169.
3. Ryrie, *Dispensationalism* 56.
4. Chafer, *Systematic Theology* 4:170.
5. Chafer, *Systematic Theology* 4:19.
6. Ryrie, *Dispensationalism* 50.
7. See chapter 7.
8. Ryrie, *Dispensationalism* 48–49.
9. Pentecost, *Things To Come* 561.

PART FOUR

Conclusions

CHAPTER TWENTY

Covenant and Dispensation

The Prescriptive Nature of the Divine Covenants

I have demonstrated in this study that the archaeological and anthropological discoveries have critical significance for our understanding of biblical covenants. I delineated the major characteristics of the ancient Near Eastern covenant types: parity, grant, and suzerainty. I defined a covenant as *a solemn unilateral obligation made binding by an oath*. Although all covenants are unilateral, I demonstrated that both parity and suzerainty covenants are inherently conditional and, therefore, non-gracious. The grant, however, is inherently unconditional and, therefore, gracious. Although all three ancient Near Eastern covenant forms are in evidence in the Scriptures, the divine covenants never use the parity form. Of the divine covenants dealing with Israel, all are grant covenants except the Mosaic covenant. These results establish that the dispensational understanding of the gracious and unconditional character of the Abrahamic, Land, Davidic, and new covenants is correct. Therefore, the scriptural data are counterindicative of the covenant theological position that the divine covenants are each administrations of the theological covenant of grace. Real differences exist in both form and purpose between these covenants. In addition, absolutely no evidence exists for the theological covenants in the Bible. Therefore, the dispensational understanding of the nature of the covenants is confirmed.

I have shown that, by means of covenant stipulations, the divine covenants prescribe God's will for the beneficiaries of the covenants. Since the covenants are not the same as ages or dispensations, more than one covenant may be in force at a time. Excepting Eden before the fall and initially under the Adamic covenant, this is always the case. It is important to realize this because the covenants often deal with different people groups (e.g., the Noahic and Davidic covenants). Additional detail is added by the realization that, within a covenant, stipulations may be instituted at differing times. Most of the covenants are eternal. However, the Edenic and Mosaic are not. *Therefore, at any given moment, the sum of the instituted stipulations of the established covenants that continue in force prescribes the will of God for the designated beneficiaries.* Dispensationalism is to be criticized in that it has not clearly, consistently, and unequivocally asserted the divine covenants as the basis of God's governing arrangements.

The purpose of the divine covenants can now be discerned. The covenant theologian is too restrictive in limiting God's purpose to salvation alone. Although certainly some provisions of the divine covenants are salvific, clearly others are not. John H. Walton advances the thesis that God's purpose in covenant is revelatory.[1] While I cannot agree with all of Walton's conclusions (e.g., single covenant and conditional rather than unconditional promises to Israel), the covenants do reveal God's will and, in that sense, are revelatory. However, Paul is clear that God's purpose is His own glory, "We have obtained an inheritance, having been predestinated according to His purpose ... to the end that we ... should be to the praise of His glory" (Eph 1:11–12). The center of history is God not man. God does reveal Himself, and that self-revelation results in His glory. *The salvific and revelatory purposes of God are but components of His doxological purpose.* Therefore, I confirm the third element of Ryrie's *sine qua non* of dispensationalism.[2]

Therefore, I conclude that

- ♦ *Covenants are defined as a solemn unilateral obligation made binding by an oath.*
- ♦ *At any given moment, the sum of the instituted stipulations of the established covenants that continue in force prescribes the will of God for the designated beneficiaries.*
- ♦ *The salvific and revelatory purposes of God are but components of His doxological purpose.*

Dispensationalism is correct in its focus on the multiple biblical covenants and assertion of God's doxological purpose. Covenant theology is in error in asserting the theological covenants without scriptural evidence. Continuity between the testaments is explained by three factors: (1) God's purpose is unified, (2) God's moral standard is unchanging, and (3) covenants may span multiple dispensations. Temporary covenants and the timing of covenantal stipulation institution account for discontinuity. Consideration of the covenantal beneficiaries results in a clear distinction between Israel and the Church as taught by dispensationalism. Dispensationalism has been deficient in that it tends to ignore the basis for the divine governing arrangements. That basis is in the divine covenants. Therefore, *covenants are prescriptive*.

The Descriptive Nature of the Dispensations

I confess that I cannot improve on Ryrie's definition of a dispensation, *"A dispensation is a distinguishable economy in the outworking of God's purpose."*[3] Dispensations are descriptions of God's chosen means of administration. They are not, as covenant theologians often misunderstand, different means of salvation. All Christians, even covenant theologians, teach at least two dispensations—Law and Grace. The dispensationalist gives proper place to the differing ways that God administers humankind. The stipulations of the governing arrangements are found in the divine covenants. Therefore, *dispensations are descriptive*.

The Complementary Nature of the Divine Covenants and the Dispensations

The divine covenants and the dispensations are complementary. The dispensationalist thinks that the covenant theologian sees too many covenants and the covenant theologian thinks that the dispensationalist sees too many dispensations. The covenant theologian focuses on the foundation, which is covenant, and the dispensationalist focuses on the structure, which is dispensationalism. The question is not, as Robertson asked, "Which structures the biblical revelation; dispensations or covenants?"[4] Covenants do structure the biblical revelation and that structure is dispensationalism. *The covenants prescribe and the dispensations describe the outworking of the purpose of God.*

What is required is a covenantal dispensationalism. Since covenant theology has commandeered the term "covenant" many would consider "dispensational covenant theology" or "covenant dispensationalism" oxymorons. Ultimately, these distinctions stem from a false dichotomy. The Scriptures are both covenantal and dispensational. *Covenants prescribe and dispensations describe the structure of the progressive revelation of God's plan for the ages.* God's administration of humankind is founded upon the bedrock of His covenant promises. To God be the glory.

NOTES

1. John H. Walton, *Covenant: God's Purpose, God's Plan* (Grand Rapids, MI: Zondervan, 1994).
2. Ryrie, *Dispensationalism* 40–41.
3. Ryrie, *Dispensationalism* 28.
4. Robertson, *Christ of the Covenants* 201–27.

◆ BIBLIOGRAPHY

Aldrich, Roy L. "An Apologetic for Dispensationalism." *Bibliotheca Sacra* 112, no. 445 (January–March 1955): 46–54.

———. "A New Look at Dispensationalism." *Bibliotheca Sacra* 120, no. 477 (January–March 1963): 42–49.

———. "Has the Mosaic Law Been Abolished?" *Bibliotheca Sacra* 116, no. 464 (October–December 1959): 322–35.

Alford, Henry. *Acts—I II Corinthians.* Alford's Greek Testament: An Exegetical and Critical Commentary. Vol. 2 of 6 vols. London: Rivingtons, 1874–5; reprint, Grand Rapids, MI: Guardian, 1976.

Archer, Gleason L. Jr. *A Survey of Old Testament Introduction.* Rev. ed. Chicago: Moody, 1994.

———. "Covenant," *Evangelical Dictionary of Theology.* 2nd ed. Ed. Walter A. Elwell. Grand Rapids, MI: Baker, 2001.

Bauer, W., Danker, F. W., Arndt, William F., and Gingrich, F. Wilbur. *A Greek-English Lexicon of the New Testament and Other Early Christian Literature.* 3rd ed. Chicago: The University of Chicago Press, 1999.

Beagley, A. J. "Scrolls, Seals." *Dictionary of the Later New Testament & Its Developments.* Downers Grove, IL: InterVarsity, 1997.

Beasley-Murray, G. R. "The Revelation." *The New Bible Commentary: Revised.* Eds. D. Guthrie, J. A. Motyer. 3rd ed. Grand Rapids, MI: Eerdmans, 1970.

Beckman, Gary. *Hittite Diplomatic Texts.* Writings from the Ancient World: Society of Biblical Literature. Ed. Harry A. Hoffner, Jr. Atlanta: Scholars, 1996.

Berger, Morroe. *The Arab World Today.* Garden City, NY: Doubleday, 1962.

Berkhof, L. *Systematic Theology.* 4th ed. Grand Rapids, MI: Eerdmans, 1977.

Berry, George Ricker. "Covenant, in the Old Testament." *International Standard Bible Encyclopedia.* Vol. 2 of 4 vols. Available in The Master Christian Library v. 8.0 [CD-ROM]. Rio, WI: AGES Software, 2000.

Biederwolf, William E. *The Second Coming Bible: The Complete Text of Every Scripture Passage Concerned with the Second Coming of Christ Plus Commentary on Each Verse.* Grand Rapids, MI: Baker, 1972.

Bierma, Lyle D. *German Calvinism in the Confessional Age: The Covenant Theology of Cas-*

par Olevianus. Grand Rapids, MI: Baker, 1996.

Blasing, Craig A., Bock, Darrell L. *Progressive Dispensationalism.* Grand Rapids, MI: Baker, 1993.

Bloesch, Donald G. "Law and Gospel in Reformed Perspective." *Grace Theological Journal* 12, no. 2 (Fall 1991): 179–88.

Bock, Darrell L. "Current Messianic Activity and OT Davidic Promise: Dispensationalism, Hermeneutics, and NT Fulfillment." *Trinity Journal* 15, no. 1 (Spring 1994): 55–87.

———. "The Son of David and the Saint's Task: The Hermeneutics of Initial Fulfillment." *Bibliotheca Sacra* 150, no. 600 (October–December 1993): 440–57.

———, Burns, J. Lanier, Johnson, Elliott E., Toussaint, Stanley D., *Three Central Issues in Contemporary Dispensationalism: A Comparison of Traditional and Progressive Views.* Gen. ed. Herbert W. Bateman IV. Grand Rapids, MI: Kregel, 1999.

Botterweck, G. Johannes, Ringgren, Helmer. *Theological Dictionary of the Old Testament.* Trans. John T. Willis. 12– vols. Grand Rapids, MI: Eerdmans, 1975–.

Bright, John. *A History Of Israel.* 3rd ed. Philadelphia: Westminister, 1981.

Brown, Collin ed. *The New International Dictionary of New Testament Theology: Translated, with additions and revisions, from the German Theologishes Begriffslexikon zum Neuen Testament.* 5 vols. Grand Rapids, MI: Zondervan, 1986.

Brown, Francis, Driver, S. R., and Briggs, Charles A. *A Hebrew and English Lexicon of the Old Testament: With an Appendix Containing the Biblical Aramaic, Based on the Lexicon of William Gesenius.* Oxford: Clarendon, 1953; reprint, New York: Oxford University Press, 1977.

Broyles, C. C. "Gospel (Good News)." *New Dictionary of Biblical Theology.* Eds. T. Desmond Alexander and Brian S. Rosner. Downers Grove, IL: InterVarsity, 2000.

Bruce, F. F. "Colossian Problems—Part 4: Christ as Conqueror and Reconciler." *Bibliotheca Sacra* 141, no. 564 (October–December 1984): 291–301.

Brueggemann, Walter. *The Covenanted Self: Explorations in Law and Covenant.* Ed. Patrick D. Miller. Minneapolis, MN: Fortress, 1999.

Chafer, Lewis Sperry. *Grace: The Glorious Theme.* Grand Rapids, MI: Zondervan, 1922.

———. *Major Bible Themes: 52 Vital Doctrines of the Scripture Simplified and Explained.* Rev. John F. Walvoord. Grand Rapids, MI: Zondervan, 1974.

———. "Soteriology." *Bibliotheca Sacra* 103, no. 411 (July–September 1946): 261–83.

———. *Systematic Theology.* 8 vols. Dallas, TX: Dallas Seminary Press, 1947.

Clemens, Samuel Langhorne. *Innocents Abroad,* in *The Unabridged Mark Twain.* Philadelphia: Running, 1976.

Cole, R. A. "Law in the Old Testament." *The Zondervan Pictorial Encyclopedia of the Bible.* Vol. 3 of 5 vols. Gen. ed. Merrill C. Tenney. Grand Rapids, MI: Zondervan, 1975.

Cook, F. C. "Deuteronomy." *Exodus to Esther.* Barnes' Notes. Vol. 2 of 14 vols. Boston: Estes and Lauriate, 1873; reprint, Grand Rapids, MI: Baker, 1998.

Couch, Mal. "Progressive Dispensationalism: Is Christ Now on the Throne of David?—Part I." *Conservative Theological Journal* 2, no. 4 (March 1998): 32–46.

———. "Progressive Dispensationalism: Is Christ Now on the Throne of David?—Part II." *Conservative Theological Journal* 2, no. 5 (June 1998): 142–56.

————. "Progressive Dispensationalism: Is Christ Now on the Throne of David?—Part III." *Conservative Theological Journal* 2, no. 6 (September 1998): 272–285.

————. "The Relationship Between the Dispensations and Covenants." *The Conservative Theological Journal* 2, no. 7 (December 1998): 405–31.

Cross, Frank Moore. *From Epic to Canon.* Baltimore: Johns Hopkins University Press, 1998.

Dana, H. E., Mantey, Julius R. *A Manual Grammar of the Greek New Testament.* N.p.: Macmillan, 1957.

Davidson, Benjamin. *The Analytical Hebrew and Chaldee Lexicon.* Grand Rapids, MI: Zondervan, 1973.

Decker, Rodney J. "The Church's Relationship to the New Covenant (Part 1)." *Bibliotheca Sacra* 152, no. 607 (July–September 1995): 290–305.

————. "The Church's Relationship to the New Covenant (Part 2)." *Bibliotheca Sacra* 152, no. 608 (October–December 1995): 431–56.

Deere, Jack. "Deuteronomy." *The Bible Knowledge Commentary: An Exposition of the Scriptures by Dallas Seminary Faculty: Old Testament.* Eds. John Walvoord, Roy B. Zuck. N.p.: Victor, 1985.

Deissmann, G. Adolf. *Bible Studies: Contributions Chiefly from Papyri and Inscriptions to the History of the Language, the Literature, and the Religion of Hellenistic Judaism and Primitive Christianity.* Trans. Alexander Grieve. Edinburgh: T. & T. Clark, 1901; reprint, Peabody, MA: Hendrickson, 1988.

————. *Light From The Ancient East: The New Testament Illustrated by Recently Discovered Texts of the Graeco-Roman World.* Trans. Lionel R. M. Strachan. Peabody, MA: Hendrickson, 1995.

Denney, James. "St. Paul's Epistle to the Romans." *Apostles, Romans, First Corinthians.* The Expositor's Greek Testament. Ed. W. Robertson Nicoll. Vol. 2 of 5 vols. Grand Rapids, MI: Eerdmans, 1990.

Dillow, Joseph C. *The Reign of the Servant Kings: A Study of Eternal Security and the Final Significance of Man.* Hayesville, NC: Schoette, 1992.

Dorsey, David A. "The Law of Moses and the Christian: A Compromise." *Journal of the Evangelical Theological Society* 34, no. 3 (September 1991): 321–34.

————. *The Literary Structure of the Old Testament: A Commentary on Genesis-Malachi.* Grand Rapids, MI: Baker, 1999.

Driver, S. R. *A Treatise on the Use of the Tenses in Hebrew and Some Other Syntactical Questions.* Grand Rapids, MI: Eerdmans, 1874; reprint, 1998.

Dumbrell, W. J. *Covenant and Creation: A Theology of the Old Testament Covenants.* Chatham, Kent: Paternoster, 1984; reprint, 2000.

Eaton, Michael. *No Condemnation: A New Theology of Assurance.* Downers Grove, IL: InterVarsity, 1995.

Elazar, Daniel J. *HaBrit V'HaHesed: Foundations of the Jewish System* [paper on-line]. Jerusalem: Jerusalem Center for Public Affairs, accessed 8 July 2001, available from http://www.jcpa.org/dje/articles2/britvhesed.htm; Internet.

English, E. Schuyler. *A Companion to The New Scofield Reference Bible.* New York: Oxford University Press, 1972.

Fee, Gordon D. and Stuart, Douglas. *How to Read the Bible for All It's Worth: A Guide to Understanding the Bible.* 2nd ed. Grand Rapids, MI: Zondervan, 1993.

Feinberg, Charles L. "Jeremiah." *Isaiah-Ezekiel.* The Expositor's Bible Commentary. Vol. 6 of 12 vols. Gen. ed. Frank E. Gaebelein. Grand Rapids, MI: Zondervan, 1990.

———. "The Virgin Birth in the Old Testament." *Bibliotheca Sacra* 117, no. 468 (October–December 1960): 313–24.

Fensham, F. C. "Covenant, Alliance." *The New Bible Dictionary.* Wheaton, IL: Tyndale, 1962. Available *Logos Library System* [CD-ROM].

Foh, Susan T. "What is the Woman's Desire." *Westminister Theological Journal* 37, no. 3 (Spring 1975): 376–83.

Freeman, James M. *Manners and Customs of the Bible: A Complete Guide to the Origin and Significance of Our Time-honored Biblical Tradition.* Plainfield, NJ: Logos, 1972.

Friberg, Timothy, Friberg, Barbra, and Miller, Neva. *Analytical Lexicon of the Greek New Testament.* Grand Rapids, MI: Baker, 2000.

Friedrich, Gerhard ed. *Theological Dictionary of the New Testament.* Trans. Geoffrey W. Bromiley. 10 vols. Grand Rapids, MI: Eerdmans, 1967.

Fruchtenbaum, Arnold G. *Israelology: The Missing Link in Systematic Theology.* 2nd rev. Tustin, CA: Ariel Ministries, 1994.

———. "Palestinian Covenant." *Dictionary of Premillennial Theology.* Gen. ed. Mal Couch. Grand Rapids, MI: Kregel, 1996.

———. "Where Are We Now? The Prophetic Plan of the Abrahamic Covenant." *The Fundamentals for the Twenty-First Century: Examining the Crucial Issues of the Christian Faith.* Gen. ed. Mal Couch. Grand Rapids, MI: Kregel, 2000.

Gade, Ralph M. "Is God through with the Jew?" *Grace Journal* 11, no. 2 (Spring 1970): 21–33.

Garlington, Don. "Oath-taking in the Community of the New Age (Matthew 5:33–37)." *Trinity Journal* 16, no. 2 (Fall 1995): 139–70.

Geisler, Norman L., Brooks, Ronald M. *Come, Let Us Reason: An Introduction to Logical Thinking.* Grand Rapids, MI: Baker, 1990.

———. "Pentateuch, Mosaic Authorship of." *Baker Encyclopedia of Christian Apologetics.* Grand Rapids, MI: Baker, 1999.

———. "Redaction Criticism, Old Testament." *Baker Encyclopedia of Christian Apologetics.* Grand Rapids, MI: Baker, 1999.

———. "Wellhausen, Julius." *Baker Encyclopedia of Christian Apologetics.* Grand Rapids, MI: Baker, 1999.

Gesenius, H. W. F. *Gesenius' Hebrew and Chaldee Lexicon to the Old Testament Scriptures.* Trans. Samuel Prideaux Tregelles. N.p.: 1847; reprint, Grand Rapids, MI: Baker, 1979.

Grudem, Wayne. *Systematic Theology: An Introduction to Biblical Doctrine.* Grand Rapids, MI: Zondervan, 1994.

Guinan, Michael D. "Mosaic Covenant." *The Anchor Bible Dictionary.* Vol. 4 of 6 vols. Ed. David Noel Freedman. New York: Doubleday, 1992.

Hague, Dyson. "The History of the Higher Criticism." *The Fundamentals.* Vol. 1 of 4 vols. Los Angeles: Bible Institute of Los Angeles, 1917; reprint, Grand Rapids, MI: Baker,

1998.

Harris, R. Laird, Archer, Gleason L. Jr., and Waltke, Bruce K., eds. *Theological Wordbook of the Old Testament.* 2 vols. Chicago: Moody, 1980.

Harrison, Everett F. "Romans." *Romans—Galatians.* The Expositor's Bible Commentary. Vol. 10 of 12 vols. Gen. ed. Frank E. Gaebelein. Grand Rapids, MI: Zondervan, 1990.

Harrison, R. K. "Deuteronomy." *The Zondervan Pictorial Encyclopedia of the Bible.* Vol. 2 of 5 vols. Gen. ed. Merrill C. Tenney. Grand Rapids, MI: Zondervan, 1975.

Hillers, Delbret R. *Covenant: The History of a Biblical Idea.* Baltimore: The Johns Hopkins University Press, 1969.

Hugenberger, Gordon P. *Marriage as a Covenant: Biblical Law and Ethics as Developed from Malachi.* Grand Rapids, MI: Baker, 1994.

Jamieson, Robert, Fausset, A. R., Brown, David. *Commentary Practical and Explanatory on the Whole Bible.* Rev. ed. Grand Rapids, MI: Zondervan, 1961.

Jenni, Ernst, and Westermann, Claus. *Theological Lexicon of the Old Testament.* Trans. Mark E. Biddle from the *Theologisches Handwörterbuch zum Alten Testament.* 3 vols. Peabody, MA: Hendrickson, 1997.

Johnson, Elliott E. "Hermeneutical Principles and the Interpretation of Psalm 110." *Bibliotheca Sacra* 149, no. 596 (October–December 1992): 428–37.

Johnson, Franklin. "Fallacies of the Higher Criticism." *The Fundamentals.* Vol. 1 of 4 vols. Los Angeles: Bible Institute of Los Angeles, 1917; reprint, Grand Rapids, MI: Baker, 1998.

Kaiser, Walter C. Jr. "The Promise Theme and the Theology of Rest." *Bibliotheca Sacra* 130, no. 518 (April–June 1973): 135–50.

———. "The Promised Land: A Biblical-Historical View." *Bibliotheca Sacra* 138, no. 552 (October–December 1981): 302–12.

Kaiser, Walter C. Jr., Davids, Peter H., Bruce, F. F., Brauch, Manfred T. *Hard Sayings of the Bible.* Downers Grove, IL: InterVarsity, 1996.

Karleen, Paul S. "Understanding Covenant Theologians: A Study in Presuppositions." *Grace Theological Journal* 10, no. 2 (Fall 1989): 125–38.

Keener, Craig S. *The IVP Bible Background Commentary: New Testament.* Downers Grove, IL: InterVarsity, 1993.

Keil, C. F., Delitzsch, F. *Jeremiah-Lamentations.* Commentary on the Old Testament. Vol. 8 of 10 vols. Trans. James Martin. Edinburgh: T. & T. Clark, 1866–91; reprint, Peabody, Mass.: Hendrickson, 1996.

———. *Pentateuch.* Commentary on the Old Testament. Vol. 1 of 10 vols. Trans. James Martin. Edinburgh: T. & T. Clark, 1866–91; reprint, Peabody, Mass.: Hendrickson, 1996.

Kent, Homer A., Jr. "The New Covenant and the Church." *Grace Theological Journal* 6, no. 2 (Fall 1985): 289–98.

Kidner, Derek. *Genesis: An Introduction & Commentary.* Tyndale Old Testament Commentaries. Vol. 1 of 18 vols. Gen. ed. D. J. Wiseman. Downers Grove, IL: InterVarsity, 1967.

Killen, R. Allan, Rea, John. "Covenant." *Wycliffe Bible Encyclopedia.* Eds. Charles F. Pfeiffer, Howard F. Vos, and John Rea. Vol. 1 of 2 vols. Chicago: Moody, 1975.

Kline, Meredith G. *By Oath Consigned.* Grand Rapids, MI: Eerdmans, 1968.

————. "Deuteronomy." *The Wycliffe Bible Commentary.* Eds. Charles F. Pfeiffer and Everett F. Harrison. Chicago: Moody, 1972.

————. "Deuteronomy." *Zondervan's Pictorial Bible Dictionary.* Vol. 2 of 5 vols. Gen. ed. Merrill C. Tenney. Grand Rapids, MI: Zondervan, 1963.

————. "Genesis." *The New Bible Commentary: Revised.* Eds. D. Guthrie, J. A. Motyer. 3rd ed. Grand Rapids, MI: Eerdmans, 1970.

————. *The Structure of Biblical Authority.* 2nd ed. Eugene, OR: Wipf and Stock, 1989.

————. *Treaty of the Great King.* Grand Rapids, MI: Eerdmans, 1963.

Koehler, Ludwig, Baumgartner, Walter. *The Hebrew and Aramaic Lexicon of Old Testament: Study Edition.* Trans. and ed. M. E. J. Richardson. 2 vols. Boston: Brill, 2001.

LaHaye, Tim and Ice, Thomas. *Charting the End Times.* Eugene, OR: Harvest House, 2001.

Lane, David H. "Theological Problems with Theistic Evolution." *Bibliotheca Sacra* 151, no. 602 (April–June 1994): 155–74.

Laney, J. Carl. "The Role of the Prophets in God's Case Against Israel." *Bibliotheca Sacra* 138, no. 552 (October–December 1981): 313–25.

Lenski, R. C. H. *The Interpretation of St. Paul's Epistle to the Romans.* Commentary on the New Testament. Vol. 6 of 11 vols. N.p.: Lutheran Book Concern, 1936; reprint, n.p.: Hendrickson, 1998.

Leupold, H. C. *Exposition of Genesis.* 2 vols. Grand Rapids, MI: Baker, 1942.

Levy, David H. *The Sky: A User's Guide.* New York: Cambridge University Press, 1991.

Lewis, Gordon R. "Theological Antecedents of Pretribulationism." *Bibliotheca Sacra* 125, no. 498 (April–June 1968): 129–38.

Liddell, Henry George, and Scott, Robert. *A Greek-English Lexicon.* Revised by Sir Henry Stuart Jones. 9th ed. Oxford: Clarendon Press, 1996.

Lightfoot, John. *Matthew — Mark.* A commentary on the New Testament from the Talmud and Hebraica: Matthew — I Corinthians. Vol. 2 of 4 vols. Oxford: Oxford University Press, 1859; reprint, Grand Rapids, MI: Baker, 1979.

Lightner, Robert P. "Perspectives on Theonomy: Part 3: A Dispensational Response to Theonomy." *Bibliotheca Sacra* 143, no. 571 (July–September 1986): 228–45.

————. "Progressive Dispensationalism." *Conservative Theological Journal* 4, no. 11(March 2000): 46–64.

Livingston, G. Herbert. *The Pentateuch in Its Cultural Environment.* Grand Rapids: Baker, 1978.

Longenecker, Richard N. "The Pedagogical Nature of the Law in Galatians 3:19–4:7." *Journal of the Evangelical Theological Society* 25, no. 1 (March 1982): 53–61.

McCarthy, Dennis J. *Old Testament Covenant: A Survey of Current Opinions.* Atlanta, GA: John Knox, 1972.

————. *Treaty and Covenant: A Study in Form in the Ancient Oriental Documents and in the Old Testament.* 2nd ed. Rome: Biblical Institute Press, 1981.

McComiskey, Thomas Edward. *The Covenants of Promise: A Theology of the Old Testament Covenants.* Grand Rapids, MI: Baker, 1985.

McDowell, Josh D. *The New Evidence that Demands a Verdict.* Nashville, TN: Nelson, 1999.

Mendenhall, George E. "Covenant." *Encyclopaedia Britannica* [book on-line]. N.p.: Britannica.com, 2001. Accessed 3 May 2001. Available from http://www.britannica.com/eb/article?eu=117214&tocid=34041. Internet.

————. "Covenant." *The Interpreter's Dictionary of the Bible: An Illustrated Encyclopedia.* Vol. 1 of 5 vols. Ed. George Arthur Buttrick. Nashville, TN: Abingdon, 1962.

————. "Law and Covenant in Israel and the Ancient Near East." *The Biblical Archaeologist* [article on-line] 17, no. 2 (May 1954): 26–44 and 17, no. 3 (September 1954) : 49–76. Accessed 26 February 2001. Available Internet. http://members.cftnet.com/chrishum/Law_Cov_Mendenhall_TITLE.htm.

————, Herion, Gary A. "Covenant." *The Anchor Bible Dictionary.* Vol. 1 of 6 vols. Ed. David Noel Freedman. New York: Doubleday, 1992.

Merrill, Eugene H. "A Theology of the Pentateuch." *A Biblical Theology of the Old Testament.* Ed. Roy B. Zuck. Chicago: Moody, 1991.

Motyer, J. A. "Law, Biblical Concept of." *Evangelical Dictionary of Theology.* 2nd ed. Ed. Walter A. Elwell. Grand Rapids, MI: Baker, 2001.

Moulton, J. H., and Milligan, G. *Vocabulary of the Greek Testament.* Peabody, MA: Hendrickson, 1997.

Murphey, Roland E. "Wisdom in the OT." *The Anchor Bible Dictionary.* Vol. 6 of 6 vols. Ed. David Noel Freedman. New York: Doubleday, 1992.

Murphy, James G. *Genesis.* Barnes' Notes. Vol. 1 of 14 vols. Boston: Estes and Lauriate, 1873; reprint, Grand Rapids, MI: Baker, 1998.

Nichols, Stephen J. "The Dispensational View of the Davidic Kingdom: A Response to Progressive Dispensationalism." *Master's Seminary Journal* 7, no. 2 (Fall 1996): 213–39.

Niehaus, Jefferey J. *God at Sinai: Covenant and Theophany in the Bible and Ancient Near East.* Grand Rapids, MI: Zondervan, 1995.

Osterhaven, M. E. "Covenant Theology." *Evangelical Dictionary of Theology.* 2nd ed. Ed. Walter A. Elwell. Grand Rapids, MI: Baker, 2001.

Payne, J. Barton. "Testament." *Wycliffe Bible Encyclopedia.* Eds. Charles F. Pfeiffer, Howard F. Vos, and John Rea. Vol. 2 of 2 vols. Chicago: Moody, 1975.

Pentecost, J. Dwight. "The Godly Remnant of the Tribulation Period." *Bibliotheca Sacra* 117 no. 466 (April–June 1960): 123–43.

————. *Things to Come: A Study in Biblical Eschatology.* N.p.: Dunham, 1958; reprint, Grand Rapids, MI: Zondervan, 1974.

————. *Thy Kingdom Come: Tracing God's Kingdom Program and Covenant Promises Throughout History.* Grand Rapids, MI: Kregel, 1995.

Peters, George N. H. *The Theocratic Kingdom of Our Lord Jesus, the Christ, as Covenanted in the Old Testament.* 3 vols. New York: Funk & Wagnalls, 1884; reprint, Grand Rapids, MI: Kregel, 1988.

Poythress, Vern Sheridan. "Response to Paul S. Karleen's Paper 'Understanding Covenant Theologians'." *Grace Theological Journal* 10, no. 2 (Fall 1989): 147–55.

————. *Understanding Dispensationalists.* 2nd ed. Phillipsburg, NJ: Presbyterian and Reformed, 1995.

Ramm, Bernard. *Protestant Biblical Interpretation: A Textbook of Hermeneutics.* 3rd rev. ed.

Grand Rapids, MI: Baker, 1970.

Rendtorff, Rolf. *The Covenant Formula: An Exegetical and Theological Investigation.* Trans. Margaret Kohl. Edinburgh: T&T Clark, 1998.

Robertson, O. Palmer. *The Christ of the Covenants.* Phillipsburg, NJ: Presbyterian and Reformed, 1980.

Rogers, Cleon L. Jr. "The Davidic Covenant in Acts–Revelation." *Bibliotheca Sacra* 151, no. 601 (January–March 1994): 71–84.

Ross, Allen P. "Genesis." *The Bible Knowledge Commentary: An Exposition of the Scriptures by Dallas Seminary Faculty: Old Testament.* Eds. John Walvoord, Roy B. Zuck. N.p.: Victor, 1985.

Ryken, Leland, Wilhoit, James C., and Longman, Tremper III, eds. "Covenant." *Dictionary of Biblical Imagery.* Downers Grove, IL: InterVarsity, 1998.

———. "Deuteronomy, Book of." *Dictionary of Biblical Imagery.* Downers Grove, IL: InterVarsity, 1998.

———. "Seal." *Dictionary of Biblical Imagery.* Downers Grove, IL: InterVarsity, 1998.

Ryrie, Charles Caldwell. *Basic Theology.* Chicago: Moody, 1986.

———. "Covenant, New." *Wycliffe Bible Encyclopedia.* Eds. Charles F. Pfeiffer, Howard F. Vos, and John Rea. Vol. 1 of 2 vols. Chicago: Moody, 1975.

———. *Dispensationalism.* Chicago: Moody, 1995.

———. "The End of the Law." *Bibliotheca Sacra* 124, no. 495 (July–September 1967): 239–47.

———. *The Grace of God: A Handbook of Bible Doctrine.* Chicago: Moody, 1963.

———. "The Necessity of Dispensationalism." *Bibliotheca Sacra* 114, no. 455 (July–September 1957): 243–54.

———. *The Ryrie Study Bible: New American Standard.* Chicago: Moody, 1976.

Sailhamer, John H. "Genesis." *Genesis–Numbers.* The Expositor's Bible Commentary. Vol. 2 of 12 vols. Gen. ed. Frank E. Gaebelein. Grand Rapids, MI: Zondervan, 1990.

———. "The Messiah and the Hebrew Bible." *Journal of the Evangelical Theological Society* 44, no. 1 (March 2001): 20.

Sanders, E. P. "Law." *The Anchor Bible Dictionary.* Vol. 4 of 6 vols. Ed. David Noel Freedman. New York: Doubleday, 1992.

Saucy, Robert L. *The Case for Progressive Dispensationalism: The Interface Between Dispensational and Non-Dispensational Theology.* Grand Rapids, MI: Zondervan, 1993.

Schreiner, Thomas R. *The Law and Its Fulfillment: A Pauline Theology of Law.* Grand Rapids, MI: Baker, 1993.

Scofield, C. I. *The New Scofield Reference Bible.* Ed. E. Schuyler English. New York: Oxford University Press, 1969.

Shanks, Hershel. "God as Divine Kinsman: What Covenant Meant in Ancient Israel." *Biblical Archaeology Review* 25, no. 4 (July/August 1999): 32.

Showers, Renald E. *There Really is a Difference: A Comparison of Covenant and Dispensational Theology.* Bellmawr, NJ: The Friends of Israel Gospel Ministry, 1990.

Tan, Paul Lee. *The Interpretation of Prophecy.* Dallas, TX: Bible Communications, 1974.

Thayer, Joseph Henry. *Greek-English Lexicon of the New Testament being Grimm's Wilke's*

Clavis Novi Testamenti. Reprint, Grand Rapids, MI: Zondervan, 1962.

Thompson, J. Arthur. "Covenant (OT)." *The International Standard Bible Encyclopedia.* Rev. ed. Gen. ed. Geoffrey W. Bromiley. Vol. 1 of 4 vols. Grand Rapids, MI: Eerdmans, 1994.

Thompson, Thomas L. "Historiography (Israelite) ." *The Anchor Bible Dictionary.* Vol. 3 of 6 vols. Ed. David Noel Freedman. New York: Doubleday, 1992.

Trumbull, H. Clay. *The Blood Covenant: A Primitive Rite and Its Bearings on Scripture.* 2nd ed. N.p.: 1893; reprint, Kirkwood, MO: Impact, 1975.

Unger, Merrill F. "Ezekiel's Vision of Israel's Restoration: Part 1." *Bibliotheca Sacra* 106, no. 423 (July–September 1949): 312–24.

———. "Ezekiel's Vision of Israel's Restoration: Part 2." *Bibliotheca Sacra* 106, no. 424 (October–December 1949): 432–45.

———. "Law." *Unger's Bible Dictionary.* 3rd ed. Chicago: Moody, 1966.

Unger, Merrill F. and White, William eds. *Nelson's Expository Dictionary of the Old Testament.* Nashville: Nelson, 1980.

VanGemeren, Willem A., gen. ed. *New International Dictionary of Old Testament Theology & Exegesis.* 4 vols. Grand Rapids, MI: Zondervan, 1997.

Von Rad, Gerhard. *Genesis: A Commentary.* Rev. ed. Trans. John H. Marks. The Old Testament Library. Gen. eds. G. Ernest Wright, John Bright, James Barr, Peter Ackroyd. Philadelphia: Westminister, 1972.

Vos, Howard F. *Archaeology in Bible Lands.* Chicago: Moody, 1977.

Wallace, Daniel B. *Greek Grammar Beyond the Basics: An Exegetical Syntax of the New Testament with Scripture, Subject, and Greek Word Indexes.* Grand Rapids, MI: Zondervan, 1996.

Walton, John H. *Covenant: God's Purpose, God's Plan.* Grand Rapids, MI: Zondervan, 1994.

Walton, John H., Matthews, Victor H., Chavalas, Mark W. *The IVP Bible Background Commentary: Old Testament.* Downers Grove, IL: InterVarsity, 2000.

Walvoord, John F. "Eschatological Problems VI: The Fulfillment of the Abrahamic Covenant." *Bibliotheca Sacra* 102, no. 405 (January–March 1945): 27–36.

———. "Eschatological Problems VII: The Fulfillment of the Davidic Covenant." *Bibliotheca Sacra* 102, no. 406 (April–June 1945): 153–66.

———. "Eschatological Problems X: The New Covenant with Israel." *Bibliotheca Sacra* 103, no. 409 (January–March 1946): 16–27.

———. *Every Prophecy of the Bible.* Colorado Springs, CO: Chariot Victor, 1999.

———. "Interpreting Prophecy Today—Part 2: The Kingdom of God in the Old Testament." *Bibliotheca Sacra* 139, no. 554 (April–June 1982): 111–28.

———. "Millennial Series: Part 7: Amillennial Soteriology." *Bibliotheca Sacra* 107, no. 427 (July–September 1950): 281–97.

———. "Millennial Series: Part 12: The Abrahamic Covenant and Premillennialism." *Bibliotheca Sacra* 108, no. 432 (October–December 1951): 414–22.

———. "Millennial Series: Part 15: The Abrahamic Covenant and Premillennialism." *Bibliotheca Sacra* 109, no. 435 (July–September 1952): 217–25.

———. "Part 3: Does the Church Fulfill Israel's Program." *Bibliotheca Sacra* 137, no. 547 (July–September 1980): 212–22.

————. "Series in Christology—Part 4: The Preincarnate Son of God." *Bibliotheca Sacra* 104, no. 416 (October–December 1947): 415–40.

————. *The Millennial Kingdom.* Grand Rapids, MI: Zondervan, 1959.

————. *The Revelation of Jesus Christ.* Chicago: Moody, 1966.

Weinfeld, M. "Covenant, Davidic." *The Interpreter's Dictionary of the Bible: An Illustrated Encyclopedia.* Vol. 5 of 5 vols. Ed. George Arthur Buttrick. Nashville, TN: Abingdon, 1962.

————. "Deuteronomy, Book of." *The Anchor Bible Dictionary.* Vol. 2 of 6 vols. Ed. David Noel Freedman. New York: Doubleday, 1992.

————. *The Promise of the Land: The Inheritance of the Land of Canaan by the Israelites.* Berkeley, CA: University of California Press, 1993.

Williamson, P. R. "Covenant." *New Dictionary of Biblical Theology.* Eds. T. Desmond Alexander and Brian S. Rosner. Downers Grove, IL: InterVarsity, 2000.

Wright, Geo. Fredrick. "The Mosaic Authorship of the Pentateuch." *The Fundamentals.* Vol. 1 of 4 vols. Los Angeles: Bible Institute of Los Angeles, 1917; reprint, Grand Rapids, MI: Baker, 1998.

Wyrtzen, David B. "The Theological Center of the Book of Hosea." *Bibliotheca Sacra* 141, no. 564 (October–December 1984): 315–29.

Yates, Kyle M. "Genesis." *The Wycliffe Bible Commentary.* Eds. Charles F. Pfeiffer and Everett F. Harrison. Chicago: Moody, 1972.

Youngblood, Ronald F. "2 Samuel." *Deuteronomy - 2 Samuel.* The Expositor's Bible Commentary. Vol. 3 of 12 vols. Gen. ed. Frank E. Gaebelein. Grand Rapids, MI: Zondervan, 1990.

Zimmerman, Charles. "'To This Agree the Words of the Prophets': Critical Monograph on Acts 15:14–17." *Grace Theological Journal* 4, no. 3 (Fall 1963): 28–40.

INDEX OF SCRIPTURES

29:18	30	16:1–63	146
30:1–31:40	168	16:8	44, 46
30:1–31:40	266	16:59	29, 30, 45
30:3–11	149	16:60	93, 169
31	175	16:62	93
31:27–40	168	17:13–19	29, 45
31:31	173	17:18	31
31:31–34	137, 171, 174, 194, 207	20:37	25, 44
		21:23	31
31:31–37	177, 182, 249	21:28	31
31:31–38	170	34:11–16	149
31:31–40	167	34:23–24	156
31:32–33	38	34:25	169
31:33–34	269	36:1–27	156
31:34	180	36:16–38	169
31:35–37	146, 181, 269	36:19–30	145
31:36	36	36:21–38	140
32:1	168	36:25–27	179
32:11	36	37:1–14	145
32:22	46	37:21–28	169
32:36–44	140	39:28	146
32:37	169	40:1–43:27	268
32:37–40	168	40:1–48:35	266
32:39–40	145	47:19	120
32:40–41	169	48:28	120
33:20	69, 94		
33:20–22	151, 163	**Daniel**	
33:25	69	9:11	30, 45, 46
34:8–20	40, 44	9:24–27	256
34:18	93, 109	9:26	260
36:37	145	9:27	27
38:16	46	12:7	46
39:10	42		
40:9	46	**Hosea**	
42:18	45	2:14–23	145
44:12	30	4:15	46
44:23	47	6:7	44, 69, 70
44:26	30, 46	8:1	44
49:13	30, 46	10:4	44
51:14	30, 46	12:2	26
Ezekiel		**Amos**	
11:16–21	140, 145	4:2	46

INDEX OF ANCIENT SOURCES

INDEX OF FOREIGN TERMS

INDEX OF MODERN AUTHORS

INDEX OF SUBJECTS

Studies in Biblical Literature

This series invites manuscripts from scholars in any area of biblical literature. Both established and innovative methodologies, covering general and particular areas in biblical study, are welcome. The series seeks to make available studies that will make a significant contribution to the ongoing biblical discourse. Scholars who have interests in gender and sociocultural hermeneutics are particularly encouraged to consider this series.

For further information about the series and for the submission of manuscripts, contact:

Hemchand Gossai
Department of Religion
Muhlenberg College
2400 Chew Street
Allentown, PA 18104-5586

To order other books in this series, please contact our Customer Service Department:

(800) 770-LANG (within the U.S.)
(212) 647-7706 (outside the U.S.)
(212) 647-7707 FAX

or browse online by series at:

WWW.PETERLANGUSA.COM